The New
BREADLINE

The New

BREADLINE

Hunger and Hope in the Twenty-First Century

Jean-Martin Bauer

Alfred A. Knopf | New York 2024

THIS IS A BORZOI BOOK
PUBLISHED BY ALFRED A. KNOPF

www.aaknopf.com

Library of Congress Cataloging-in-Publication Data
Names: Bauer, Jean-Martin, author.
Title: The new breadline : hunger and hope in the twenty-first century /
Jean-Martin Bauer.
Description: First edition. | New York : Alfred A. Knopf, 2024. |
Includes bibliographical references.
Identifiers: LCCN 2023031559 | ISBN 9780593321683 (hardcover) |
ISBN 9780593321690 (ebook)
Subjects: LCSH: Food security. | Food security—Government policy. |
Food supply—Government policy. | Hunger—Social aspects.
Classification: LCC HD9000.5 .B347 2024 | DDC 338.1/9—dc23/eng/20231020
LC record available at https://lccn.loc.gov/2023031559

Jacket design by No ideas
Chapter opener art by No Ideas
Ornament art © Qualit Design/stock.adobe.com

Manufactured in the United States of America

First Edition

To the Masters of the Dew

Timeo danaos et dona ferentes.

Beware of Greeks bearing gifts.

—VIRGIL, *THE AENEID*

Contents

The New
BREADLINE

Introduction

"They're inside. They got over the wall. I can see them," Paul whispered to me over his phone. I heard him swallow hard. A heavy silence followed, and he hung up.

A few months earlier, I had been appointed the World Food Programme's (WFP's) country director in Haiti. Paul, a Haitian agronomist, was the head of our office in Gonaïves. That September morning, we were losing the battle to save our office from a mob that had come to plunder the food stocks in our warehouse. Paul had just called to warn that attackers had breached our perimeter.

Over the previous days, we had barricaded the compound after demonstrators tried to force their way in. We pleaded, in vain, with the police and local authorities to protect us. We even used a forklift to move a twenty-foot-long shipping container across the main gate to reinforce it. That morning, the mob forced its way in. In the next hours, they vandalized our office, carried away all the food from our warehouse, and burned it to the ground.

Footage of the fire went viral on social media. It showed dark pillars of smoke rising from our warehouse, and crowds carrying away heavy bags of rice. I was disheartened, but not surprised, when I saw that Twitter accounts cheered on the destruction of humanitarian food stocks. That day, the attackers made off with enough food to feed 100,000 children. Although Paul was shaken, he was safe, as was the rest of our team in Gonaïves.

In Haiti, not a single voice spoke out publicly against the attack. This was perhaps because people feared becoming targets themselves if they condemned the events. Whatever the reason, the silence testified to the climate of impunity in the country.

The attack on the WFP warehouse occurred as the global food crisis took a turn for the worse. The Haitian people were suffering more than ever. Experts estimated that half of the country's population was facing acute hunger as food prices took off and as violence took hold in much of the country. In September 2022, violent demonstrations against *lavi chè*—the high cost of living—broke out. The worst riots since the fall of Jean-Claude Duvalier in 1986 shook the entire nation. Over several weeks, angry crowds targeted banks, supermarkets, government offices, and even humanitarian facilities. To the starving multitudes of Haiti, stocks of humanitarian supplies were fair game—regardless of the consequences for their community's schoolchildren.

It's easy to imagine desperate citizens justifiably looting a warehouse with idle stocks of surplus relief items. This was not the case in the attacks we suffered in September 2022. The men and women who attacked us had been manipulated, egged on through slogans that spread like wildfire over FM radios and WhatsApp. Hunger left the people open to manipulation and receptive to their worst instincts. Suffering citizens turned into brazen rioters.

Being a humanitarian worker in Haiti has long meant being treated with skepticism by the local people. By 2022, we had become targets, facing the open hostility of the communities we are meant to help. How are we supposed to fight hunger when the people we're meant to help turn on us?

The sacking of the WFP warehouse in Gonaïves hit me like a gut punch. It felt personal because my mother was born in Haiti. As a teenager she had left the troubled country for the United States, where I was born and raised.

I joined WFP in 2001, right after college, and spent my early career managing food programs in the West African Sahel, a front line in the fight against global hunger. During the early part of my career, I planned food distributions to poor communities with our local partners. I purchased food at local markets and negotiated logistics with trucking companies. I also monitored projects to ensure food got to the intended beneficiaries. It was a demanding task that my energetic and curious young self embraced.

In 2008, I became an analyst. For the next decade, the role brought me to Afghanistan, the Central African Republic, Syria, and many other war-torn countries. I wrangled data about crops, food markets, and family-level dynamics. I explained the stories the numbers told to other humanitarians. In doing so, I became intimate with the systems that create and sustain acute hunger in the most fragile parts of the world.

When I was assigned to lead WFP's office in Haiti in 2022, I was both enthusiastic and uneasy about what I'd find. When I got off the plane, I was saddened to see that broad, sandy gullies now scarred the once-green mountains that ring Port-au-Prince. It looked like the island was well on its way to becoming a Sahel in the Caribbean.

The land was badly wounded, and that was the least of it. Port-au-Prince was in the throes of an undeclared civil war. Heavily armed gangs were vying for territory, killing and maiming count-ess civilians. Ruelle Waag, the quiet middle-class street where my mother had grown up in the 1950s, was now a no-go area, one that the neighborhood militia periodically barricaded to keep the gangs at bay. Millions of Haitians had been plunged into hunger as armed men cut off supply lines. Farmers could not bring their produce to the market. Food prices spiraled upward, making essentials unaffordable to many. People had seen all this before, and it seemed to me there was a fatalism in their attitude. Far from a relic of a bygone era, hunger remains an everyday ritual for millions of Haitians.

"We're Haitian. We're used to hunger," a young mother told me softly in Cité Soleil, a seaside slum.

It's not just Haiti. All over the world, hunger has proven hard to beat.

Believe it or not, for a moment at the turn of the millennium, it seemed the world was winning the battle against hunger. Famines had been virtually eliminated. As technology advanced, and as government programs reached more people than ever, deaths from starvation fell sharply in the second half of the twentieth century. Trends were so encouraging that in 2015, the world's governments publicly committed to eliminating hunger by 2030.

But instead of being eradicated, hunger has surged because of escalating global food prices, even as conflict and climate change continue to decimate livelihoods. Experts estimated that in 2023, more than 250 million people would be facing acute hunger—double the number in 2020.

What was long regarded as a problem facing only the poorest nations is now pressing in on us here in the United States, where more than 13 million families are food insecure. During the early months of the COVID-19 pandemic, we saw on the news the snaking lines at food banks around the country, after millions of people lost their jobs. Even generous government aid was not enough to stop hunger from rising among minority groups in America, a fact that reminds us that all over the world, hunger is the outcome of deep-rooted social inequality.

There is plenty of food in the world to feed everyone. And yet even in a country like the United States, endowed with abundant food supplies, people don't have enough food to eat. This paradox can be explained only by our society's deep structural inequalities and the shortcomings of our systems of production and distribution. In other parts of the world, conflict and corruption are added to the mix. But if, as has been said, hunger is a political condition, then it is, like all political conditions, something we can change.

Political systems can exacerbate or drive hunger by disenfranchising a society's most vulnerable groups—the Haratin caste of formerly enslaved people in Moorish society, landless farmers of the arid Sahel, or Indigenous people of central Africa's rainforests. And when a food crisis strikes, the population at large also suffers. Nobel economist Amartya Sen argued that the most extreme food shortages have almost always been the result of rulers' neglect and indifference to the plight of their people. "No famine has ever taken place in the history of the world in a functioning democracy," he wrote in 1991.

The current crisis should motivate us to reassess our food production and distribution systems as well as our social safety net. To stanch hunger's worldwide resurgence, we need to think big, and think differently, about the causes of hunger and famine and how to combat them more effectively. Those of us working in the humanitarian space can improve aid delivery by, for example, embracing emerging technologies—digital payments, robotics, advanced analytics, and artificial intelligence—and other disruptive developments that promise to produce more food with less waste and enable food deliveries in high-risk settings. Technology, as we know, is a double-edged sword, and our use of these systems will require care, but their potential is undeniable.

Technology alone won't solve our problems. In the war against hunger, it is people who use the tech, who make the decisions and perpetuate (or disrupt) hierarchies and inequality. From America's inner cities to refugee camps in various countries, food programs involve unequal power relations between those who provide aid and those who receive it—inequalities often abetted by race and colonial histories. Even as workforces of humanitarian agencies have become increasingly diverse, it has remained taboo to discuss the racial dynamics shaping aid delivery.

There are times when the lack of concern about hunger is infuriating. In the summer of 2021, as the number of people facing food shortages rose around the world, we saw billionaires compete to be the first in space. There's nothing wrong with people making money and spending it as they see fit, including on private spaceships. But if our society can launch people into orbit, it should also be able to feed its own.

The artist Tupac Shakur called out this jarring juxtaposition of ostentatious wealth and hunger in America: "There's no way Michael Jackson, or whoever Jackson, should have 100 million dollars and there are people starving," he stated, adding, "That's not idealistic, that's just real." For public opinion, mass hunger seems to be an acceptable by-product of society, tolerable as long as it only affects others. It's an attitude fraught with risk: throughout history, famines have been breeding grounds for revolution and war.

In early 2022, just when we thought we'd turned the corner on the worst of the pandemic's impacts, Russia invaded Ukraine and spurred the global food crisis to new heights. The all-out war in the fertile Black Sea basin, a key global grain source, caused food prices all over the world to spike. The price of gas soared too. And once more, working-class people near my home in West Virginia were facing an impossible choice, between filling their gas tanks to commute to their jobs, heating their homes, or buying food. It looks as though the breadlines that returned to America in early 2020 will be here for a while.

When will it end? Or, at least, when will things get better? The answer is "not anytime soon." We're facing a slow-motion disaster that could lead to a lost generation—kids who have grown up not knowing where their next meal will come from, disillusioned about or even hostile toward a society indifferent to the suffering of its own. We need to wake up to the fact that these recurrent emergencies have now taken on a more global dimension. I fear that worse is to come.

These food crises are not just self-contained events that hurt people a world away. We are in a broad, resurgent emergency that is unfolding because of extended conflict, emerging diseases, resource scarcity, and climate change. The global food crisis threatens millions who suffer from hunger, just as it undermines social progress and national security in better-off parts of the world. So far, our responses have not been coordinated, far-sighted, or effective enough. Our global food security is too important to be managed on a crisis-to-crisis basis. We must commit to building a better food future for all of us, for the long term. And it requires both ambition and humility: we need to be bold enough to demand action at the global scale, and humble enough to acknowledge that local initiatives can be transformative and lifesaving.

've read a lot about hunger, and one of the books that left a lasting imprint on me was a novel published in 1944 that I first read as a teenager. *Masters of the Dew*, by the radical Haitian author Jacques Roumain, is set in the fictional Haitian community of Fonds-Rouge. The novel shows how humble family farmers—the eponymous "Masters of the Dew"—are oppressed by their leaders and hindered by their own divisions.

The novel's protagonist, Manuel, returns to his hometown

after fifteen years abroad. He comes home to find his community drought-stricken, hungry, and hopeless, his aging parents penniless and starving.

Back home, Manuel resolves to find a way to irrigate the area's parched fields and finds an abundant water source high up in the mountains, enough to relieve the drought. But soon after his discovery, one of Manuel's jealous rivals murders him. Roumain draws parallels between Manuel's death and the Passion of Christ. In the end, the community overcomes its divisions to dig a channel, and cool water flows down the mountainside to the thirsty fields of Fonds-Rouge.

Masters of the Dew lays out the tenacious forces that are now propelling hunger's global resurgence. Drought and violence certainly contribute to rising food insecurity. But its root causes are corruption, exploitation, and poverty. Roumain's work echoes Amartya Sen's argument that hunger is "related, ultimately, to economic disparity and political disempowerment."

The novel portrays men and women who turn their starving community into a place of hope and possibility. Before coming back to Fonds-Rouge, Manuel had worked on a sugar plantation in Cuba. It belonged to Americans who exploited both the land and their workforce. From his time cutting cane in Cuba, Manuel brought back a sense of right and wrong, and of the strength of humble people when they unite.

Roumain tells us that ending hunger requires leaders who, like Manuel, are clear-eyed, determined, and able to bring people together. He portrays Manuel as a diplomat who expertly bridges the divide in his community, and as champion who's able to stand up to the unconcerned officials and ruffians who thrive at the expense of the population.

In my decades as an aid worker overseas, I have worked in many countries I didn't know much about. I offered only my expertise and good intentions as they struggled with food shortages. Manuel is a very different person: he returns to his own community to save his kin. In Roumain's novel, there is no white savior parachuting in to save Fonds-Rouge from the clutches of starvation. Solutions come not from a rotating retinue of experts brought in from afar, but from the Masters of the Dew themselves.

Roumain's account echoes what I have seen in my career: hunger as the by-product of an unequal, corrupt, and dysfunctional society, but also as a condition that can be cured by courage, determination, and sacrifice. The fictional Haitian community in *Masters of the Dew* is like so many real villages I have seen, in the Sahel, the Middle East, or central Africa—deeply troubled by food shortages, sometimes in desperate straits, but never places or people to be given up on. This book aims to place those struggles in historical context, and to show how, by making better political choices and creating more equitable and humane systems of aid, we can reduce or even eliminate hunger.

Young Haiti

From Failed Rebellion to Mass Hunger

Can a man desert the soil?

—Jacques Roumain, *Masters of the Dew*

I t had been decided they would die by firing squad. The two young men, Marcel Numa and Louis "Milou" Drouin, were tied to posts next to the stone wall at the entrance of the National Cemetery in Port-au-Prince. Marcel, a tall, athletic Black man, and Milou, a wispy mulatto, were the only members still alive from an ill-fated expedition to overthrow President François Duvalier. Their public execution would serve as a warning to anyone foolish enough to threaten the regime. Duvalier had ensured there would be a massive crowd for the execution of the captured rebels by ordering all government workers to attend and trucking in people from the countryside.

Police officers in khaki shirts signaled the start of the proceedings, pushing the onlookers back. Some in the crowd were silently praying, holding out hope that the dictator might change his mind and spare the condemned men. A white Catholic priest appeared, Bible in hand, and approached Marcel and Milou. Stoic and resolute, both men refused the last rites. Soon after, the nine members of the firing squad raised their rifles, aimed, and fired; the commanding officer delivered the coup de grâce with a pistol. It was November 12, 1964.

The story looms large in Haitian history. The execution, which was recorded for television, is proof of the brutality the Duvaliers inflicted on the Haitian people for decades. The fate of the young rebels also looms large in my own family history. Many of my relatives supported Duvalier, just as others quietly plotted the regime's overthrow.

One of the latter was my uncle Serge Picard. It turns out Serge nearly found himself alongside Marcel and Milou that day in 1964. In fact, Serge had seen their deaths coming. A few years earlier, as a recent high school graduate, Serge had left the country for New York, where he began studying sociology. In New York, he naturally reconnected with other members of the growing Haitian diaspora, including his childhood friends Marcel and Milou, who hailed from the same town in southern Haiti. They were all part of a group of young exiles in the city who'd known one another from their days as Boy Scouts and who had formed a rebel group called Jeune Haiti, or Young Haiti. They were fiercely opposed to Duvalier's regime, which had been responsible for the arrest, torture, and murder of many of their friends and relatives. Like Serge, many had felt compelled to join when Duvalier declared himself president for life in April 1964.

Jeune Haiti occasionally met at Serge's apartment on 77th Street on the Upper West Side, opposite the American Museum of Natural History. The group soon hatched a bold plan to overthrow Duvalier: they would buy weapons, rent a boat, sail to Haiti, and land in their hometown of Jérémie. They would take over the town's barracks and armory, and set in motion the downfall of the dictator, just as Fidel Castro and Che Guevara had done with Fulgencio Batista in Cuba a few years before. Serge was initially on board with the plan. But as he listened to his friends, he knew in his gut that they were doomed. He pleaded with them to cancel the plan, but it went ahead without him.

According to Serge, Jeune Haiti's failure was the result of a combination of betrayal, errors, and bad luck. Its members had talked so much that their plan had become an open secret in New York. Inevitably, informants infiltrated the group. In August 1964, thirteen Jeune Haiti members set out for their homeland aboard the *Johnny Express*, a Miami-based freighter whose mysterious skipper refused to land in Jérémie as planned, instead dropping them off like packages farther west, out of reach of their supporters. The missed landing was a disaster for the expedition. The young exiles, used to the comforts of New York, found themselves facing the fight of their lives high in the towering mountain ranges of southern Haiti.

In the years following, Serge was able to piece together some of their ordeal. He met a Catholic priest who had risked his own life to shelter the young men on the night of the landing. The area was crawling with Tontons Macoutes, Duvalier's ruthless militia, who were looking for the already demoralized rebels. The priest gave them coffee and sent them on their way before sunrise, knowing their attempt was certain to fail. A few days after they set out, the expedition found itself facing the fury of Hurricane Cleo, a powerful storm that hit Haiti in late August. As Serge searched for evidence of what had happened to his friends, he spoke to a farmer in the countryside who said he'd given them shelter in his isolated mountain hut as the storm raged. The men were drenched and cold, the farmer said, and one was coughing uncontrollably, while the hurricane toppled trees and torrential rain fell. One of the group, probably Marcel, according to the farmer's description, seemed convinced that Duvalier himself had used his diabolical powers to summon the storm.

Betrayed, unlucky, and unprepared, the Jeune Haiti members

were also brave and resourceful: over the weeks of their attempted insurrection, they trekked two hundred kilometers through rugged mountains and managed to shoot down a Haitian Air Force plane. But in the end, short of water, famished, and out of ammunition, the men were reduced to fighting off Duvalier's soldiers with stones. At a series of engagements that September, the dictator's forces picked off the rebels one by one. Only Marcel and Milou were captured alive to face the firing squad.

The regime didn't execute just the rebels. Duvalier's men also murdered their families in cold blood, including twenty-seven elders, women, and children, all from Jérémie's embattled and largely mulatto upper class. The mulatto families that had long dominated business and politics in the port town were opposed to Duvalier's brand of radical, anti-elite politics. Duvalier built his following by opposing the rule of a tiny light-skinned minority. To those who committed them, the massacres were revenge—visited upon a hated bourgeois class who despised people like them. Jeune Haiti's landing had given them the perfect pretext to unleash their fury and get even.

The killings took place near the airport, where the victims were buried in a mass grave. The murders were atrocious. It is said that two of Duvalier's henchmen tortured a four-year-old girl in front of her mother, throwing the child in the air and impaling her on a knife. They put their cigarettes out in the eyes of crying babies. The massacre took place over a series of nights, and people living in the nearby hills could hear the shouts of soldiers and the echoing screams of their victims. Soon after the killings, the assassins were seen driving the cars of the people they had just murdered.

As for Serge, he was tormented by guilt and grief for the rest of his life.

The executions of Marcel and Milou, and the murder of the rebels' families, were only some of the innumerable sins of the Duvaliers, father and son, who ruled Haiti from 1957 to 1986.

The regime's ideology was *noirisme,* a form of Black fascism, a reaction to the light-skinned elite's domination of Haitian society. Haiti's mulatto bourgeoisie had rigged society to their benefit. They controlled the government and institutions and amassed great wealth, while the darker-skinned masses moldered in abject poverty. Haitian-American writer Edwidge Danticat calls the arrangement "social and economic apartheid." For all his revolutionary swagger, Duvalier didn't end the hated system.

Papa Doc, the elder Duvalier, created a corrupt and murderous police state in which the entire nation was kept in a state of terror, and a hideous personality cult that had schoolchildren reciting a modified version of the Lord's Prayer: *Our Doc, who art in the National Palace for life, hallowed be Thy name . . .* Like most dictators, Duvalier became increasingly paranoid as the years went by. At one point he ordered that every black dog in Port-au-Prince be killed, after one of his adversaries was said to have used a voodoo spell to turn himself into one.

The regime's top priority was to survive; it crushed opposition movements like Jeune Haiti. Although the elder Duvalier came to office on a populist platform, he was obsessed with power. The younger Duvalier kept a stable of sports cars, while his wife had a huge refrigerator built in which she stored her fur coat collection. The Duvaliers' ruthlessness and greed had a profound, long-term impact. The country lost its skilled class as educated professionals emigrated. Illiteracy, poverty, and malnutrition were rife.

Both Duvaliers, father and son, let hunger metastasize into the full-blown crisis it has become today.

Journalists routinely describe Haiti as the first Black republic, or they might say it's the poorest nation in the Western Hemisphere. As I write this in 2023, the hunger facing Haitians is especially dire; there are even pockets of famine-like conditions in the capital. The United Nations estimates that nearly half of Haiti's 12 million people need food assistance, while 100,000 children suffer from malnutrition each year. In Haiti, misrule, violence, and starvation have gone hand in hand. But hunger in the country is not a single man's legacy: over the centuries, an unconcerned bourgeoisie and self-serving foreign "friends" also played a large part. It has become a sobering case study of the man-made forces that lay the groundwork for hunger.

Things in Haiti had once been different.

Soon after independence in 1804, when the country's population was only a few hundred thousand, there was, for a time, a modicum of political stability—and, importantly, enough land for everyone. In the south of the country, President Alexandre Pétion broke up the French colonial plantations that had produced a bounty of sugar, coffee, and indigo. He distributed the land to his soldiers, creating a nation of small farmers at the stroke of a pen. The move allowed the free Blacks to establish a multitude of family homesteads focused on subsistence farming, sometimes on the very land the French had forced them to work. Haiti even had enough land to offer refuge to thousands of African Americans fleeing racism and slavery at home.

As in Africa, nineteenth-century Haitian farmers grew corn, beans, sorghum, sweet potatoes, coffee, and bananas, and kept goats, pigs, and chickens. In the African way, they lived in multigenerational family compounds, or *lakou*. With their hard-won freedom secure, the nation's farmers kept to themselves, avoiding the cities and their arcane politics.

But it wouldn't last. In 1825, Haiti was forced to pay an outrageous "indemnity" to France in exchange for diplomatic recognition. The ransom of 150 million gold francs was meant to "compensate" former colonists for the loss of their plantations and property, including the people they'd enslaved. The agreement would become a drain on Haiti's finances for the next century, stymieing the country's investment in its own infrastructure and people. Corrupt members of the Haitian elite played along, agreeing to repayment terms that enriched themselves and French banking interests.

Over the course of the nineteenth century, a French-speaking, politically influential mulatto bourgeoisie cornered the coffee trade, then the nation's main export. With the profits, the elite began to acquire land from small farmers, plot by plot. In time, many Haitian farmers were driven into sharecropping, while population growth meant the *lakous* were subdivided into ever smaller plots.

By the late nineteenth century, Haiti had run out of land to feed its burgeoning population, forcing legions of young, able-bodied men to seek work cutting cane in Cuba or the Dominican Republic. One can only imagine how hard it was for independent-minded Haitians to work abroad in conditions that looked a lot like slavery. Migration became a rite of passage. Migration and exile remain at the core of the Haitian experience; my family's departure for New York in the 1960s is but one story among many.

Haiti entered the twentieth century both financially crushed by its former enslavers and suffering from an acute land shortage. The seeds of hunger had been sown. And politics turned from bad to worse. Rebellion after rebellion shook the country. The country had five presidents between 1910 and 1915. In July 1915, the last of them, Villebrun Guillaume Sam, ordered his predecessor murdered, along with 167 other political opponents. When news spread of the bloodbath, riots broke out in Port-au-Prince. A mob pulled the hapless Sam out of the French embassy, where he had sought refuge, tore his body limb from limb, and paraded his remains around town. All this was too much for President Woodrow Wilson, who sent in the Marines. The United States would occupy Haiti for the next nineteen years.

A turning point in Haiti's ability to feed itself came in October

1954, when Hurricane Hazel hit the south, a productive farming area, leading to an influx of food aid. The powerful storm drowned hundreds of people, devastated the crops, and flooded the cities of Les Cayes and Jérémie. The USS *Saipan*, an aircraft carrier, was the first vessel to bring American food surpluses to Haiti, just months after President Eisenhower's new Public Law 480 formalized food aid as a foreign policy instrument. For weeks, the people of Jérémie owed their survival to the food rations the ship's helicopters ferried over. While the *Saipan* brought much-needed aid, its visit heralded the start of Haiti's fractious relationship with food aid that persists to this day.

As a child, my uncle Serge saw the USS *Saipan* at anchor off Jérémie and saw how the food it carried saved lives. It might have inspired him, because he became a manager of food aid programs in Haiti and, later, an independent rice farmer. Serge ultimately struggled to realize his vision of sustainable farming in Haiti, and the problems he faced provide insight as to why Haiti lost the ability to feed its own people.

After earning his sociology degree in New York, Serge spent more than a decade working in the United States and for international organizations, before resettling in Haiti in 1977. By then, things had changed on the island. Papa Doc had died, and his son was now president. There was less tension and violence than in the 1960s. Still, Serge steered clear of the kind of activity that had doomed his friends. "I don't do politics," he would grumble in his deep voice to anyone gauche enough to ask. Serge was first the director of Catholic Relief Services and later of other U.S. nongovernmental organizations (NGOs).

Serge and his wife, Nelly—a Haitian woman he'd met in New York, who also worked for international NGOs in the country, including Save the Children—became rice growers in Patte Large, a remote corner of the south, farming a hundred hectares of paddies bordered by steep mountains that plunged straight into the sea. The estate, called Kay Ben, was well watered and fertile, but extremely isolated. I was delighted when Serge took me to Kay Ben as a teenager in the summer of 1997. At the time, I hadn't been to Haiti in a decade.

I remember it took two days to get there from Port-au-Prince. You had to navigate the busy, badly rutted road to the port town of Miragoâne, to the west of the capital. From there, you boarded an open boat with an outboard engine that weaved for hours through a blurry maze of shallow coral reefs before reaching its destination.

There was another, much less pleasant way to get to Kay Ben: the ferry. I took it myself in 1997. The *Agnes* was a decaying triple-decker behemoth from the former East Germany that, after decades of service in the Baltic, had found a second life in the Caribbean. It was always hopelessly overcrowded, and its engines were oppressively noisy and hot. Travelers—families, market women, and a few foreigners—paid a few dollars for passage and were all jammed together with their luggage, sleeping wherever they could find space on the decks. Bottles of warm soda and ripe bananas were passed around. Passengers relieved themselves in plastic buckets whose contents were thrown overboard. The *Agnes* gave off a distinctive, sour stench that hung in the air wherever it docked. Not only was the trip to Kay Ben long and uncomfortable, it was also risky: in 1993, the *Neptune*—the *Agnes*'s sister ship—went down in a violent storm, drowning hundreds.

Kay Ben had been built on the ruins of an eighteenth-century French sugarcane plantation. The big house, a fortress-like two-story structure, remained intact, though only the walls were left of the *guildive*, the circular sugarhouse where the cane was crushed, turned into juice, and cooked into molasses, crystals, and rum. The colonial French had made a fortune exporting these delicacies until the Africans they had enslaved rebelled in 1791, forcing them to flee.

Serge and Nelly had a passion for farming: they wanted to transform Kay Ben into a productive, modern, state-of-the-art rice farm. It was the project of a lifetime, an attempt to bring the "Green Revolution" in agriculture to their corner of Haiti, where traditional farming was considered backward because it relied mostly on manual labor, which was expensive, and unproductive seeds. The Green Revolution promised huge gains in productivity to those who adopted a package of innovations, including improved seed varieties, chemicals, and mechanization.

This approach, pioneered by the American agronomist Norman Borlaug, had already paid handsome dividends in other parts of the world. After Borlaug's wheat varieties arrived in Pakistan in 1965, production took off, and the country became self-sufficient three years later. Similar results were seen in India and Brazil, both of which became top agricultural exporters. Borlaug won the Nobel Peace Prize in 1970. His ideas could work in Haiti too, Serge and Nelly thought.

Nelly, an energetic woman with a fabulous smile, tackled the irrigation network first. The springs at Kay Ben needed to be brought under control. She directed laborers to lay down a network of canals and channels so that the water could be used when the rice needed it. She and Serge purchased improved seeds from abroad that promised to raise yields, and hired planters from the Artibonite, the north central valley known as Haiti's breadbasket, who were experienced in commercial rice farming. They even brought in a small, motorized tiller. My uncle and aunt sank all their savings into the farm, doing everything their agronomists prescribed.

But keeping the farm afloat was hard. Every year, the seeds, fertilizer, pesticides, and fuel became more expensive as the Haitian currency lost value against the U.S. dollar, while the land grew more acidic with each harvest—meaning that more chemicals were needed to restore the soil as the years went by. It seemed the land itself was unforgiving of the brutal past, stubbornly refusing to yield to the promises and persuasions of the Green Revolution. The winners were still the foreign dealers who sold agricultural inputs to my uncle and aunt. Ultimately, these choices had a direct impact on Serge's and Nelly's health. Late in her life, Nelly suffered from a rare neurological condition her daughters believed was a result of her exposure to pesticides.

Despite their dedication to the project, it seemed that they were conflicted about the Green Revolution's methods. Serge and Nelly, along with many others, knew a better way was possible. I once noticed they kept a paperback copy of E. F. Schumacher's *Small Is Beautiful* on the shelf at Kay Ben, a book that questioned the consumerist excesses of contemporary society. They had also read Masanobu Fukuoka, the Japanese farmer-philosopher who had shown that small farms could achieve high rice yields without the chemicals and machinery the Green Revolution prescribed. Fukuoka was adamant about the limits of chemical farming. "If we throw mother nature out the window, she comes back in the door with a pitchfork," Fukuoka is said to have warned. The statement captured Serge and Nelly's predicament perfectly. And yet they continued farming with chemicals.

For all their struggles with farming techniques, international power politics proved to be the real kiss of death for my uncle and aunt's rice farming project. In 1994 Serge and Nelly went out of business almost overnight when President Bill Clinton forced Haiti to drop its tariff on imported, subsidized rice. The Haitian market was suddenly flooded with cheap rice imports—"Miami Rice," which was mostly shipped in from Florida. Serge and Nelly couldn't compete. While they never lost Kay Ben, they drastically scaled down their ambitions and returned to their office jobs in Port-au-Prince. When, a few years later, Serge, who had become the director of Feed the Children, an NGO, found himself distributing containers of surplus cornflakes from Oklahoma to Haitian schoolchildren, the irony was painful.

The lowering of the rice tariff in 1994 stands out as the moment when Haiti lost control of its food supply. After this, outside interests triumphed over the country's food economy, paying little attention to the needs of Haitian farmers or citizens. The nineties were an especially turbulent decade for Haiti. After a chaotic few years following the fall of Jean-Claude Duvalier, a round of democratic elections was held in late 1990 and early 1991. They ushered in a civilian regime led by Jean-Bertrand Aristide, a popular leftist firebrand priest who proposed redistributing land and investing in social programs. Right-wing members of the Haitian military deposed him in a coup seven months later and fostered such a climate of terror that a mass exodus to the United States began. The military harassed Aristide supporters and stole their grain reserves and livestock. Thousands of people were imprisoned, tortured, and murdered. It was the Duvalier years all over again. Haitians left by the thousands in sailboats, many picked up by the U.S. Coast Guard and taken to Guantanamo Bay, others somehow managing to evade the dragnet, landing on the beaches of south Florida.

From 1992 to 1994, Haiti fell under a near-total international trade embargo. Intended by global powers to put pressure on the military junta, the embargo instead delivered a knockout blow to the economy, destroying more than 140,000 manufacturing jobs and plunging the country into yet another food crisis. In the slums of Port-au-Prince, people had become so poor that women were buying rice by the half cup. A Haitian economist who chose to remain anonymous noted that for "the majority of Haitians, it's been one meal a day. Now it's one meal every other day." Thousands of people understandably chose to leave the island.

The flow of starving migrants out of Haiti was so large it forced the United States to send in the Marines again. In October 1994, President Jean-Bertrand Aristide returned to ecstatic crowds who hoped things would change for the better. But the embargo had shattered the economy, and the fleeting sense of hope quickly faded. Haitians found out that as a condition of U.S. support for his return, Aristide had agreed to liberalize the economy, including agriculture, and to slash the rice tariff. His return should have been a new beginning, an opportunity to start afresh. Instead, Haiti found itself once again in turmoil.

The pain of the embargo and its aftermath was of course not shared equally. While it was in place, a small, savvy, westernized elite had made money hand over fist, controlling imports of lucrative contraband. The existing economic inequality had only been magnified by the embargo: while millions had gone hungry, elites bought fine French cheeses smuggled in from Miami at luxury supermarkets with armed guards at the door. After the embargo, these Haitian families added to their fortunes by leasing land and facilities to the international force that joined the Marines and kept the peace. They also made fortunes importing food from abroad after local farming had collapsed. It was as though they couldn't lose.

By the late 1990s the embargo was over, but Haiti still found itself in a downward spiral of food shortages. I realized just how bad things were in Haiti when one day Serge and I visited the Cayemites, two low islands off the southern peninsula, to meet a boat that would take us back to Port-au-Prince. I was tagging along with Serge as he visited projects his NGO was implementing in the area.

When we got to shore, there was a commotion. A small crowd had gathered around a disconsolate and thin old man, who was bleeding from a head wound. Holding his head in his hands, he described in a high-pitched voice how he had nearly killed his own son moments before. His Creole was so fast I couldn't catch everything, but I understood that he had found his son working on land they'd been arguing over. A fight ensued, and he had picked up a boulder and thrown it at his son, hitting him in the head. The old man was breathing quickly, the veins on his temples throbbing, his expression a grimace of pain. I didn't know how the man's own head had been bloodied, but I could imagine.

Eking out a living on the Cayemite islands in the 1990s was difficult: the islands were tiny, without electricity or a phone network, and with only limited fresh water. But that incident could have happened anywhere in Haiti. There just wasn't enough land to go around for families to feed themselves, and so the smallest patch could be bitterly fought over. Subsistence farmers had reached a breaking point. A crushing trade embargo and the forced opening of the island's economy had sent them over the edge.

Around this time, Serge, fuming at his struggles growing rice and the collapse of local agriculture after 1994, penned a sharply worded op-ed in the *Nouvelliste*, Haiti's most widely read newspaper. As I recall, its title was "The Food Aid We Don't Want." Instead of taking shipments of subsidized rice, Serge argued, Haiti should support its farmers and rebuild its agriculture. "Food aid is the cancer of national production," he wrote bitterly. How, he asked, could Haitian farmers compete against heavily subsidized American farmers, especially after the embargo? His questions fell on deaf ears.

The forced opening of the Haitian market to U.S. food imports at a time of political upheaval seems a textbook example of what Naomi Klein calls the "shock doctrine": moneyed interests taking advantage of a disaster to advance a neoliberal agenda. Haiti's leaders were under duress, focused on their personal safety and political survival. Food policy was simply not the embattled government's priority, and it consented to slashing the rice tariff. But Serge saw clearly what was going on, as Haiti's agricultural production shriveled in the face of unfettered food imports. Haiti is now one of the top three importers of U.S. rice, buying $200 million worth of the commodity every year. The country—largely self-sufficient in food until the mid-1980s—now imports half its food, and 80 percent of its rice supply.

When Bill Clinton insisted that Haiti open its markets to food imports, his intentions were no doubt largely good. He and Hillary had honeymooned in Haiti and taken a liking to it. And who looks at a nation devastated by poverty and natural disasters and sets out to make things worse? But good intentions aren't enough. After an earthquake killed hundreds of thousands in 2010, Clinton finally admitted it had been a mistake: "I have to live every day with the consequences of the lost capacity to produce a rice crop in Haiti to feed those people." Clinton, then a private citizen, took a leading role in the botched reconstruction of the country, a notoriously ineffective and wasteful enterprise. With friends like these, a Haitian might think, who needs enemies?

I grew up on a quiet street in the suburbs of Washington, D.C.—a world removed from Haiti's woes. During my childhood, the country's unending tribulations were a regular fixture on the evening news. But thanks to my Haitian heritage, I also knew the country was an enchanting place of rich culture and history, home to people who deserved better.

My family had fled the island for the United States in 1967, when they ran afoul of the Duvalier regime. Until then, my family was close to those who terrorized Haiti. My forebears' most public declaration of fealty came in 1963, when one of my relatives, Doctor Jacques Fourcand, stood before the dictator himself in Port-au-Prince and delivered the speech of his life.

My great-uncle Jacques was Duvalier's personal physician and longtime friend, as well as the president of the Haitian Red Cross. But that day, with a pistol on his hip, the good doctor was threatening carnage. In a peroration delivered in impeccable French, he warned the international community that if anyone tried to prevent Duvalier from staying in power, the regime would lay waste to Haiti:

> Blood will flow in Haiti like a river. The land will burn from the north to the south, from the east to the west. There will be no sunrise and no sunset, just one great flame licking the sky. There will be a Himalaya of corpses, the dead will be buried under a mountain of ashes. It will be the greatest slaughter in history.

The crowd cheered; conch shells sounded. When Jacques had finished, Duvalier rose and hugged him. It was the doctor's finest moment, the pinnacle of his public life. Later, Jacques would fall into disgrace when he was suspected of plotting against Duvalier, prompting my family's hurried departure from Haiti.

Jacques had rehearsed this frightening speech in front of his cousin's teenage children in their family home. I know this because one of those children was my mother, who was then thirteen. As her older siblings applauded, my mother hesitated. She was well acquainted with the tumultuous world of Haitian politics. On an election day a few years earlier, she had gone to the polls with her mother and a senior regime official. As onlookers cheered, she, a child, was given a ballot and cast her vote—for Duvalier, of course, who was about to win another rigged election. Now she wasn't so sure about it all; her uncle's harsh, threatening words made her uneasy.

I picture my mother in the house on Ruelle Waag, her brothers and sisters rapt as the man they called Uncle Jacques rehearsed his lines. I see in her misgivings a nascent awareness of right and wrong, a distaste for violence acquired in the years after she cast her first ballot. It is in that hesitation that I see the seeds of who I am and what I have chosen to do with my life. My mother's moment of doubt created the possibility for her and her children to choose their own future, far from Jacques Fourcand's fire and brimstone. It was an intuition that another way existed.

The doctor's speech—forty-nine minutes, delivered without notes—was recorded by the West German embassy in Port-au-Prince, thanks to a microphone hidden in a flowerpot. A Red Cross diplomat later smuggled the recording out of the country. To this day, the Geneva-based International Committee of the Red Cross (ICRC) uses the speech as a case study in the failure of the Red Cross to uphold its values. The recording is posted on the ICRC website, along with a notice explaining that under my uncle Jacques's leadership, the Haitian Society of the Red Cross was expelled from the International Red Cross movement.

Jacques wasn't the only notorious member of my family. My great-grandfather General Champana Bernard was a ruthless fighter during Haiti's civil wars in the early twentieth century. He and his men battled *Caco* insurgents in the rugged mountains of the north. It was said that Champana ordered his troops to maim their prisoners, using their machetes to sever the tendons behind the knee so they couldn't fight ever again—a punishment similar to one meted out to runaway enslaved people more than a century earlier. As he was running for public office, the general was murdered, another victim of Haiti's long history of poisoning.

My family has dealt with its tumultuous history in different ways. My siblings, cousins, and I are Haitian Americans like any others, and we have largely moved on from the sins of our fore-fathers. But until her death in 2002 in Maryland, our grandmother would disapprove of any criticism of François Duvalier in her presence.

But in my family, there were also those who had the courage to push back, including Uncle Serge and Aunt Nelly. Uncle Jacques often acted as Serge's overbearing protector, but Serge refused to follow in his uncle's footsteps. After Serge failed his admission exams for medical school, Jacques abused his authority as dean of the college in Port-au-Prince and arranged for his nephew to start the next semester. Serge wanted no part of his uncle's plans and decided to take up the U.S. embassy's offer to study in America, an offer commonly extended to bright young Haitians.

Serge flatly rejected the corrupt system of patronage that his uncle represented. Undaunted by their country's trauma, Serge and Nelly were advocates for a more just system, and they inspired me to become a humanitarian worker.

So I come from two ways of looking at the world: as a place to be dominated and plundered, and as a place in need of uplift and succor. I've had a life of privilege, but I've also spent my life trying to solve problems of hunger and inequality. When I step into a taxi in New York City, any Haitian cabbie hearing my belabored, Frenchified Creole will immediately peg me as a member of the Haitian upper class—a predatory elite unwilling to recognize people's aspirations for something as simple as a square meal. Until our exile in 1967, my family was part of a political system that resulted in mass hunger, while Haiti itself has been the victim of a global system that has encouraged debt, dependence, and food deficits. When I joined the UN as a young man in 2001, I hoped to take on these problems and, perhaps, come to terms with my family's history.

The Duvalier regime's legacy is one of oppression, exile, poverty, and hunger. Graham Greene once wrote that he hoped that after Duvalier's tyranny, the country would be ruled by heroes, like the Jeune Haiti thirteen. It was not to be, and Haiti's slide into misrule and food insecurity continued.

The pattern of exploitation, alongside a dismal string of natural disasters, has brought Haiti to the brink again and again, right up to the present day. When Tropical Storm Jeanne dumped 13 inches of rain on Gonaïves in 2004, there were hardly any trees left on the hills above the city to slow the downpour. Terrifying mudslides tore through Gonaïves, flooding out 80,000 people, killing more than 3,000, and wiping out that season's rice crop. The January 2010 earthquake killed at least a quarter of a million people. In October 2016, Hurricane Matthew destroyed 80 percent of food crops in the south; in its aftermath, nearly 1 million people required emergency food aid.

In recent years, questions have begun to arise about the proliferation of foreign NGOs in Haiti, and to what extent their presence benefits Haitians. Why was local expertise not called on in the aftermath of the 2010 earthquake? Why was that relief effort so poorly managed? The American Red Cross raised an astonishing $500 million from the public for earthquake relief but achieved little—an investigation in 2015 showed that only six permanent houses had been built in the five years since the disaster. Once again, outsiders found a way to take advantage of the country, reinforcing the same narrative that has been playing out for centuries. Haiti's long and distressing history with foreigners—including humanitarians—reminds us that we need to always ask ourselves who really benefits from aid, and whether our intended help does harm.

We find echoes of Haiti's painful experience in other parts of the world. Ireland's nineteenth-century potato famine involved colonial rule, the exploitation of the rural poor, and mass emigration. After being pushed to open their markets to food imports in the 1990s, many other countries in the Global South have been flooded with the equivalent of Miami rice. Mexico, Nigeria, and Senegal now find themselves importing millions of tons of grain each year from America, Europe, or Asia. Just as in Haiti, local farmers were crushed; the collapse of smallholder farming contributed to hunger and migration.

As I write this in 2023, Haiti is spiraling out of control as armed groups bludgeon one another for control of the capital and the nation's prime farmland. Experts fear that Haiti is on the verge of becoming a failed state, a Somalia just seven hundred miles from Florida. Thousands of Haitians continue to board rickety sailboats and set out into the blue Caribbean, fleeing a familiar mix of civil strife and food shortages. Hunger's resurgence in Haiti is a symptom of deep-seated dysfunction, a mirror held up to a society that has, for generations, been unwilling and unable to look after its own.

Desert Blues

Generational Hunger in the Sahel

The food speculators live on us like fleas.

—Jacques Roumain, *Masters of the Dew*

In biological terms, food is fuel. When deprived of food, the human body initially taps into its existing stores, converting the fat around our organs or under our skin into glucose, a mechanism that early humans developed to make it through periods of famine. Humans can survive on reduced rations and their energy stores for weeks, entering a state called *ketosis* that can cause the lethargy and foggy state of mind that is familiar to dieters. When the body's fat stores are exhausted, it begins breaking down muscle protein into energy, leading to the "wasting" of body mass only seen in starving people. This is essentially the body digesting itself, redirecting what nutrients remain to the organs. Chronic diarrhea sets in, as the body lacks the vitamins and minerals needed for digestion. Protein and micronutrient deficiencies cause the skin to crack. Hair and nails become brittle. Hunger weakens the immune system and organ function. Ultimately, starving people die of disease or cardiac arrest.

In her memoir *The War*, the French novelist Marguerite Duras describes nursing her husband back to health when he emerged from the Bergen-Belsen concentration camp nearly dead from starvation. She could feed him only teaspoons of watery gruel, as the weight of food would have lacerated his stomach. His heart was beating so fast it was as though it were trembling in terror. As she writes, "He couldn't eat without dying. But he couldn't go on not eating without dying. That was the problem."

Death by starvation is an extreme phenomenon. A quarter of a billion people in 2023 suffer from acute hunger—when lack of food is life-threatening. Chronic hunger, when someone has just enough food to survive, but not nearly enough to thrive, affects more than 700 million people. This everyday want of food, and the malnutrition that follows, deforms bodies and minds in highly specific ways. When people eat the cheapest calories available, and don't have enough of high-quality foods that deliver essential nutrients, immediate and longer-term health problems result. For example, overreliance on corn causes pellagra, a skin condition that became a scourge in rural areas of Europe and the southern United States in the late nineteenth and early twentieth centuries. Exposure to long-term hunger also makes some diseases more likely—research has brought to light a correlation between food insecurity, high blood pressure, and diabetes. In young children, lack of food leads to stunted growth, and negatively affects brain development, resulting in cognitive deficits that can never be made up.

Of course, food is more than just fuel for the body. Hunger can devastate mental health; those who experience hunger describe suffering from anxiety and depression. Neuroscientists believe that long-term exposure to hunger can cause "toxic stress," a prolonged activation of the body's defenses that affects the very architecture of the brain. Researchers Mariana Chilton and Jenny Rabinovitch argue that exposure to toxic stress in childhood "may be the key to what fuels child food insecurity across generations." Children growing up in a food-insecure household are more likely to suffer from poor mental and physical health later in life, leaving them less able to find decent work and care for their own children. In other words, hunger's psychological impacts can be lifelong and generational.

Both acute and chronic hunger are especially rife in the West African Sahel, an arid belt of land between the sands of the Sahara and the savannahs. As I write in 2023, the area is a front line in the battle against global hunger. At least 20 million of its people require emergency food assistance every year, and malnutrition remains a leading cause of death for children. And unfortunately, the numbers keep rising. With its many countries, cultures, and colonial histories, the region offers a rich case study in the reasons for hunger and how it becomes entrenched.

As a young humanitarian worker, I was posted to the World Food Programme's office in Niger, before moving to nearby Mauritania and Guinea-Bissau. During those years I was an eager young aid worker as I learned the ropes of food assistance programs. I felt that every day I was helping thousands of people access the food they needed so much. I believed that solutions to hunger were in our grasp. I later worked as a roving advisor in Senegal until 2012, a role that took me to many remote corners of the Sahel, and made me witness the underlying forces that were slowly pulling increasing numbers of its people into hunger. By then it was clear to me just how difficult it would be for anyone to stem the tide of rising food insecurity in the Sahel.

The region's protracted battle with food scarcity and an increasingly hostile climate matters because it's a harbinger of a hunger nightmare to come, one that will affect us all. It is debated whether the region will remain habitable as our planet heats up. It is one of the areas most vulnerable to climate change, with temperatures forecast to rise by 3 to 5 degrees Celsius by 2050. With 80 percent of the region's land already degraded, the outlook is bleak. As our changing climate makes rainfall less predictable, the Sahel is the canary in the coal mine. Other nations of the arid tropics—in places like southern Africa or Central America—are watching the region closely, because they might be next.

Vladimir Lenin called war an "accelerator of history," a force that propels a nation toward its destiny. In the Sahel, the threat of drought has always been the black swan that can trigger famine and topple governments. In April 1974, with the country enduring another dry year, Niger's army staged a coup, ousting an unpopular and corrupt civilian government whose members had been accused of pilfering food aid. Similarly, Mauritania's army overthrew its president in 1984, after a severe drought that killed 75 percent of the country's livestock. Niger's army again deposed its president during the food crisis of 2010, and the doubling of grain prices in 2012 contributed to a coup in Mali. No wonder that in the Sahel, rainfall totals are watched as closely as the Dow Jones index.

During the 1970s and 1980s, rainfall in the Sahel was 30 percent below average. One of the worst droughts of the twentieth century, it decimated farming and herding. In fact, the drought of 1973 was so devastating that the people who experienced it still talk about it today in hushed tones. "That year," an older Senegalese colleague told me, "we ate what animals eat." He meant grass and bark; there were no alternatives.

The droughts of these years were especially painful for the Sahel's herdsmen. The trauma of the experience often intruded into my conversations with people who'd lived through those times. I was once working with a Mauritanian government official named Sid'Ahmed on the response to the 2003 drought, the worst in years. One morning, in his office, we were discussing the government's plans, which largely involved subsidizing cattle feed. Sensing I was curious about why the country was making such large investments to save the country's cattle, Sid'Ahmed told me that cattle were life; they needed to be saved, no matter the cost.

That day, over tiny cups of sweet mint tea, Sid'Ahmed proceeded to describe the harrowing journey he had taken thirty years earlier with his uncle, a herdsman. Sid'Ahmed was from Brakna, a southern part of the country east of the capital, Nouakchott, reached after navigating a hundred-mile-wide sea of undulating dunes.

Sid'Ahmed was a teenager in 1973, the summer he helped his uncle drive his cattle. That year, the rains had never made it to their hometown of Cheggar, so they marched the herd south in the hope of finding water and pasture. They even crossed into Senegal, but there was no water there either, so they turned around and headed back. By that point, the cows were so weak, Sid'Ahmed said, that he and his uncle had to physically prop them up. "If the weakest cows sat or fell on the trek home, we knew we would never get them to stand again. We spent weeks trying to get my uncle's cows home alive. It was a death march; I saw cow after cow die that year. We had left home with hundreds of cattle in the summer of 1973, and we came back with a dozen. My uncle was wiped out and lost his mind."

It is not surprising that Sid'Ahmed's uncle plunged into despair after seeing his cattle die, one after the other. In the Sahel's herding communities, a man's worth was measured in livestock. The herds trekked across great distances in search of water and grazing land, and the fresh milk they provided nourished the community. "I was born in milk," a colleague would say, referring to the abundance that had existed in his childhood. Livestock kept in this way were a source of generational wealth. They were admired, looked after, used to pay dowries, or ritually sacrificed at the Eid, but rarely sold for cash. Disdainful outsiders dismissed the nomads' management of their herds as "contemplative," a way of life that, at first glance, could seem idle, even unproductive.

The dry 1970s and 1980s profoundly disrupted herding. Until then, nomads had maintained large, mobile herds, while farmers focused on growing food crops, keeping a few livestock on their homesteads. Repeated droughts, and the hardening of national borders throughout the Sahel after independence in 1960 (which created distinct nation-states where none had existed), dealt a blow to the ancestral nomadic way of life.

All over the Sahel, the nomads seemed eternally mistrusted and misunderstood. Mistrusted because of their past as a ruthless warrior class that raided farming communities until the late nineteenth century. Misunderstood because their ways put them in a world apart. Nomads such as the Tuaregs, Moors, or Fulani are people who modern states always view with suspicion. How could anyone survive on just sweet tea and milk, as it seemed many nomads did? Was it not true that they craftily obtained identity papers in all the countries they set foot in, making their loyalties uncertain?

The governments of the Sahel eventually tried to settle the nomads near markets or wells. As a result, ramshackle encampments, dating back to the 1970s and 1980s, now line the roadways throughout the region. Because these communities lost their herds during the droughts, the generous flow of milk that once nourished them has dried up. Their descendants who've given up the nomadic lifestyle now buy cartons of ultra-pasteurized milk, or cans of milk powder, commonly imported from Europe. Often thickened with palm oil, these products offer nowhere near the nutritional value of fresh milk. But their importation into West Africa has only accelerated in the past ten years, as the region's nascent milk industry fails to keep pace with demand.

The herders of the Sahel were up against a force that has profoundly reshaped the land. I saw the scars in my travels for WFP as a young aid worker. Nguigmi, a town in eastern Niger, a bumpy three-day drive from the capital, is where the tarmac disappears into the Sahara. In front of the *sous-prefecture,* a dilapidated mud-walled building, a bleached elephant skull stands at the entrance for all to see. Back in the 1930s, a French administrator had bagged the creature, then left the trophy behind. The climate must have been much more humid. By the time I visited the town in 2001, the rains had retreated far to the south. The town was dust, thorn trees, and sand. There were many camels and donkeys, but the nearest elephants were hundreds of miles away, across an expanse of fine white sand that covered the area where the northern section of Lake Chad had once been.

Vast swaths of the Sahel have suffered a similar fate, losing their ability to sustain wildlife, crops, and perhaps, eventually, people. "See all this desert?" a seasoned French agronomist asked me, as we drove through an especially bleak stretch of Mauritania. "Put a fence around it, turn it into a park." The tongue-in-cheek comment hinted at a stark truth: the experts were doubtful this once-fertile land could ever again feed its people.

For all the energy experts devote to analyzing rainfall patterns and desertification, climate is only part of the story of the Sahel's struggle with hunger. Other less obvious factors that have nothing to do with drought are in play. A major one is population growth, a thorny issue that has been debated for hundreds of years.

Thomas Malthus, the eighteenth- and nineteenth-century English economist, feared that industrial Britain was destined for famine, disease, and war, the only mechanisms that could regulate the nation's "surplus" population. He advocated for population control, and questioned Britain's Poor Laws, which provided aid to deprived people and, in Malthus's view, irresponsibly encouraged people to have large families.

Malthus's grim scenario never came to pass in Britain: the

industrialization of agriculture led to robust food surpluses, and population growth eventually declined as contraception became widely available. In the academic community, Malthus became a figure of derision. One of the teaching assistants in an economics course I took at Harvard had named her dog Malthus; it was certainly not a compliment.

Most people know Charles Dickens's *A Christmas Carol* as a holiday parable, but when it was originally published in 1843, Scrooge was meant to be a scathing caricature of Malthusian theories about population control and thrift. The miser attempts to heat a freezing office with a single lump of coal, works by the light of a single candle, and lives on thin gruel. On Christmas Eve, he refuses to give money to a charity, saying of the poor: "If they would rather die . . . they had better do it, and decrease the surplus population." Scrooge embodied the Maltusian mindset of Victorian Britain, where the poorest were confined to squalid workhouses in exchange for meals. With the rise of organized labor in the late nineteenth century, Malthusian approaches were forgotten as government policies became less hostile to the working class.

In the 1960s and 1970s, something of a Malthusian revival occurred in the West. Books called *The Population Bomb* and *Limits to Growth* warned of impending food shortages. Again, the dark scenario did not come to pass, as agricultural production took off in Asia.

Today, fragments of Malthusian thought persist in the "degrowth" community. It challenges Western society's commitment to economic growth at any cost, and the waste, environmental damage, and social inequality it creates. Its radical members are sometimes derided, as Malthus was, as Scrooges who would deny others basic material comforts, such as air-conditioning, or hamburgers. And demographers are increasingly vocal about the imminent risk of population collapse in many countries, rather than about the risks of a global population explosion. But anyone looking at the Sahel's ongoing struggle with the twin forces of rapid climate change and population increase could be forgiven for thinking that there may be some merit to degrowth theories.

The aid community in the Sahel knows that tackling population growth represents a solution to the hunger, poverty, and instability in the region. To counteract the phenomenon, aid agencies are working to empower women. They have been championing girls' education, enabling access to family planning, and promoting economic opportunities for women. All over the Sahel, UN agencies have launched public information campaigns to change perceptions and make teenage marriages taboo. But in the region, as in many others, birth control remains a sensitive topic. To make matters worse, ongoing violence and political instability in the region has put some of this important work on the back burner. Until the Sahel addresses the root causes of hunger, much of the aid it receives will focus on responding to recurring food emergencies— like trying to put a Band-Aid over a gaping wound.

All over the world, resource scarcity and growing demand create opportunities for someone to make money. As the Sahel's population grows, and farming reaches its limits, more food than ever is being imported to feed the region. Enter the traders.

I met the wealthy millet trader that I'll call Mamane Kaka when I was on assignment in southern Niger to assess the impacts of the 2009 drought. Friendly and goateed, Mamane also had a well-deserved reputation as a shady character. When his scrapes with the law turned up in the local press, a local colleague of mine rolled her eyes and said, "He's just like his father. The thought of going to jail has never scared him."

Mamane plied many trades, but excelled at one: importing millet, Niger's staple food, a tall grass that produces long wands of golden grain. West Africans are thought to have domesticated the crop more than four thousand years ago. A summer crop, millet is tolerant of drought, heat, and poor soils, thriving where corn, rice, and wheat cannot. Even today when Niger's long-awaited first annual rains fall, people stop what they're doing to plant as much millet as they can in the wet soil. The habit is so hardwired that hardly a spot of ground goes unplanted. Even in the capital, Niamey, vacant lots or unpaved areas are turned into impromptu millet fields.

Until the early 2000s, Niger was able to feed itself if the rains came on time. But in the 2020s, if the annual rains start late, or end early, disaster awaits. Each October, at the end of the harvest, government experts anxiously tally up how much grain the country's farmers were able to produce and compare that amount to what the population needs. If the calculation shows a large deficit—and there is one nearly every year now—anxious bulletins are dispatched to the country's leaders. Prices start rising. This is when people like Mamane spring into action.

Mamane, a member of Niger's majority Hausa community, knows how to supply thousands of tons of millet every week. The Hausa have always been traders, heirs to a tradition that once spanned the Sahara. Through the nineteenth century, camel caravans from the Hausa city of Kano would regularly make expeditions to Tripoli, on the shores of the Mediterranean. This rich history left a legacy: the Hausa embraced Islam, and their language includes a smattering of loan words from Arabic, including numerals. Over the centuries, trips to Mecca allowed Hausa traders to develop networks that they were able to leverage for finance and long-distance commerce.

By the 1990s, Hausa grain traders like Mamane were applying their skills to secure Niger's food supply. They contended with—or, some might say, took advantage of—one major obstacle: the fact that Niger's main source of grain is located across the border in northern Nigeria. The French and British had drawn a border straight through the heart of Hausaland in the late nineteenth century, dividing communities that shared a language and history. Colonization and independence created two artificial entities with different governments, laws, and currencies—and disrupted a centuries-old trading network.

But people like Mamane knew how to operate on both sides of the border. Mamane would hedge against sudden fluctuations in the naira, the Nigerian currency, by moving funds and assets from one side of the border to the other. He used his family ties on both sides of the border to pull strings as needed. He had informants all over northern Nigeria's grain belt and in the wholesale markets of Niger, and he never missed a beat. Because he had his own trucks and warehouses, he was able to buy up millet when it was cheap after the harvest and sell it when prices rose six months later.

Mamane had mastered all the hacks for smuggling millet from Nigeria into Niger. When Nigeria banned millet exports in 2008, Mamane said, "I told my people to hide bags of millet under bags of beans in the trucks. It was still legal to export beans, so customs waved us right through."

Back in Niger, Mamane had to be careful. Trucks with foreign license plates get into trouble, so all of his trucks were registered in both countries. When they crossed from Nigeria into Niger, he simply removed the Nigerian plates and replaced them with Niger plates, without unloading the cargo. For stealth runs, Mamane used a blue Mercedes Benz Unimog, a truck with high clearance and four-wheel drive that could take the sandy back roads known only to locals, operating at night without headlights to avoid detection.

Mamane played the market with ease, like a video game. In drought years, the millet trade was especially lucrative, and people like him amassed fortunes. When prices spike in the dry season, some starving Nigeriens pay more for a pound of millet than a Westerner does for a pound of wheat flour at the supermarket. Sometimes double the price, during all-too-common seasonal shortages. Often, people borrow cups of precious grain at extortionate interest rates because they have no choice. They need to eat.

In the Sahel and many places like it, dysfunctional markets stoke food shortages. They keep families on the cusp of hunger, while making fortunes for traders and moneylenders. Markets that hurt the poor are one of the many systems that contribute to hunger in the Sahel and other regions. As the world has become more urbanized, more of us rely on fickle markets to feed ourselves than ever before. While the rich might shrug when the price of a staple food rises, for the poor, it can mean cutting down on meals.

The Sahel's unforgiving social structures mean that millions of people find themselves locked into generational inequality, land poverty, and food deprivation. An example is the Haratin caste of Mauritania, a Black population that had been enslaved by the ruling Moor group.

Mauritania was the last country in the world to abolish slavery. It did so in 1981, after a Haratin girl was put up for sale in a market in the northern town of Atar, causing an uproar, but legislation to criminalize slavery was only passed in 2007. Now, although slavery is illegal, to be born Haratin is tantamount to being sentenced to a lifetime of poverty and hunger. The Haratin may be nominally free—as were Black Americans in the Jim Crow era—but in practice, they still struggle to access land to grow crops or to secure anything other than menial jobs working the fields or driving cattle.

Not surprisingly, the burden of hunger in Mauritania falls on the Haratin. In 2004, I met a woman named Binta, a member of the caste. It was a tough year in southern Mauritania, but she was determined to survive. She and her children lived under a patched-up canvas tent by the dry Karakoro riverbed. They were struggling mightily to get by, and all too often, Binta had nothing to give her children for dinner. So she invented a routine to trick them into falling asleep on empty stomachs. "At night," she told me, "I gather the pots and pans, and build a fire. I pour out water into the large pot. I act just as though I am making dinner. And if my kids become suspicious and start asking me when dinner is ready, I snap at them and tell them: 'Quiet! Can't you see I am cooking?'" Only when the children had fallen asleep would Binta stop the show. She hoped that somehow, the next day, she might have the means to fix them a meal.

Because of their lesser status, Haratin communities farm only the poorest, most marginal land. One settlement I visited was little more than a cluster of ragged low tents, barely managing to scrape by on the rocky plateau south of Tidjika. Hidden in a fold in the barren landscape, the community survived thanks to a large natural depression that supports a few acres of beans, a crop that grows just fast enough to mature before the water is gone. The day I was there, entire families were busily tending the bean crop, which clung to the dark brown rocks like a carpet. Under the beating sun, men, women, and children were crouched over, trying to get rid of the aphids that were sucking the bean plants dry.

As hard as the Haratin work, they don't own the land. Customary law dictates that a share of their beans go to their former masters, the Moors. Confined to the poorest land, their crop devoured by insects, the profit from their labor confiscated because of feudal landholding arrangements, the Haratin community is stalked by hunger. It's an accepted fact of life in Mauritania that the Haratin should make do with dregs.

Caste is a powerful predictor of hunger in the Sahel. Gender is another. The burden of feeding a household falls squarely on the shoulders of overworked and undervalued women, many of whom live in extreme poverty. While men do support their families, they must often migrate for work, keeping them away from home for months on end. And polygamous marriages remain common in rural Niger, meaning that income from men is divvied up among different spouses. There is no fat, no protective cushion. All it takes is a stroke of bad luck—an illness, an accident, a drought—for an entire family to tip into hunger. In such a harsh risk-prone and unforgiving environment, it's no wonder so many young children are malnourished.

I first traveled to Niger in June 2000, to start a microfinance scheme for Trickle Up, an NGO headquartered in New York that gave $100 grants to women who ran small businesses. The sum doesn't sound like much, but in Niger, it could change someone's life: women in Niger lived in a world of microtransactions and microprofits, selling fried dough or fruits and vegetables on the sandy verge of Niamey's streets. They sometimes made less than a dollar a day, the meager sum somehow allowing a family to get by.

One day in front of Niamey's General Hospital, I met women who sold fruit, sitting on the ground, with small piles of mangoes arranged in front of them. There were two categories of vendors: the women, sitting on the ground, in the sun, and the men in their produce stands, in the shade. "If I were a man, I would be over there," one of the women told me softly, glancing at the men a few yards away. This gender hierarchy is present in virtually every aspect of Nigerien society. According to UNICEF, 76 percent of girls are married before age eighteen. Only 14 percent of women can read and write, compared to almost half of all men. Trickle Up was a first step toward helping these women deprived of opportunity. But the deck was stacked against them, and a $100 business grant only went so far.

Well before the sun rose each morning, while the air was still cool, a gang of sinewy women could be seen, some with babies strapped to their backs. They were hauling heavy buckets of gravel to central Niamey's construction sites. The gravel came from the dry riverbed, and needed to be hauled a mile uphill. At the riverbed, each woman would fill two enamel buckets with gravel. The two buckets were attached to a carrying pole. Having balanced the load across their shoulders, the women would slowly trudge up the hill to central Niamey, following one another in heavy silence. It looked like they were undergoing a form of punishment. The men in charge must have thought it not worth paying for an excavator and a truck for the job. Mercifully, the hauling stopped when the sun rose.

Such scenes were not meant to exist in twenty-first-century Niger. The country had once dreamed of propelling itself into modern consumerism. In 2000, I saw the imagined utopia on display at Niamey's outdoor national museum, where a rectangular white building stood—the "Uranium Pavilion," named in honor of the country's number one export. The 1970s exhibit featured a uranium-fueled future that never came to be. It stood unchanged, as if frozen in time. Inside the pavilion, there were pictures of the neatly laid out towns then being planned near the new mines. Niger's future was to include prefabricated homes, tennis courts, and supermarkets with brightly lit aisles. For a moment in the 1970s, when the price of uranium was booming, it all seemed possible: Niger was poised to vault into great wealth, like the countries of the Persian Gulf. New buildings went up in Niamey, and a wave of French expatriates moved in. But when new uranium deposits were discovered in Australia, the price of the mineral crashed. Niger's uranium mirage vanished into thin air.

Almost forty years ago, a large-scale experiment got under way in Niger, where the government was desperate to save its people from the advancing Sahara. Keita, an area in central Niger so desolate agronomists called it a "moonscape," would be where human beings stopped the desert in its tracks. In 1983, the initiative received substantial backing from donor countries, including Italy.

Under the firm leadership of the agronomist Renato Carucci, the Italians brought in bulldozers, graders, and tractors to refashion the desolate landscape. The project area covered four hundred villages, home to many of the lower caste. Wells were dug and dams were built. Hillside trenches were planted with trees to slow erosion. In all, more than 20 million trees were planted over the next twenty-five years. It wasn't all accomplished with machinery: much of the anti-erosion work was done by hand, by women wielding hoes and shovels. The workers recovered nearly 35,000 hectares of degraded land this way.

The aim of the Keita project was nothing less than terraforming the Sahel to make it habitable again. Although it's no oasis, Keita came alive, its landscape studded with sturdy, mature trees and its villages boasting granaries and gaggles of goats and sheep. The bottomlands were rich with dark soil, planted with tomatoes and onions. Its markets were busy with traders. People who knew the Keita of the 1970s told me that desperate communities had been brought back from the brink.

When I started working with WFP in Niger in 2001, however, the Keita project was already a faded glory. After almost two decades of support, the donors were pulling out. A sense of decay hung in the air. In the project's heyday, staff used to bump around the valley in boxy open-top Fiat Campagnolas, the Italian answer to the Jeep. Now, many of the vehicles sat idle at the project compound, covered in a thick coat of orange dust.

One day I headed out with a team to meet a group of women who had been working on one of Keita's land restoration sites. The women, from a caste of formerly enslaved Tuareg, were given WFP food as an incentive to participate; it would help tide them over until the next harvest. Work took place during the dry season, at a time when most able-bodied men had migrated. Food was distributed under the supervision of project staff.

At a nearby food distribution site, I saw women lined up to collect the rations they had earned. A frail-looking mother with a baby on her back had just received a few scoops of millet, beans, and oil. Keeping her head down to avoid eye contact, she cupped her hand and silently returned a measure of grain to the woman carrying out the distribution.

"Why did she give back part of her ration?" I asked the staffer who'd been showing me around. I had naively hoped that the women who had worked so hard planting trees would not have to share what they'd earned.

"It's to acknowledge that that woman is her master," he said, shrugging. "It's to thank her." He said the word *master* without a second thought; I was flabbergasted at the open acknowledgment of a social system with masters and slaves, in the twenty-first century.

Once again, caste mediated all aspects of life, even in this well-intentioned project to stop the desert. Keita was a society in which a caste of formerly enslaved people was struggling to survive on the economic and social margins, and Keita's bulldozers and graders had done nothing to dismantle this legacy of deep inequality.

In her book about the Keita project, *From Slavery to Aid,* Benedetta Rossi describes how former Tuareg masters in Keita continued to exert influence over the lower caste during the 2000s. Because of their subservient status, male members of the caste still paid hefty "ransoms" to their traditional masters to "buy back" their wives and daughters. Rossi describes the heavy burden that fell upon women, who worked on the erosion-control projects while caring for their families; they were often alone during the dry season as their husbands had migrated to Nigeria for work. The very structures that had caused poverty and hunger in

Niger were impeding the country's progress in addressing those ills. The landscape might have been healing, but the people were still suffering.

I t is apparent to all that the Sahel is locked in a hunger trap. In 2023, more than 40 million people were acutely food insecure in the Sahel and West Africa, a record number. To reverse the trend, think tanks in the West are calling for a long-overdue surge in investments in agriculture. In 2021, France's president Emmanuel Macron announced $14 billion in funding for the Great Green Wall, an attempt to plant trees from Dakar to Djibouti and create a living buffer against the Sahara. The funding is meant to reinvigorate the troubled project; it has made slow progress since its creation in 2007.

The Sahel does need much more investment in agriculture, especially for irrigation systems in this era of increasingly erratic rainfall. And, yes, planting trees will be of great benefit if communities are involved at the grassroots level. But it's not enough. Drought and desertification are but the tip of the hunger iceberg. All the wells, dams, and trees in the world won't feed anyone in the Sahel as long as its caste system and gender inequalities keep so many of its citizens on the margins of society.

Perhaps it's easier to plan and execute agricultural and forestry schemes on a large scale than it is to confront deeply entrenched social inequality, or challenge rigid systems in need of change. In the Sahel, and in other parts of the world, food insecurity should be recognized and addressed as the social justice issue that it is. The fact is that extreme poverty and inequality lie at the root of the region's tenacious hunger. Ensuring opportunity for all, including women and people of lower caste, is the battle the societies of the Sahel urgently need to wage.

3

To Deal with the Devil
The Global Rush to Grab Land

And farmers, are there farmers like us, over there?

—Jacques Roumain, *Masters of the Dew*

Nations have always needed to control food supplies to wage war, seal alliances, and punish rivals. "Grain was to antiquity what oil is to the world today," wrote the historian Lionel Casson. "Few of the larger cities of the Mediterranean could rely solely on what was grown locally, most were compelled to eke this out with purchase from these favored lands that had a surplus."

Ancient Rome relied almost exclusively on wheat shipped from overseas. From the days of the republic through those of the empire, each Roman man was entitled to a free ration of wheat. This "grain dole" was key to preserving peace in the capital. Each spring, hundreds of ships, large and small, would sail from Italy to Egypt, the empire's breadbasket. The vessels hugged the coast, taking as few as six days to sail from Ostia to Alexandria, and weeks or even months to come back in the summer, laden with precious grain. During the winters, when the weather made the seas unnavigable, Rome's wheat supplies dwindled; in some years, famine loomed. The philosopher Seneca described the excitement that would sweep Italy when the year's first wheat vessels from

Alexandria were sighted off Pozzuoli, near Naples. "The Campanians are glad to see them," he reported. "All the rabble of Puteoli [Pozzuoli] stand on the docks." The arrival of the fleet heralded freedom from hunger until the next winter.

Rome's addiction to Egyptian wheat had wide-ranging political consequences. A period of political instability in Egypt that compromised the vital wheat shipments pushed Julius Caesar's legions to invade the country. After this land grab, Egyptian agriculture flourished, and the province provided as much as a third of all of Rome's wheat. The wheat supply chain was so important to the ancient Romans that it had its own goddess, Annona, who was represented on coins as a woman holding ears of grain, with ships in the background.

Concerns about high prices and scarcity may make the world's great powers just as protective of their food supply as the Romans once were. A global land rush is on, as nervous nations scramble to acquire farmland abroad. Geopolitical tensions in Ukraine and the Middle East are only adding to the trend.

There is a clear pecking order in the geopolitics of food. At the top are the major food exporting nations (the United States, Argentina, Brazil, Australia, Canada, France, Russia, and Ukraine). In the second tier are the rich food importers, such as the countries of the Persian Gulf or South Korea, who can afford to pay when prices rise. Third are poor but self-sufficient countries, such as India, Uganda, the Democratic Republic of Congo, and Tanzania, who might become food importers in a few years because of population and economic growth. And finally, at the lowest rung, are the poor and chronically import-dependent nations that can't afford higher prices, such as Yemen and Haiti. These last two groups are urgently seeking to develop their domestic agriculture, even if it means signing away rights to large swaths of their farmland to unscrupulous investors.

In November 2008, the *Financial Times* broke a startling story that made it obvious the world was entering uncharted waters. The South Korean company Daewoo Logistics had acquired a mind-boggling 3 million acres of land on the island nation of Madagascar to grow corn and palm oil for export. The deal was a ninety-nine-year, no-cost lease that covered an area as large as Belgium. Madagascar had just signed away the rights to half of its arable land to a foreign corporation.

Daewoo made no attempt to hide its motives: it was securing South Korea's food supply for decades to come. Hong Jong-wan, a manager at Daewoo, put it starkly: "Food can be a weapon in this world. We can either export the harvests to other countries or ship them back to Korea in case of a food crisis."

The people of Madagascar were baffled by the decision to hand over such a large share of their nation's land to foreigners. Shock turned to anger and, a few months later, the president of Madagascar and his government were thrown out of office.

Daewoo's land acquisition in Madagascar, and a flurry of similar deals involving other entities purchasing land in Ethiopia, Mali, and Sudan, occurred in the aftermath of the 2007–2008 global food crisis. A "super spike" in commodity prices led to spiraling food costs the world over. A sense of alarm spread as food riots broke out across the world, and experts whispered among themselves about which fragile government the crisis would topple first.

As policymakers scrambled to find solutions, savvy investors scrambled to secure farmland. In 2009 alone, buyers expressed interest in acquiring more than 140 million acres of farmland in Africa, Latin America, and Asia—an area larger than all of the corn and wheat fields in the United States combined. Many of these deals took place in nations facing food shortages. When governments approve these contentious land acquisitions, they rarely publicize them, probably because of the fraught trade-offs they involve. Moneyed, often foreign interests push out struggling farmers for their own gain—but in return, they provide sorely needed investments, like irrigation infrastructure, that could help nations become self-sufficient in the long run.

As one-sided land acquisitions continue, we have to ask: Who is benefiting from them? Is it ever fair to sacrifice small farmers today to feed future generations?

Whether they are exploited by an international conglomerate or by local elites, the losers in this land rush are the people who subsist on the world's 500 million family farms. More than 2 billion people—nearly one in three humans on the planet —depend on small farms, typically established on fewer than five acres. And they produce one-third of the world's food. Many smallholder farmers live on $2 a day or less, and experience hunger themselves, their farms being too small or not productive enough to reliably feed a family.

Do these farms have a future, as private investors buy up more and more land? It's easy to be nostalgic for a fantasy of small-scale family farming, which is, in reality, a harsh and grinding existence. But we should be concerned about what the crowding out of small farmers by private interests might mean for food security. And we should all be worried about the trend's potential to ignite violence.

t is hard to overstate the shock that the 2007–2008 global food crisis inflicted on food-importing countries. For decades, global markets had been deceptively stable, as large food stockpiles in the European Union and the United States kept prices in check. After World War II, the United States did everything it could to make the hardships of wartime food rationing a distant memory. In the UK, rationing of bread continued into 1948, and many foods, including sugar and meat, were rationed until 1954. These countries modernized their agricultures, replacing farmhands with machines that dramatically reduced the amount of labor needed to grow grain. They also provided generous subsidies to farmers to incentivize them to grow as much food as possible. Production soared, and, by the 1970s, "lakes of milk and mountains of butter" had accumulated. In the 1990s, the West pressured developing countries to open their markets to food imports, to help absorb the glut.

The West's surpluses ushered in an era of low global food prices that for a long time looked like a win-win arrangement: as Western farmers produced more and more food, newly independent countries could easily afford to import the surpluses. Flows of cheap food from abroad—whether as commercial imports or food aid—were a safety net of sorts for the developing world. Imports of low-quality foods, like the rice that flowed from Florida into Haiti, became common in some countries. In Senegal, one of the largest rice-import markets in the world, people have developed a taste for broken rice, a by-product commonly used in Asia for brewing or animal feed. It is perfectly healthy and tastes just like regular rice, but it is sold at a price point that the nation's price-sensitive consumers can afford.

For a time, rock-bottom food prices were a boon for food-importing countries, even as they hurt local farmers and stunted local agriculture. But the comforting illusion that the international market would forever provide a manna of cheap grain was obliterated when food prices skyrocketed.

Times have changed: we are now in a "risk society," a term coined by German sociologist Ulrich Beck in the 1980s following the Chernobyl disaster, which meant that society's choices were coming home to roost in unpredictable and disruptive ways. I would argue we now live in a "food-risk society," where ongoing problems like climate change, market failures, or pandemics expose our supply to critical disruption. The global food crisis of 2008 made it plain that past overreliance on food imports was short-sighted, corrosive, and dangerous.

Land grabbing is a reaction to the mounting risks that now pervade the global food system. Lester Brown, of the Earth Policy Institute, fears that global food scarcity looms. The world's population has doubled since 1970, and demand for food is escalating rapidly. We need to feed 80 million more people each year. Rising standards of living in many parts of the world are increasing demand for eggs, dairy, poultry, and meat—and for the grain needed to feed all the livestock. At the same time, some of the world's largest producers are increasingly using grain to make fuel that fuels cars, trucks, and buses.

Supply is also at risk as the world warms. Agronomists warn that each degree Celsius rise in temperature will reduce grain yields by 10 percent. We have seen how devastating a warmer climate can be for food production: the 2010 drought in Russia caused a 40 percent drop in wheat production that year.

Brown worries that artificial and unsustainable "water-based food bubbles"—food-production systems that rely on overdrawing water reserves—are ready to pop. After putting in place a farming system that relied on the overdrawing of water from nonrenewable sources, Saudi Arabia was briefly producing enough grain to feed itself. It was a mirage, however: after a few years, the nation was forced to ban domestic wheat production to protect its aquifers. Similarly, hundreds of millions of people in arid parts of India and China rely on water-based food bubbles, the collapse of which will put additional strain on tight global food markets.

To make matters worse, as the war in Ukraine has made clear, belligerents are now ready to weaponize the supply chains that feed the world by seizing farmland and attacking key grain export ports.

The upshot is that there is now much more risk in the food system than in previous decades. As Brown explains, "From the mid-twentieth century until 1995, the United States had either grain surpluses or idle cropland that could be planted to rescue countries in trouble. When the Indian monsoon failed in 1965, for example, President Lyndon Johnson's administration shipped one-fifth of the U.S. wheat crop to India, successfully staving off famine. We can't do that anymore; the safety cushion is gone." It is this context of risk and high stakes that explains why a global land rush is on.

The land acquisitions have proven to be political lightning rods that aggravate social tension. In 2007–2008, when food prices shot through the roof, experts I met when I was an analyst for WFP worried about a neo-communist revolution in fragile countries. The subsequent land grabs that resulted in mass dispossession of land may have the same effect. "Few things are more likely to fuel insurgencies than taking land from people," Brown notes.

When supply chains fail, rich food-importing countries are able to get creative to avoid shortages. In 2017, Qatar, a gas-rich Gulf emirate that imports 90 percent of its food, flew in four thousand dairy cows from Germany after Saudi Arabia put it under a trade blockade. But countries like Haiti, Yemen, or Liberia have fewer options; they can't dial up a food airlift when they need one.

I had been working in the West African Sahel for seven years when the global food price crisis hit in 2008. Until then, my work had involved implementing food assistance programs: I'd set up cereal banks in Niger, supported rice farmers in Mauritania, and delivered school meals in Guinea-Bissau. As global food prices spiked in 2008, WFP thought I would be a good fit as a market analyst in our bureau in Dakar, Senegal, and I jumped at the chance. I'd spend the next years wrangling data and helping others understand the relationship between markets and hunger.

In 2008, I flew from Dakar to Monrovia in Liberia for one of my first assignments in my new role. The country, which had relied on food imports for decades, was especially affected by the crisis, and the international community was concerned for the fragile peace in the country. The capital had been slowly emerging from a years-long war, its dark, potholed streets patrolled by squads of silent UN soldiers. Postwar Liberia spent half its GDP on food and fuel imports, making it uniquely vulnerable to the impact of the unfolding crisis.

My job in Liberia involved working on a UN team to estimate the impact of the food crisis on the population. We organized surveys in Monrovia and analyzed what economic and social data was available. Although it was my first visit to Monrovia, the city felt strangely familiar. Perhaps it was the Liberians' soft accents, which sounded like those I heard in the southern United States, a vestige of African American migration in the nineteenth century. Maybe it was the names of its neighborhoods, with "Virginia" to the north, near the sea, and "New Georgia" to the east. Or it might have been the town's hulking, columned Masonic temple, which looked like those in my native Washington, D.C.

The parallels ended there. The country was reeling from the crisis, and what rice remained was being hoarded like gold. Its cost had gone up by 40 percent, slamming an impoverished population that had recently lived through cycles of violence and displacement.

I visited the sprawling market at Red Light, a district on the outskirts of town that got its distinctive name from the traffic signal there. Crowds of enterprising teenage boys sold imported rice by the cup out of beat-up wheelbarrows. Realizing that they could not increase the price of a cup without losing their cash-strapped customers, the wheelbarrow boys turned to trickery to protect their profits. The subterfuge was simple: the boys tampered with the tin cans they used to scoop and measure out the rice, carefully hammering in the bottoms of the cans to reduce their volume. The customers shelled out the same amount of money but took home less food. Monrovia's people were already struggling; with food prices high, many were so poor they could only afford to buy one meal at a time

The rice import business was organized in a way that reflected—and contributed to—Liberia's position at the lowest rung of the global economic order. A small group of international trading companies, many operating from Switzerland, called the shots. Unlike their Liberian counterparts, the traders had access to the financing needed to arrange to import a cargo of rice—at a marked-up price. The Swiss traders purchased the rice from Asia in advance of any orders and shipped it to West Africa. The vessels waited off the coast, poised to call at the port that offered the most profitable trade. Once the ship had docked, the traders' agents sold the rice to local distributors, who paid in cash. The Liberian distributors would truck the rice to markets like Red Light. And from there, it would find its way into countless beat-up wheelbarrows and dented tin cans. This convoluted arrangement was far from unique to Liberia; the Swiss rice traders also held sway in Guinea, Senegal, and Côte d'Ivoire.

In May 2008, the Liberian rice dealers of Monrovia patiently worked their phones in their smoky, windowless downtown offices. They knew that as surely as global prices had spiked, they would sooner or later tick down. And they suspected that even in those tense days, international traders would offer stocks of rice—from South America or perhaps Myanmar—that could be brought in and sold at a price low enough for their price-sensitive customers and acceptable to the ever-watchful government.

As the months went by, domestic rice stocks continued to dwindle, and just as consumers at the market were buying food hand to mouth, Liberia itself was importing just enough to keep going.

Although outright shortages were averted, price increases seriously harmed the poorest Liberians, many of whom were spending most of their budget on food. Many cut down on meals, or switched to cheaper foods, replacing fish and vegetables with a monotonous and nutritionally poor diet of "butter" rice—a cheap Chinese variety eaten with a dollop of margarine—or plain cassava. The assessment I worked on in Monrovia concluded that "severe" food-insecurity levels doubled in the capital during 2008, from 4 to 8 percent of families.

But as is true the world over, the city had two economies. While the poorest Liberians starved, those who could afford it—mainly expats and a few wealthy locals—dined at one of two new air-conditioned sushi bars, where Filipinos in black robes served raw marlin. In May 2008 the expat community in Monrovia was abuzz with talk about a *Washington Post* article that pointed out that the cost of a meal for two at these sushi bars easily exceeded the monthly salary of most Liberians. The expats I met there were uneasy. They found the obvious inequity awful and guilt-inducing, but also seemed paralyzed about how to help. The jarring juxtaposition of starvation and sushi reflected what was going on worldwide: in 2008, consumers in the West shrugged off the global price increases, while in poor countries they were a matter of life or death.

The Liberian authorities were under pressure to do something, *anything*. The situation in 2008, unfortunately, felt too familiar—in 1979, an ill-advised, government-mandated rice price increase had triggered riots, events that marked the opening act of the civil war, from which Liberia was only just recovering. Everyone hoped that a similar outcome would be avoided.

In 2008, at a public rally, the government unveiled a plan to respond to the crisis. It was held at the Samuel K. Doe Stadium, an aging Chinese-built venue in Paynesville, just outside Monrovia. Large banners that read "Eat What You Grow, Grow What You Eat" hung outside in the blazing sun. The people attending the event had been given white T-shirts that read "Back to the Soil" in bold green letters. Inside the stadium, a slate of officials spoke, proclaiming to the cameras that Liberia would weather the food crisis. They solemnly called on the nation's farmers to grow more food locally. And they called on Liberians to eat more local food.

The rally was meant to convince Liberians that their leaders were doing what they could to address the emergency. The government also announced it had temporarily lifted taxes on rice imports and taken other measures to contain price increases. But the reality was grim: aside from symbolic measures, there was little anyone could do to counteract the powerful forces that had compromised the nation's food supply—volatile international food markets, and decades of underinvestment in local agriculture.

It is well known that what goes up must come down, and although they never said so openly, the government of Liberia chose to simply wait out the crisis. Liberia and other food-import-dependent nations let out a collective sigh when rice prices came off their midyear peaks in the fall of 2008 as that year's harvest came in.

After the crisis, though, the Liberian government was spooked—in 2009, they signed over a chunk of land to a multinational that promised to farm it. When I returned to Monrovia that year on another assignment in the country, the rumor mill was buzzing with stories about Sime Darby, a Malaysian company that had signed a sixty-three-year lease for a whopping 220,000 hectares of land. Sime Darby announced that it would invest more than $3 billion over fifteen years—almost double Liberia's GDP at the time. It seemed that Sime Darby meant business: when passing their office in town, I saw a row of shiny green John Deere combine harvesters lined up out front.

But those who hoped the investment would boost local rice production were set up for disappointment. The government had agreed that Sime Darby would grow palm oil for export. The venture would not increase the food supply in the country. Then, in 2020, Sime Darby pulled out of Liberia, citing lackluster financial results. The task of growing food crops would remain a chore left to the country's small farmers.

Liberia is lush and green and has plenty of arable land. The nation ought to be able to feed itself. The cruel irony—or dirty secret—that explains why Liberia's agriculture has never taken off is that in Monrovia's markets, rice imported from Asia is still cheaper than the rice produced by local farmers. The reason for this paradox is that Asia's rice-exporting countries consistently support their politically influential farming cooperatives with public spending and tax breaks, while Africa's stunted supply chains and infrastructure make it difficult to sell local rice at a profit. Under such conditions, why would any farmer in Liberia bother growing any food at all?

As long as the international trading system remains stacked against Liberia and countries like it, they will find it hard to feed themselves. "Pity the nation that wears a cloth it does not weave, eats a bread it does not harvest, and drinks a wine that flows not from its own wine-press," wrote the Lebanese poet Kahlil Gibran. Such nations are at the whim of fickle markets and unscrupulous intermediaries, never fully in control of their destiny.

One of the most controversial cases of land grabbing was Libya's acquisition of a massive swath of Mali's best farmland in 2008. In early 2010, I saw the impacts of this deal firsthand when I traveled to Niono, a struggling farming community a few hours' drive east of the capital, Bamako. The town is at the heart of the Office du Niger, a struggling agricultural district that is largely a pancake-flat, barren landscape of cracked, dry rice pad-dies, crisscrossed by empty water channels. The people there lived in squat, windowless mud-and-wattle houses. With water, this arid land could flourish again, but it was the dry season, and the area was temporarily a dust bowl.

I met a group of four Malian elders in a nearby hamlet. They sat in a row in the shade of a low wall, their keffiyehs and ample robes protecting them from the dust. Their expressions were grim and their words bitter. Their farmland had just been sold to investors from Muammar Gaddafi's Libya, and it wasn't clear they'd get any compensation. In 2008, the presidents of the two countries had launched the Malibya project, a joint venture between Mali and Libya's sovereign wealth fund, the legal entity the Libyan state uses to invest abroad. The project covered an enormous 100,000 hectares—an area larger than Singapore or Bahrain. The Malian government conceded the land for fifty years, free of charge, and it included water rights.

The deal had been done over the elders' heads. They were furi-ous at their leaders who'd signed away their land. "We will go and find them in Bamako," one of the elders declared. "We will bring our axes," he added ominously.

Libya's motives were clear: like many other arid nations, it des-perately needed to secure farmland abroad to feed its people. For the Libyans, Mali's Office du Niger was a natural place to stake a claim for land. Mali was a friendly country where the land was going begging. Through the Malibya deal, Libya had secured a potentially productive slice of the Office, a region that stretches from the Niger River nearly as far as the border with Mauritania, more than a hundred miles to the north. The area's slope is such that it could be entirely irrigated without pumps: an agronomist's dream. The Libyans intended to build the infrastructure needed to turn this dusty corner of the Sahel into verdant acres of rice.

On hearing news of the deal, Malian activists immediately castigated the government for selling out the country's prime land to Libyans, who, they argued, were sure to put rice on cargo planes back to their own country while Malians starved.

Not only did the deal with Libya ignite hostility from the farmers it displaced, it was also controversial among Mali's agricultural experts. I saw this when I attended a meeting that the UN had called to discuss the situation. The conversation quickly turned to the Malibya project, and the experts began to spar. A hydrologist in a kufi cap reminded everyone present that the Niger River didn't flow as it once had. "Water has become scarce," he said. "If the Libyans ever try to irrigate all that land, we all know there will not be enough water for everyone, especially in the dry season when the river is low." Many of his peers nodded. Questions flew: How would the water be shared? Would family farmers stand a chance, or would the deep-pocketed Libyans outbid them for the water they needed?

Water was the key concern for everyone around the table that day. *Aman, iman* is a Tuareg saying often quoted in Mali and throughout the Sahel. It means "Water is life." The fact that there might not be enough water for everyone after the Libyans took their share struck a powerful emotional chord.

Others in the room that day disagreed. "We all know the Libyans won't take the canal they have promised to build back to Libya," said an official from the Ministry of Agriculture. "We have been waiting a long time for this." A heavy silence fell over the room: the truth had finally been spoken. A deal was needed for the greater good—Mali's long-term food supply. Foreign investors would be handed a large slice of prized farmland so that they could make the investments Mali couldn't.

The Malibya deal raised a host of conundrums and trade-offs that many other land-rich but food-insecure countries now face. In Mali, the government granted foreigners prime farmland at a time when more than a quarter of Malian families didn't have enough to eat, and when nearly 40 percent of children were chronically malnourished. The deal would displace thousands of farming families, and compensation arrangements were unclear.

It looked as though a community of small farmers was being sacrificed, their hopes dashed, their needs ignored, displaced in the name of progress and to enable—it was hoped—a food-secure future. Perhaps the authorities thought it would all be worth it in fifty years, when the Malibya concession lapsed. But for now, the deal suggested that hunger in Mali was a problem so deep-rooted as to be beyond immediate resolution. It was a tacit admission that the country could not possibly feed its citizens and develop agriculture at the same time. The lack of transparency about the deal also led to whispers about corruption. Although no evidence of fraud ever came to light, there was a sense that it would be easy for a leader to turn over his people's prime farmland in exchange for a large enough bribe.

These issues were never openly debated—and they would never be resolved, because the Malibya project was soon in trouble. At the time of the Arab Spring in 2011, civil war broke out in Libya, and Gaddafi was toppled. All work on the Malibya project stopped, and the Libyans went home, never to return. Amadou Toumani Touré, the Malian president who had signed the contract, was himself overthrown in 2012. All that was left of the project were fading roadside billboards and crumbling infrastructure. While the local farmers are now back in their fields, the collapse of the Malibya project is cold comfort: they know unscrupulous outsiders can take their land at a moment's notice.

After years of seeing land grabs happen again and again—at the expense of local farmers—I was curious to meet the people who worked the land after it was sold. When I worked in Congo for WFP from 2017 to 2020, I got to know a group of South African farmers who had decided to move there. While their arrival caused disruption, they turned out to be a far cry from the stereotype of big corporate interests I had in mind. It seemed I had stumbled on an exception to the exploitative narrative about land grabbing that unfolded elsewhere in Africa.

Fred Daly and his associates were white commercial farmers who were looking for opportunity abroad. Since the end of apartheid, South Africa's white farmers have been at the center of a politically charged debate about control over the nation's farmland. Since 1994, the South African government had been redistributing farmland by purchasing it from willing whites and selling it to Black Africans. But the policy has left many farmers unsatisfied: Black South Africans think the process is too slow, while white South Africans find it hard to acquire land in their own country. Short of options at home, some white commercial farmers began leasing land in other parts of Africa. Congo needed expertise and capital, while the South Africans needed land. A match was made, and ultimately thirty farmers joined Daly in Congo, creating a company called Todi River Farms.

In late 2011, an advance party of ten South Africans arrived with a convoy of four trucks and seven vans, having made the long, rough drive north through Namibia, Angola, and the Democratic Republic of Congo. When they reached the Congolese border, authorities gave them a hero's welcome: a succession of besuited officials made flowery speeches as cameras rolled. The celebrations took Daly by surprise. After all, he and his associates were there to farm, not to hobnob.

Daly was there because Congo imports more than two-thirds of its food. During the decades following independence in 1960, the country became a crude oil exporter. Oil revenue allowed Congo to import whatever it needed, including food, leaving its domestic farming sector stunted and archaic. Similarly to other developing countries in 2008, when food prices spiked, the Congolese government brought in outsiders to develop the country's agriculture. Authorities conceded 40,000 hectares of land to the South African farmers, who planned to grow corn and soybeans in the south's fertile Niari valley and sell them locally. The concession was granted on the condition the South Africans farm the land.

I visited Daly on his farm, which was based on an abandoned estate that the French had set up almost a hundred years earlier near the village of Malolo II. In the 1940s, French colonists had attempted to grow jute, a fiber crop, in the area. The project never lived up to expectations and was soon shut down, the land reverting to wilderness. Decades later, the South Africans set themselves up in the stone houses the French colonists had built. The one Daly occupied, on a ridge high above the valley, enjoyed a spectacular view of the wide Niari river basin below.

Daly saw Congo as a land of opportunity. "They need every foodstuff you can imagine. They are paying huge prices for imported food. The market is there. And of course you've got two rainy seasons, so if you are planting grains, you've got double the potential you have in South Africa." Daly had grand plans to develop a commercial farm in Malolo II, a tiny community of just a few hundred people. Getting there involves traversing a forested gorge on an unpaved track. Life there is slow—subsistence farming, a one-room elementary school, and not much else. There is no running water or electricity. Just beyond the village are the gates to the South African farmers' base.

Inevitably, the arrival of the South Africans created tension. As was true of the local people in Mali and Madagascar, those who held customary land rights in the area had not been consulted.

When the South Africans moved in, the people of Malolo II lost access to land they had used for hunting and foraging. To make matters worse, some of the village's sacred sites were located on the concession. Thankfully, with the help of the NGO Cercle des Droits de l'Homme et du Développement, a dialogue took place.

Alvin Koumbhat, a coordinator for the local NGO, recalled how Todi River Farms began to engage with the community. "The locals said, 'You have a camp for your workers. That camp is electrified, yet our whole village is in darkness.'" Todi River Farms agreed to provide solar panels to households. They drilled a well in the village, built a health center, and provided jobs on the farm. The commercial farmers and community found common ground.

What Daly and his companions achieved in their corner of southern Congo was startling. They converted a vast acreage of African savannah into a flat landscape of endless parallel furrows that looked a lot like Kansas. They brought in tractors that they could control remotely by GPS, even when they were in Cape Town. Their farm covers a few thousand hectares, a common size for a commercial operation in South Africa, but which dwarfs other farms in Congo. The day I was there, I could see thousands of tons of corn from the previous harvest stuffed into horizontal silos that spread out like linked sausages.

Getting started had not been easy. People tend to assume that the land in Congo is fertile, but Daly and his team discovered otherwise: they had to bring in tons of lime to reduce the acidity of the soil and make it suitable for farming corn. Their initial harvests were disappointing, and morale was low. Dangerous dry spells slashed yields, while bureaucracy meant that critical supplies such as spare parts and fertilizer—items that could not be bought in Congo—spent months at the port waiting to clear customs.

Daly explained that farming in Congo is not for everyone. Some of the men who came with him from South Africa in 2011 had dreamed of instant riches: "The ones who came thinking they'd make a quick buck are all gone," he told me. Those who remain are committed to hard work, and to creating a farm that would succeed over the long term. "The key here is to develop your market," Daly told me. Over the years he had patiently woven a web of customers—the local mill, the emerging poultry industry—

building a roster of reliable local partners. While the South Africans' arrangement in Malolo II was unequal and problematic, this was not the exploitative project that I had feared.

While the ethics of land grabbing are always murky, the investors behind these deals come in different stripes. International conglomerates like Daewoo, who repatriate foods across oceans, are one type of actor. Daly and his fellow farmers, who found a way to coexist with their host community and who are helping a local farming ecosystem emerge, are another.

Governments of the Global South, short of options, are making deals with shady entities that could transform their nations' agriculture in the short term, in the hope of an ultimate redemption. For a few decades, some of their land will be under foreign control, but will thereafter revert to the nation, improved with infrastructure and technology.

One thing is clear: many hunger-prone nations urgently need investments in agriculture. Unless their farming systems become more productive, they will face the full force of the devastating food crises that a changing climate makes more likely. Unless they boost their food supply, they will have no choice but to go on bended knee to those reigning over the new geopolitics of food—nations with surpluses to sell, or private companies with the financial capacity to arrange imports.

These governments don't want to be victims. But if they intend to survive politically, they will need to find a way of building up their farming systems without dispossessing their own citizens.

4

Starving in a Land of Plenty

Misrule and Greed in the Central African Republic

You don't have to invite misfortune in. It comes anyhow
and sits at your table without permission. It eats and leaves
nothing but bones.

—Jacques Roumain, *Masters of the Dew*

An hour before midnight, on December 31, 1965, a young Central African colonel named Jean-Bédel Bokassa led an army coup to overthrow his own cousin. "Reasons of State prevail over family reasons," he would later say dismissively. Bokassa, who had once been an officer in the French army, would remain in power until 1979. He was a vain man: he once ordered his uniform strengthened to support the weight of all the medals he had given himself. But being a seven-star general and president for life was not enough, and in 1977, he chose to crown himself Bokassa the First, Emperor of the Central African Empire.

By virtue of his military service, Bokassa held French citizenship. He looked up to Napoleon, perhaps because he, like the French emperor, had risen from obscurity to take the reins of his country. His coronation in the capital, Bangui, was modeled after Napoleon's in 1804, and it was an extravagant affair. A crown of gold and ermine was ordered from a jeweler outside Paris. The towering, eagle-shaped imperial throne, made of gold, bronze, and red velvet, weighed three tons. Bokassa rode to the ceremony in a gilded carriage drawn by a team of eight white horses that had been flown in from France for the occasion. Like Napoleon, he wore a Roman robe and gilded wreaths and carried a six-foot silver scepter. A detachment of Hussars—cavalrymen in ornate uniforms and tall, plumed busbies—escorted the newly crowned monarch.

To Bokassa's dismay, the pope dispatched a cardinal to attend in his stead. The Japanese emperor Hirohito and Shah Pahlavi of Iran both stayed home. African heads of state also shunned the ceremony, as did Valery Giscard d'Estaing, the French president. Relations with France were already fraught: years before, Charles de Gaulle had openly called Bokassa "a roughneck," "an asshole," and "an idiot." The press, on the other hand, turned up in force to report on the spectacle, ogling in disbelief at this absurdly ostentatious display of wealth unfolding in one of the world's poorest countries. A French TV crew documented it all: the crowds that had been made to line the streets, cheering on command and wearing specially made cloth bearing the emperor's likeness; the ridiculous stuffed panther carried by bare-chested hunters; the splendid white horses that collapsed while pulling the emperor's carriage in the tropical heat. Out of sight of the cameras, armored cars stood at the ready, in case there was trouble. The *Independent* summed it up nicely in Bokassa's obituary three decades later: "Surely no public occasion in the twentieth century has been more lurid or insane."

As befits an imperial coronation, prodigious quantities of food and drink were served. That evening's state dinner began with Iranian caviar, crayfish dumplings, and Nile perch, followed by an intermezzo of pear and champagne sorbet. Then antelope in a cognac and red wine sauce. There were foie gras and hearts of lettuce. The "imperial cake," a towering masterpiece of a dessert, had been baked in Paris that very morning. Tens of thousands of bottles of Chateau Mouton Rothschild wine and Moët & Chandon champagne were on hand. There was much waste, of course, and a lot of food was thrown out. The French TV crew reported that the waiters who served the gargantuan meal had not eaten that day.

The event cost about $50 million, and as France was still providing support to its former colony, much of that money came from the French taxpayer. It was the equivalent of the annual Central African budget. The U.S. ambassador in Bangui at the time witnessed the excess, and America canceled its aid to the country the very next day.

Bokassa's hold on power crumbled less than three years later. His ultimate downfall came after he greedily introduced a rule that forced schoolchildren to buy expensive uniforms from a company that belonged to his family. A group of kids had the audacity to throw rocks at his Rolls-Royce in protest. The imperial gendarmes killed dozens of schoolchildren in response, and mass protests broke out. France, which continued to wield extensive influence in its former colony, sent in its special forces to topple the emperor and replace him with a mild-mannered bureaucrat.

There were rumors that Bokassa was a cannibal. A French minister famously recalled the emperor saying to him after the sumptuous coronation dinner—he hoped jokingly—"You did not realize it, but you just ate human flesh." Once he had been chased out of power, Bokassa was lampooned in the press as the Butcher of Bangui, a man who had fed his enemies to wild animals in his private zoo.

Bokassa was sentenced to death twice, once in absentia in 1980, while he was in exile in France, and once in person in 1986, after he had returned to his country. But in a startling indication of how far the Central African Republic (CAR) has fallen in recent decades, people now see his reign as a high point for the country, even though he drove the economy into the ground. When people long for the dictatorial rule of a megalomaniac, life is bad. But to some Central Africans, the days of Bokassa had offered hope of progress, a vision—or a fantasy—of a better future. And if the country remained desperately poor, at least there was some stability. A movement began to rehabilitate Bokassa, and President André Kolingba granted an amnesty to the former emperor, who was freed in 1993 in Bangui. Bokassa died three years later, and in 2010, he received a posthumous pardon.

If I asked you to think of sites of global hunger, the arid Sahel might come to mind. Or conflict-stricken Somalia. Perhaps the densely populated Ethiopian highlands, or the plains of northern India. Central Africa, a forested, well-watered tropical area, probably wouldn't spring immediately to mind. Even the experts don't see it as a likely place to be prone to starvation. In private conversation, I often heard them say that farming in the area is easy: that if you drop a stick on the ground, a tree grows. That people don't need to work all that much to eat. That the fish there die of old age.

While it's true that the CAR doesn't battle the terrible droughts the Sahel sees, the country is going hungry because of the systems human beings have built, the mistakes they have made, and the selfish excesses in which they've indulged, even after Bokassa was gone. If a government is spending the annual budget on a gargantuan celebratory feast, then it's probably not the sort of government that's prioritizing its hungry citizens. It isn't just drought that turns a bountiful tropical garden into a wilderness of hunger. Greed can do it too.

CAR stands out for its severe and long-lasting food crisis, like Somalia and South Sudan. The nation's trajectory makes us wonder: how did a relatively quiet country so suddenly tip into a raging food emergency? The crisis in CAR sheds light on the limitations of humanitarianism: when extreme violence breaks out, international organizations pull out, and people are left to starve. The CAR tragedy forces us to ask what can be done to ensure such disasters never happen again.

F ood shortages are nothing new in CAR; it's a place where hunger was manufactured and wielded as a tool of oppression.
In the early twentieth century, the people of what is now CAR
suffered years of famine that resulted from the brutal and exploitative colonial system that milked the land of its natural resources.
Estimates say that between 20 and 30 percent of the population
died during those years, because of either violence or malnutrition. Under colonial rule, the threat of starvation was a way to
coerce the colony's population into forced labor.

Private enterprise was the engine of what became known in
central Africa as the Big Starvation. In the colonial era, governments granted private businesses generous "concessions," exclusive rights to loot natural resources in specific areas in exchange
for a fixed fee and royalties. By the late nineteenth century, concessions had become an established device of colonization. The British colony of Rhodesia was a concession to a company chartered
by the mining magnate Cecil Rhodes. Powerful U.S. corporations
such as the United Fruit Company (now Chiquita Brands International) carved out gigantic concessions in Central American countries, which then came to be known as "banana republics." The
concession regime would bring unprecedented hunger to colonial
central Africa.

French Equatorial Africa, which includes the Oubangui-Chari
colony that would become the independent CAR, was so poor
in the nineteenth century that it was known in France as "the
Empire's Cinderella." The French Republic did not have the resources to develop its new colony. Soon after it took over the
area in the 1880s, an ugly form of unrestricted capitalism was
turned loose on the tropical land. Completely disregarding the
people who lived there, colonial authorities ceded vast tracts
of land to private companies, granting them exclusive rights to

harvest rubber, copper, and ivory, and to export their products to France proper. More than 700,000 square kilometers of land—an area larger than France itself—would be granted to almost forty companies.

The system in the Oubangui-Chari was modeled on the ruthless and lucrative methods that Belgium's King Leopold used on the other side of the Ubangi River. Leopold managed the Congo Free State as his own private property, an exercise in exploitation and madness that Joseph Conrad describes in *Heart of Darkness*. The novel portrays the moral corruption of greedy colonial agents who brutally assault locals to procure ivory for export. As the nineteenth century ended, the Europeans who had organized the pilfering of the Congo Free State crossed the river and brought their ruthless methods to the Oubangui-Chari.

The tacit agreement was that the French civil service would not interfere with the activities of these private companies. In any case, there were hardly any French civil servants in the Oubangui-Chari to begin with. In each concession, a handful of Europeans would force thousands of Africans to bring in quotas of rubber obtained from wild vines in the forest. To the colonizers, it didn't matter that the rubber tappers cut right through the vines, killing them in the process. Short-term profit was the priority.

The Mpoko concession, located near Bangui and incorporated in 1899, covered an area as large as the state of Maryland, or Belgium. It stands out as an especially egregious example of the use of hunger to achieve financial gain. A climate of terror reigned at Mpoko concession. A private army of four hundred *touroucous,* African mercenaries, dragooned workers and punished those who would not comply. They routinely held women and children as hostages until an arbitrary rubber quota was met. The *touroucous* raped women while their men were out collecting rubber. Murder was common. Through bribery, the operators of Mpoko co-opted local leaders into backing the company's interests.

The impact on food production was staggering. The *touroucous* burned villages and cut down banana trees by the thousand, ensuring people would starve. Just a few years earlier, in 1897, Émile Gentil, who later became governor general of the Oubangui-Chari colony, had visited the north and seen generous fields of millet and cassava, and had come away with an impression of prosperity. But when Savorgnan de Brazza, the French founder of the Congo, visited the same area in 1905, he found the fields reverting to bush. The population had vanished. "Everywhere," writes the Belgian historian Daniel Vangroenweghe, "there was wilderness and hunger."

The Africans of Mpoko had begged company officials to postpone the rubber harvest by a few months to enable them to grow food, but their pleas had been denied. In some places, the food shortages were so severe that people were reduced to eating the trunks of their banana trees. As conditions became increasingly dire, there were reports of cannibalism. An official at the French Ministry of Colonies described what happened to a boy who had escaped his cruel master and been recaptured: "A *touroucou* has him taken prisoner, attaches him to a pole and [has him] promptly shot. He then immediately negotiates with the villagers about the sale of the body that is eaten the same day." Another heinous practice: "When the *touroucous* in charge of the recruitment of laborers did not have enough food to feed them, they killed passers-by with their guns to give to the men."

In 1908, French authorities, who had caught wind of atrocities at Mpoko, sent a magistrate to Oubangui-Chari to investigate. The magistrate brought to light this appallingly inhumane system that used violence and starvation to coerce the population to collect rubber from the forest. Touring Mpoko, the investigating magistrate visited villages that produced a bounty of valuable rubber but where the people still wore clothes made from bark. He established that 1,500 people had died at the hands of armed men who were in the service of the Mpoko concession. At one point, the magistrate overheard the director of the concession upbraiding his deputy for agreeing to let the Africans plant crops: "As soon as the natives have food, they will not harvest rubber anymore."

Starvation in the Oubangui-Chari was not merely a by-product of conquest; it was also an instrument of social control. The companies starved people to quench the French industry's thirst for latex. In the Oubangui-Chari, colonial capitalism steamrolled the systems that kept people fed.

In other places and at other moments of history, the triumphant emergence of capitalism coincided with the appearance of new forms of deprivation and hunger. Economist Karl Polanyi describes this time of great dislocation when there was "a miraculous increase in production, accompanied by the starvation of the masses."

The dismantling of Britain's Poor Laws in the nineteenth century is such a case. Under the Poor Laws, which had been in place for centuries, parishes had the obligation to provide a safety net for the nation's poor. They supplied meals and shelter for orphans and the elderly. This protective system kept people attached to their parishes and made wage labor unattractive. As England began to build factories that required more and more workers, the Poor Laws stood in the way of economic expansion.

Joseph Townsend, a physician and vicar opposed to public provision of relief, campaigned to modify the system. The doctor argued that for their own good, the nation's workers needed to experience hunger. In 1786, he wrote his influential *Dissertation of the Poor Laws,* where he argued that only hunger could push the poor to work; it was a "natural" incentive that kept people both motivated and docile. A helping of hunger, he explained, is good both for the poor and for society at large. Townsend's ideas gained currency and were turned into policy. Government reformed the

Poor Laws in 1834 and required paupers to work in squalid work-houses to earn a living.

In industrial Britain and in colonial central Africa, profits and hunger soared concurrently. The dehumanizing and exploitative systems that relied on hunger as a means of social control would soon be exported to many of Europe's colonial territories, including the CAR.

Until about a decade ago, many aid workers didn't pay much attention to the CAR. It was an unfamiliar, distant, chronically unstable place at the mercy of an alphabet soup of rebel movements. In 2013, that changed when the CAR escalated to a major crisis, complete with mass hunger and warnings of a possible genocide.

The current hunger crisis began with the emergence of the Seleka, a previously unknown rebel group, in late 2012. A slew of insurgencies had broken out across the CAR over the preceding years, and it seemed that the Seleka—the name means "alliance" in Sango, the national language—was a conglomeration of the armed groups that riddled the distant, disinherited north, the area of the country that borders the troubled nations of Chad and Sudan. The alliance's motorized columns began sweeping through the vast country.

By December 2012, Seleka columns were just 70 kilometers from Bangui. The only thing keeping the rebels from entering the capital was a detachment of two hundred South African troops, who had deployed to protect their country's mining interests in the CAR. I remember that the South Africans cut quite a sight in Bangui, where their tan shorts and white socks were entirely out of place. But they allowed a fleeting sense of normalcy. Although the Seleka were not far away, the front line had at least stabilized.

Observers whispered that the events could lead to a partition of the country.

I took my first trip to the CAR in early 2013. My years in the Sahel were over and I was working as an analyst at WFP headquarters in Rome. I was part of the agency's food security analysis department, a role I was well suited to because of my penchant for numbers. I worked to analyze a battery of household food statistics and local markets. My work helped estimate how many people humanitarian programs should reach, and where they lived. Being a French speaker, I was sent on assignment for a few weeks to Francophone CAR. My job there was to assess how humanitarian needs had changed in the north, an area that had recently fallen under Seleka control. We were also hoping to learn more about this mysterious rebel movement that had come out of nowhere.

I traveled by plane from Bangui to Kaga Bandoro with a small team of UN staff. It was the first time my Central African colleagues would come face-to-face with the new rebellion. As protocol required, we reported immediately to the rebels' command post. The Seleka detachment in Kaga Bandoro had set up its quarters at the local gendarmerie, a beat-up concrete bungalow surrounded by trees. Two brand-new Toyota Land Cruiser pickups were parked outside. This was no ragtag guerrilla force that had materialized from the bush.

The Seleka commander in Kaga Bandoro was a tan, stocky Arab man, dressed in spotless desert camouflage fatigues, his head swathed in a white turban. Behind him, a brand-new CAR flag hung on the wall, its creases still showing. It looked as though it had just been taken out of its packaging.

The commander sized us up from behind a small wooden desk. He said nothing as the Central Africans on the team explained to him in French why we were in town that day. With a slow nod, he silently dismissed us. He was not being aloof; he probably spoke no French. Back outside, we passed a clutch of thin teenagers, who looked like the shepherd boys I had seen in the Sahara years before. They were milling around the freshly painted pickup trucks, speaking in Arabic. The equipment, the light complexions, their use of Arabic—everything showed these soldiers were not from the CAR.

My Central African colleagues, all Sango-speaking Christian southerners, were horrified. The exchange with the commander had confirmed their worst fears. They had just seen, with their own eyes, evidence that the rebellion was a horde of raiders who had crossed the faraway desert to pick apart their country—a novel phenomenon different from the home-grown rebellions that had popped up in the CAR in the previous decade.

After meeting with the Seleka commander in Kaga Bandoro, we visited a nearby settlement typical of the forested and sparsely settled interior. The town was little more than a cluster of shacks. The church was a set of wooden benches set out in the open. An air of impermanence hung over it, perhaps because the people living there knew that if shooting started, whether from the Seleka, the CAR's national army, or any other armed group, they would once again flee.

We met a family in a ramshackle clapboard house there. The father told us that in this part of the north, which was not far from the border with Chad, the people had seen rebel armies come and go for the better part of a decade. When the Seleka rebellion began in late 2012, the family had done what they usually did at such times: they abandoned their house and fled the village, leaving the Seleka to plunder what little they had left behind.

The family of four had once again retreated to a place deep in the forest, isolated and safe from the rebels. They slept out in the open and spoke to no one for weeks. The father told me they lived on small wild yams they found in the forest until things calmed down. The yams were so bitter that they needed to soak them in water for days before cooking them. If they were lucky, they'd find honey in the forest.

For as long as the Seleka were around, it was too dangerous for the family to farm. They had left their crops untended for weeks, and they knew that finding enough to eat would be difficult in the months to come. Their survival skills, honed over years of conflict, kept them alive. What was striking about this family was that surviving on bitter yams and wild honey for weeks was an accepted fact of life. Farmers all over the world deal with drought, flooding, and pests. This family, and many others like them, also faced the ever-present threat of armed groups. This is how a nation of small farmers, like the CAR, plunges deep into a food crisis in times of civil strife. I recall that we estimated that fewer than a million people in the country were food insecure at the time.

When the Seleka burst on the scene in the CAR in late 2012, the disruption caused a national food crisis. Over the next few months, the nation would become one of the world's most dangerous places.

It turned out the Seleka were merely biding their time. After a stalemate that lasted three months, they smashed through South African lines and rolled into Bangui in March 2013, ousting the president and setting off days of frenetic plundering. The situation had just changed drastically.

I wasn't in the country then, but of the many accounts I heard, that of a colleague I'll call Sally stands out. Sally was in Bangui with the Baltimore-based Catholic Relief Services (CRS), one of the few international NGOs working in the CAR. Sally knew about the rebellion in the north but was still taken by surprise. "Bangui was a sleepy little river town," she said. "We had no idea what was coming."

The night the Seleka approached Bangui, Sally stayed in a safe house with the CRS manager and their security officer. Copious gunfire signaled the arrival of the dreaded Seleka columns. The next day, a UN security team rolled up with an armored vehicle to get the group to safety. A Texan with a gray ponytail was in charge, flanked by his West African colleague. The two patiently negotiated with a group of brooding Seleka soldiers positioned right outside the compound.

Sally and the others paid the soldiers off with whatever cash and jewelry they had on them. They were not allowed to take any bags, so they buried their satellite phones in the backyard and hid their passports in their underwear. The UN detail signaled for them to board the armored vehicle, and as they were walking out, Sally felt someone push her in the back, causing her to stumble. When she looked up, she saw a Seleka soldier, about fifteen years old, with an AK-47, looking down at her.

The armored car took the group to the main office of what was then the UN mission in the country, where expatriates were being taken before evacuation. Sally found the others there as distraught and shell-shocked as she was. Sally and her companions were each given an eight-ounce bottle of water and a ration of white rice, which briefly made the humanitarian workers feel like they were refugees.

By that point, the situation in CAR had deteriorated to the point where even the most committed humanitarian workers, who work under the most difficult circumstances, were forced to leave the country to save themselves. When violence is that extreme, there is little aid workers can do to stave off starvation. The only solution was to wait it out and hope for the situation to improve.

In the mayhem that followed the Seleka's entry into Bangui, civilians ran for their lives, fearing summary execution or murder.

Tens of thousands converged on the grounds of Bangui's Mpoko airport, establishing a colossal camp that became the symbol of the crisis engulfing the country. The camp was impossible for anyone arriving by plane to ignore, and that was perhaps the point: every passenger would see out the window a desperate tide of humanity lining the runways, standing cheek by jowl and staring up at the Air France and Royal Air Maroc airliners.

The makeshift camp at Bangui airport had just appeared when I next landed there in December 2013. Crude tarpaulins sheltering displaced families had been tied to the frames of dilapidated planes that dotted the edge of the runway. A mass of boys in rags lined the tarmac as planes taxied up to the terminal, and UN peacekeepers held them back. At the peak of the displacement crisis in 2013 and 2014, Mpoko airport camp held more than 100,000 people. By then, 800,000 Central Africans had fled their homes—a staggering number for a country of 4 million. Those who weren't crowded into the camp were in church compounds around the country or refugee camps in Cameroon or Chad.

People in these camps left behind all their belongings and found themselves confined with little more than the clothes on their backs. The overwhelming majority were down to one meal a day, usually a meal of corn or cassava paste—the cheapest calories available—with no greens or protein. Our assessment showed 2.6 million people in the country needed emergency food assistance—double the number a few months before.

By December 2013, the conflict had taken an ugly turn. The UN was warning that a genocide was brewing; a well-armed group of militias from the south called the "anti-balaka" (a name whose origin isn't clear) had materialized, challenging the Seleka who had swept in earlier in the year. In the months that followed, pressure from the anti-balaka militia and international forces led the Seleka to withdraw to the north. Soon, scores were being settled in Bangui and the rest of the south: the anti-balaka targeted Muslims, and thousands fled to Chad and Cameroon. In the chaos, others were left behind.

Conditions were especially extreme for Muslims in "enclaves" that were surrounded by anti-balaka forces. These enclaves were fortified ghettos where they could find protection from sectarian violence, but they were cut off from food supplies. Those in the enclaves faced a terrible choice: either leave and risk attack from the anti-balaka or stay and face starvation or disease.

An established, diverse community of Muslims lived in CAR among a Christian majority. Many of the Seleka's leaders were Muslims, and the conflict soon took on a sectarian dimension. Most Muslims had nothing to do with the rebellion, but the entire community soon found itself under attack. This included the Fulani, herders who had been in the country for generations. As the conflict took root, Christian militias chased them out of CAR, to Cameroon in the east. There, some Fulani would create an armed group that fought to reclaim their grazing lands in the north and west of CAR. There was another group of Muslims whose families came from Chad, a trading class that had lived there for decades. They too were forced back to their ancestral home. In time, all Muslims would be seen as adversaries, isolated in ghettos or forced out of the country.

Before the war, Bangui was desperate to shed its image as a quiet town and become a thriving, modern city. The government looked with envy at nearby African capitals like Yaounde in Cameroon, Dakar in Senegal, or Abidjan in Côte d'Ivoire, with their landmarks that exuded optimism and progress. Many boasted an enormous airport terminal, connected to town by a brightly lit highway. In some, an imposing presidential palace, or a monumental place of worship, dominated the city. Others had a swanky business district, where men in suits and shiny shoes strutted in the shadow of glass buildings. Bangui, by contrast, felt almost frozen in time. If it weren't for the mobile phone towers, it would probably look just as it had during Bokassa's rule.

And then the Ledger was built, to cater to the business elite. A five-story, sparkling luxury hotel, it was surrounded by a giant parking lot and high walls and powered by large generators. It opened in September 2012, just as the Seleka rebellion was brewing in the north. In early 2013, the Ledger was almost entirely empty, its oppressive elevator music playing for no one.

But when the Seleka arrived in Bangui in March 2013, they made the Ledger their seat of government, and the hotel's fortunes rose as the country slid into chaos. The Seleka leader, Michel Djotodia, now the president, stayed in a poolside bungalow listed at $3,850 a night, while his ministers occupied penthouse suites. The Ledger was also home to what the anthropologist Louisa Lombard called "the good intentions crowd"—staff from the embassies, UN agencies, and NGOs who wanted to help. It was not unusual for humanitarian workers to meet armed Seleka soldiers in the Ledger's elevators, where the two groups would ride to their respective floors in silence.

Because periodic fighting made it dangerous to leave the Ledger, the hotel became the de facto base for many aid workers. In the mornings, they converged on the poolside terrace with their laptops. In the evenings, strategies were discussed around the sumptuous buffet, as tracer fire lit up the night sky.

Western reporters had come to cover the crisis, and out of all of the guests at the Ledger, they seemed to be the most stressed by the circumstances. One evening when the gunfire in Bangui had been especially intense, I spotted a young white journalist splayed out on the marble floor in the hotel lobby. He wore a heavy flak jacket emblazoned with the word PRESS in large white letters. He looked like he was overheating, panting as his chest heaved. The sweat made his hair stick to his face, and his forearm rested on a helmet. Others sat on the floor next to him. It made for a jarring sight. The plush lobby was not meant to be a place for young, sweaty journalists to crash out. As exhausted as they were, the journalists were ready to jump into their rental cars to chase the action. They kept a close eye on their phones, waiting for someone to tell them where the shooting was coming from.

The journalists had made a calculation: they would come to CAR to tell the world what was happening there, and in doing so, they would make a name for themselves. They would live through the thick humidity, the power cuts, the malaria, the bad food. They would tell the story, even if it meant putting themselves at personal risk. These journalists were in Bangui for a reason both timeless and universal: a shot at the big time.

For war reporters, just as for aid workers, working amid acute human suffering in places like Bangui is a career opportunity. And that raises ethical questions, including whether it's right to profit from others' misery to make a living, or to advance in your career. Many aid workers rationalize what we do by saying our work helps people in desperate need. While the motivations may at first seem opportunistic, many of us are driven by the mission, and the hope—although it sometimes feels like an illusion—that we will somehow make a difference.

Those nights in Bangui I slept lightly. There were brief, intense eruptions of staccato gunfire in the distance, punctuated by the sound of grenades exploding. I kept my handheld radio switched on throughout the night. Once, in the middle of the night, I heard an expat calling UN security, sounding very agitated: "Sierra base, do you read me?" A deep voice came back: "Sierra base here. Move to channel 3 please."

Wide awake and curious, I switched my radio to channel 3 to hear the rest of the exchange.

"Sierra base," the caller said, "there is a dead body in front of my house."

"Roger," the man at UN security said. "We will come to you when the sun is up."

It sounded as routine as a visit to the dentist. I turned off the radio and went to sleep.

When I think back to those moments, I realize how numb I was then to the trauma of the Central African people. I focused on my spreadsheets and reports, impervious to the upheaval around me. It's how I kept going.

In times of war, a community's resources shift to supporting the military effort—and away from meeting civilians' basic needs. Wars foster parallel economies that revolve around smuggling, speculation, and large profits; hunger is often a by-product. The conflict in CAR devastated agriculture: two-thirds of the livestock were lost, killed, or stolen. In 2014, with its trading routes in disarray, its markets broken, and its farmers harassed by armed men, the nation's food production shrank by 58 percent. Agriculture shifted toward subsistence, leaving the cities undersupplied. Prices crept up in Bangui, and food scarcity loomed.

By 2014, many farmers in CAR had Seleka-proofed their crops. They planted cassava, a hardy root, rather than corn, which can easily be stolen by marauding rebels. Cassava, on the other hand, is harder to pilfer: it needs to be dug up before being carted away, and even then, the root requires days of processing before it is edible.

CAR's main road west to Cameroon is the nation's windpipe. It was also the corridor through which most food imports entered the country. Even before the crisis, it could take a week for trucks to get from the Cameroonian port of Douala to Bangui. But in early 2014, the flow slowed to a trickle as robbers and rebels took to hijacking trucks. The highwaymen lived in bush camps where they gorged themselves on stolen meat. Some were soldiers on the lam, others Fulani outcasts. The food supply to the capital was cut off. The military organized convoys so traders could keep food imports flowing in.

The food markets that people normally relied on had collapsed. In many Central African cities, Muslim traders operate the corner stores, "les boutiques," which could be anything from a small kiosk to a twenty-foot-long converted shipping container. Just like a bodega in New York City. The corner stores are open all day except during Friday prayers and sell everything from single eggs and tomato paste to cell phone credits. As the conflict escalated, however, the Muslim traders who had operated these ubiquitous stalls moved to PK5, the Muslim ghetto in the west of the capital, or fled the country altogether. Their disappearance from Bangui led to the emergence of food deserts, entire neighborhoods where food was difficult to come by.

No matter how dangerous CAR became, the war economy offered profits for traders. I visited the eastern mining town of Bambari and met traders from Sudan who continued to brave the badly rutted roads. At the town's market, a warren of wattle shops and thatch stands, an orange Nissan truck with Sudanese plates pulled in. The lower body of the truck was covered with dried mud. The driver, a wiry old Arab trader in a blue robe, told us that he had been on the road for twelve days, making his way from Nyala, in the Sudanese Darfur. The Nissan had brought a bounty from Sudan. Shrink-wrapped packs of orange and yellow soda in eight-ounce plastic bottles. Stacks of flip-flops held together by large rubber bands. Spare motorcycle parts, wrapped in cardboard boxes bearing the logos of Indian manufacturers. Bags of sugar. I saw nothing illegal in the cargo, but trucks like this one were rumored to be bringing weapons, in addition to these sundry supplies.

The man had come to Bambari to trade his goods for the bitter robusta coffee beans for which this area was famous. I didn't realize it at the time, but the coffee trade with Sudan was one of the factors driving the conflict in CAR. The armed groups that controlled roads, checkpoints, and markets could tax a trade worth millions of dollars. The old Arab and other traders like him had to pay their way through a gauntlet of roadblocks. Those waging war were looking to milk this lucrative trade. The United States Institute for Peace called coffee CAR's "Green Diamond."

"This is the price at which you eat sugar in Europe," Voltaire wrote in an essay about the atrocities of eighteenth-century slavery in the Americas. The Sudanese weren't enslaving their Central African neighbors, but their taste for coffee was fueling the deadly and destructive conflict.

But as wars do, the conflict in CAR also cultivated resourcefulness and creativity. In the late summer of 2014, I met a farmer outside Bangui who was known for his skill at raising pigs. However, during the chaos that followed the Seleka's arrival, armed men had taken all of his animals. Determined to find a new source of revenue after the plunder, he began raising gerbils in a cellar. They were reproducing quickly, and he would sell them at the market for $3 apiece. He had no trouble selling the gerbils he raised. "As soon as I save enough money," he told me, sounding undaunted, "I'll buy pigs again."

Other men in the town of Yoko, about twenty-five kilometers from Bangui, were brewing potent moonshine. They used a still that had been improvised from rusty oil drums and old inner tubes. Inside the drums, a fermented cassava and corn mash cooked slowly over hot coals. The vapors snaked through the contraption until they condensed, honey-colored moonshine dripping from a long cooling tube. The Central Africans called the drink "Boganda," after an independence-era politician said to have had a taste for it. The Reverend Boganda—a relative of Bokassa—had looked likely to become the first president of independent CAR, but his plane exploded shortly before the elections. At a few cents a shot, a hit of Boganda was the cheapest drink available in Bangui.

War-weary soldiers and civilians alike were in need of some numbing, and demand for the stuff was through the roof.

The crowds that gathered in the streets of Bangui in March 2013 to watch the humanitarians withdraw were right to be concerned. They were being abandoned, left behind in their sleepy river town that had turned into a hell on earth. CAR was left to unscrupulous outsiders and their homegrown allies whose plays for power choked trading systems, endangered food production, and deprived people of their livelihoods, dragging an entire society into a food crisis.

As 2013 wore on and as the Seleka withdrew from Bangui, aid workers trickled back into the country and a provisional government was seated. Although the Seleka had retreated to the north, there was still a lot of violence in Bangui. Gradually, the provision of assistance was scaled up, but the damage had been done: a Pandora's box of violence had been opened, with mass displacement and hunger the result.

CAR has not been a land of milk and honey for generations, but its widespread hunger is only increasing. It has gone through more than a decade of war and instability since 2012. In 2023, a record 3 million people, half the population, were in a food crisis that had engulfed every district in the country. CAR is teaching us the lesson we have already learned in Somalia, South Sudan, and elsewhere: it's easy to start a food crisis, but much harder to end one.

In CAR, I saw how conflict fueled acute hunger. Aid workers like me were adamant that something, *anything,* had to be done to stop the suffering. What was especially galling was that international law regarded starvation of civilians as a legitimate, if ugly, tactic of war. Holding people accountable for starving their enemies in wartime is extraordinarily difficult, but decades of advocacy are beginning to change that.

During the Nuremberg trials in the aftermath of World War II, the court examined the case of Germany's Field Marshal Wilhelm von Leeb, who had pleaded not guilty to charges of war crimes during the brutal 1941–1944 siege of Leningrad. During the siege, which von Leeb had initially led, starvation and cold killed a million Soviet citizens. In the siege's darkest days, armed gangs roamed the city and killed people for their ration cards—or to eat their corpses. Survivors described wandering past half-eaten bodies as German bombs fell. There was so little food in Leningrad that the city's rats migrated en masse to the well-supplied German lines.

Despite the mass starvation that was a direct result of his action, the U.S. court exonerated von Leeb. The court stated that "a belligerent commander may lawfully lay siege to a place controlled by the enemy and endeavor by a process of isolation to cause its surrender . . . the cutting off of every source of sustenance from without is deemed legitimate." The Hague Conventions of 1899 and 1907, which established internationally accepted rules of war, were the basis for the ruling. The conventions banned the use of chemical weapons and forbade looting and the bombing of undefended cities—but somehow, they did not prohibit the deliberate starvation of civilians.

While von Leeb's actions to starve out Leningrad were considered legal, the terrible famines of World War II and the mass death they caused were a turning point, for both scholars and public opinion. Through fits and starts, changes in the norms of war would unfold over the next decades.

Accountability for starvation in war came up again during the conflicts of the Cold War. The televised war in Biafra of 1967–1970, which pitted Nigeria's Federal Military Government against secessionists, brought the question right into Western living rooms. The Federals set up a naval blockade and besieged the secessionists, with the explicit objective of starving out rebels and civilians. They also denied access to aid agencies, who resorted to risky night flights to bring in aid. The situation was dire. In his poem "Refugee Mother and Child," Chinua Achebe wrote of the ghastly conditions in Biafran camps, of children "with washed-out ribs and dried-up / bottoms . . ."

The suffering sparked widespread indignation in the West, but the Federals were unapologetic: "Starvation is a legitimate weapon of war," declared one Nigerian official. Brigadier Benjamin Adekunle of the Nigerian army said, "I want to see no Red Cross, no Caritas, no World Council of Churches, no Pope, no missionary, and no UN delegation. I want to prevent even one Ibo having even one thing to eat before their capitulation." Biafrans were faced with a stark choice: surrender or starve. They fought on for almost three grueling years. Two million people died.

While nothing like the Nuremberg trials followed the Biafran war, the conflict galvanized the world's nascent humanitarian community. New interventionist and politically engaged actors—including the organization that would become Médecins Sans Frontières (MSF)—emerged. They challenged the traditional state-centered humanitarian paradigm embodied by the Red Cross, whose policy in Nigeria had been one of non-interference. The emboldened humanitarians would challenge the status quo—including the tacit acceptance of starvation in war.

The Geneva Convention's 1977 Additional Protocols represented progress. They explicitly prohibited the starvation of civilians in war and the destruction of what was necessary for their survival, including crops, farmland, and irrigation infrastructure. It was hoped that this measure could be legally enforced, but when the International Criminal Court was established in 2002, its foundational statute had a critical loophole. The ICC would only prosecute cases of starvation during war in "international" conflicts, leaving it without jurisdiction over civil wars. This was a significant omission—civil wars constitute the bulk of contemporary conflicts and are where most acute hunger occurs.

The re-emergence of conflict-induced famine in civil wars in the 2010s—including in South Sudan, Yemen, and Syria—provided impetus for action. Activists, academics, NGOs, UN agencies, and European governments came together to amend international humanitarian law. In May 2018, the UN Security Council passed Resolution 2417, which condemns starvation as a form of warfare, and condemns the blocking of relief for civilians, regardless of whether violations occur in international or non-international conflicts. The adoption of Resolution 2417 opened the door to action by the ICC, whose members unanimously voted in 2019 to amend the court's foundational statute to extend its jurisdiction. With the loophole closed, it is time to move from intention to action.

The jurisprudence around Resolution 2417 is evolving, but there have thus far been no prosecutions. An amended legal statute alone won't avoid another Leningrad or a new Biafra. The legal framework is new and untested, and the standards for evidence are unclear. Should a latter-day von Leeb ever be brought to justice, a prosecution will be far from straightforward, because a trial can last years and cost millions of dollars. And armed groups like the Seleka of CAR couldn't care less about international statutes. Torching crops and food reserves now lies beyond the pale of what is legal in conflict, but that doesn't mean that such tactics aren't still used. It's a long journey from amending legal statutes to holding people accountable for the use of starvation as a tactic in war.

Forever Famines

The Middle East's Descent into Hunger

If a man won't think with his head, he'll think with his belly—
especially if it's empty.

—Jacques Roumain, *Masters of the Dew*

Occasionally, the brutality of starvation intrudes into the minds of the well fed. In October 2018, a *New York Times* story on the war in Yemen included a graphic photo of a starving seven-year-old girl. The close-up shot shows Amal Hussain laid out on a black gurney. Long wisps of red hair frame her face. Amal's emaciated left hand covers her throat; her right hand rests on her protruding rib cage. Her head is tilted to the right, as she gazes intently at something outside the frame of the shot. The caption reads "Amal Hussain, 7, is wasting away from hunger. The Saudi-led war in Yemen has pushed millions to the brink of starvation." Amal died seven days after the photo appeared.

The article, an account of the extreme hunger tormenting war-torn Yemen, explains how a naval blockade and the destruction of the country's infrastructure threw vital food supply chains into chaos. It outlines how currency depreciation made food so expensive that even middle-class people struggled to buy enough for their families. And it tells of women selling their jewelry to survive, of the elderly begging, of grieving families burying their young.

More than any data or carefully chosen words, it was the image of Amal Hussain that shocked readers. After angry readers wrote outraged letters to the editor, the *Times* felt the need to explain why they published such a graphic image. The *Times* editors published a follow-up article that invoked their journalistic duty to bear witness, to give voice to the victimized and the forgotten. "The tragedy in Yemen did not grow out of a natural disaster," the editors explained. "It is a slow-motion crisis brought on by leaders of other countries who are willing to tolerate extraordinary suffering by civilians to advance political agendas."

The sight of an innocent child sentenced to a preventable death forces the viewer to confront uncomfortable truths, and offers a searing indictment of our culpable indifference and inaction. The fact is, photo or no photo, Amal would have died. But there *was* a photo, and her agony—and our guilt—became impossible to ignore. How many of us wrote a check to relief organizations, or phoned our elected representatives to demand an end to the suffering in Yemen? Probably a few more than would have without the image of Amal, but still not enough to matter. It's hard to argue that publishing the photo of Amal did much good in the long term.

Starvation made visible exerts a potent effect on the human psyche. This is why hunger is such an effective weapon in war, not only waged by those with the power to control resources or impose a siege, but also by those who are otherwise powerless—the hunger striker.

An example is the death by starvation in 1981 of Bobby Sands, a member of the Irish Republican Army (IRA), at the infamous Maze Prison. He and other IRA members went on a hunger strike to campaign for political prisoner status. Sixty-six days into his hunger strike, Sands lapsed into a coma and died. Nine more men would die on the hunger strike while Prime Minister Margaret Thatcher refused to buckle.

Bobby Sands's agony galvanized the Irish Republican movement. Shortly before he died, he was elected to the British Parliament. At least 100,000 people attended his Belfast funeral. Bobby Sands's death turned into a political victory for the IRA: a surge in recruitment followed, and the nationalist Sinn Fein party received an increasing share of the vote over the next two years.

When I think about the stories of Amal Hussain and Bobby Sands, they remind me of the paradoxes of what I do. How do we individualize suffering? And how do we counter widespread public apathy and helplessness? Hunger strikers are using their bodies to bargain for the greater good, and their lives can be saved at the stroke of a pen. But what do we do about the 12.4 million acutely food-insecure people in Syria? Or the 13.5 million who need urgent aid in Yemen?

Amal Hussain and Bobby Sands have very different stories, but both offered an image of starvation so compelling, and horrifying, it was impossible for the public to ignore. We seem able to respond to a single starving person, but not to millions. Statistics, however grim, aren't enough to spur meaningful action against hunger.

We live in a world of selective empathy, where there are good disasters and bad ones. Some crises are met with an immediate outpouring of global solidarity—and money—while others are ignored or conveniently forgotten. After the tsunami of December 2004 in Southeast Asia, relief organizations raised more than $6 billion. The tide of money was such that less than a week after the tsunami hit, the French NGO Médecins Sans Frontières controversially announced it would stop taking donations. In just a few days, it had raised $40 million, enough to cover its immediate operational needs. But even so, money kept flowing in and the NGO soon found itself with more than $100 million on its hands. Rather than engage in a questionable race to spend surplus funds,

MSF asked their donors to redirect the funds to other "forgotten" emergencies.

The West is capable of great empathy, but its generosity is fickle: it is easier for governments, companies, and citizens to reach for their checkbooks when blameless populations suffer an undeserved stroke of bad fortune. Raising funds to help people enduring years of grueling war—such as those in Syria and Yemen, where societies face a large, conflict-induced hunger burden for which no quick fixes exist—is much more difficult.

The 2020 annual UN humanitarian appeal called for $3.8 billion for Yemen but received only $1.8 billion in funding. In Syria, needs stood at $4.2 billion, and only $1 billion was raised. While funding is but one of many challenges aid workers face, these relatively meager resources make it impossible to make lasting change. And widespread acute hunger is a ticking geopolitical time bomb.

History teaches us that hunger and revolution go hand in hand. Most famously, the French Revolution occurred after harsh winters and lackluster harvests sent the price of bread soaring in Paris, sowing widespread discontent. Legend has it that, when told of the people's suffering, Queen Marie-Antoinette replied, "Let them eat cake." While it's almost certain she never uttered those words, the phrase captures the monarchy's indifference to its subjects. Ultimately, Marie-Antoinette and her husband, King Louis XVI, were guillotined. The collapse of the French monarchy plunged Europe into decades of war and misery.

This intimate link between hunger and instability is one of the reasons why the rulers of Syria go to extraordinary lengths to feed the masses. The nation's painful history of hunger is another. In 1915, during World War I, Britain, France, and Russia blockaded Syria's ports and the Ottoman province went through a catastrophic famine.

The Levantine poet Kahlil Gibran, then in the United States, tried to muster relief for his famine-racked homeland, but the Allies would not let any aid through the blockade. "They perished from hunger / In a land rich with milk and honey," he wrote of his countrymen in the 1916 poem "Dead Are My People." Historians estimate the famine killed up to 500,000 people. Lebanon alone, then a part of Greater Syria, lost a third of its population.

In the aftermath of the wartime famine, access to farmland in Syria remained deeply unequal. During the French Mandate in the 1920s and 1930s, Syria's bourgeoisie was allowed to buy up land. In time, the wealthy cobbled together large farming estates, where they often became absentee landlords. The business elite controlled much of Syria's farmland, and two-thirds of the country's poor farmers became landless.

This legacy of famine and inequality shaped Syria's food policies. After independence in 1946, nationalist leaders sought to weaken the landowning aristocracy's political influence and began redistributing their land. The Baath Party, which has ruled the country since the late 1960s, made land reform and food security top priorities. President Hafez al-Assad, father of current president Bashar al-Assad, placed much of the nation's agrifood system under government control. As journalist Annia Ciezadlo wrote, "For the Assads, controlling wheat and bread was an excellent way to keep unruly peasants and bedouins—or anyone else who posed a threat to central state power—in line."

In the 1960s and 1970s, the government forced farmers to join cooperatives through which it provided subsidized seeds, fertilizer, fuel, and irrigation. A state agency established production quotas and held a monopoly on purchases of "strategic crops," such as wheat and cotton, at set prices. Over time, the authorities built a network of silos capable of storing 3 million tons of grain—a stockpile equivalent to one year's worth of consumption. By the late 1970s, Syria's agriculture had become a state-dominated, command-and-control system that hoarded grain to keep the nation fed.

While the Baathist system led to a rapid increase in food production in the 1970s and 1980s, the trend turned out to be short-lived. Like contemporary Saudi Arabia, Syria was another "water-based food bubble." Over time, salinization, a by-product of excessive irrigation, began eating away at Syria's farmland. As a result, arable land declined from well over 6 million hectares in the 1960s to approximately 4.5 million in the 2000, a loss equivalent to the area of Connecticut, or Northern Ireland.

In the Levant, bread is commonly called "liqmet aeesh"—a morsel of life. The food's symbolic value explains why the Syrian regime ensured it was available in ample supply to all its citizens—similar to the arrangement described in chapter 3 that had ensured stability in ancient Rome. To do so, the government regulated the wheat-milling industry, and provided a nationwide network of public bakeries with subsidized flour to make a cheap flatbread that was the lifeblood of the working class.

While this mechanism was prone to corruption and waste, it did bring a considerable measure of security to the population: in Syria, government bread accounted for 40 percent of the calories the typical family ate each day. Versions of this scheme exist in many other countries in the Middle East, where being able to buy subsidized loaves of government flatbread for a few cents is regarded as a right, as freedom of speech is in the West. For all its faults, the Baathist system guaranteed that people were fed.

Then, in the 1990s, Western experts criticized Syria's state-managed economy for being expensive and inefficient. The International Monetary Fund put pressure on the government to "streamline the extensive subsidy system." This was the era when the U.S. government, the IMF, and the World Bank advocated for free markets and democracy—a movement that led countries all over the world to open their markets to international food trade, with disastrous results for their small farmers.

Syria, which needed external support to weather an economic crisis, obliged and began cutting back on the safety net it had built over decades. It reduced fuel subsidies, and lowered price guarantees. Farmers were squeezed, as their costs for irrigation and transportation rose and their income fell. Farmers once protected from price swings were now on their own. Years of drought between 2006 and 2010 only made the situation worse. That prolonged drought, the worst in at least nine hundred years, exposed the Syrian farming system for the house of cards that it was: food production collapsed, forcing the country to start importing wheat to feed its people. Mass internal migration followed, as up to 1.5 million people moved from the beleaguered countryside to the cities, where they mostly settled in slums, where they subsisted on bread and tea alone. This population would later become a ready target for recruiters during the Syrian civil war.

As the nation curtailed its support for farmers in the 2000s, the guarantee of cheap flatbread for the cities was all that remained of what had once been an expansive national safety net. As far back as 1970, Syrian officials had declared that raising the price of bread was a red line they wouldn't cross. But authorities could not hold the line in the face of drought, creeping inflation, and a yawning food deficit. The price of bread crept up. As Syria's decades-old systems teetered in the 2000s and food insecurity rose, unrest became more and more likely.

The causes of Syria's plunge into war are multiple, but rising food prices loom large. The Arab Spring—demonstrations against authoritarian regimes that spread throughout the region in 2011 and that turned into outright war in Libya, Syria, and Yemen— occurred at a time when high wheat prices plagued the Middle East's food-importing nations. When masses took to the streets of

Cairo, they demanded "bread, freedom, and social justice." People were prepared to put up with an autocratic regime, as long as it delivered cheap bread. The dismantling of the Syrian food safety net ahead of a multiyear drought and growing volatility in global food markets was very bad timing. The decision had massive and unpredictable consequences.

A decade of war since then has turned Syria's farming sector—once the envy of its neighbors in the Middle East, countries to which it had exported grain, livestock, and vegetables—into a shell of its former self. Wheat production has plunged by half, from more than 4.1 million tons per year in 2011 to 2.2 million in 2019. Those bakeries that somehow are able to keep operating sell bread at much higher prices, and people wait hours to buy it. Syria's breadlines—like those in the United States in the 1930s or the Soviet Union in the 1980s—have become a national embarrassment, symbolic of a broken system unable to fulfill basic promises to its citizens.

Syria's journey, from breadbasket to food crisis, shows that food secure nations and regions can easily tumble back into vulnerability when their farming systems and safety nets collapse, reversing in just a few years what took generations to achieve.

By the mid-2010s, the conflicts of the Middle East had become one of the global humanitarian community's biggest challenges because of their large scale and protracted nature. The Syrian conflict was the most complex. Four million Syrians had fled the country, while humanitarian agencies were providing food rations or cash to 7 million people inside Syria—an astounding number, considering that the nation's prewar population was 21 million.

In 2014, WFP began sending me on regular trips to the Middle East, then an emerging hotbed of global hunger. The experience

I'd gained as an analyst in Africa proved useful in the Middle East as WFP programs expanded there. In the spring of 2015, I went to Syria for a few weeks with UN colleagues to assess the country's food assistance needs. By then, the nation had sunk into the civil war that pitted the government against a plethora of armed groups, including Islamic militants, secular revolutionaries, and Kurdish separatists. We were able to travel outside Damascus and see for ourselves the toll that four years of conflict had taken on the country. The war in Syria had mangled the food system that the Baathist regime had built over decades. Factions clashed over the rich wheatlands of the northeast. They battled to control the industrial grain mills in Aleppo. They bombed bakeries that civilians relied on for their daily bread.

One morning, I was being driven on a highway overpass in the war-ravaged city of Homs, when something caught my eye. A boy in a red sweater, his little sister in tow, stood at the bottom of a rusting yellow dumpster, picking through garbage. My colleagues and I got out to talk to them. The boy looked to be about twelve, his cheeks pink from exertion. The dumpster looked difficult to get into, but the pair was resourceful; the boy said they were able to find their way in to look for food, perhaps scraps of bread. He told us that his father had died at the front the year before. Like so many other children, the boy now needed to provide for his family.

The boy told us that he and his family lived on stale bread and sweet tea. At the time, though, there were relief distributions in Syria, and millions received monthly food parcels. That the boy's mother had been reduced to sending her children out to pick through dumpsters made me wonder why the family was not receiving any assistance. It was possible that the family faced delays getting registered with aid agencies. Or perhaps there had not been enough food for all the people in need around Homs.

For an instant, I thought about how easy it would be to hand over a few dollars to the boy so that he and his family could eat a proper meal that day. Just then, the colorful Syrian banknotes I carried burned in my pocket. But I chased the thought from my mind immediately, because I knew that trying to help them could cause them harm. Onlookers seeing a mysterious man handing out cash to street kids could easily misunderstand the situation. The most responsible thing for me to do was to help ensure food aid got to where it was needed.

The outskirts of Homs looked deceptively normal. The four-lane highway to Damascus was open. The university was bustling with throngs of students, its well-watered lawns invitingly green. But the center of the city had been completely shattered by years of war. Mere minutes away, the districts of Baba Amr, Khalidiya, and the Old Town had been blown to smithereens by the three years of fighting that had begun in 2011. The siege had been so intense that block upon block of the city had been reduced to gray rubble. Tall concrete buildings were gutted. Others had collapsed, their floors on top of one another, stacked like pancakes. Twisted rebar poked out of the mangled remains. The result of air strikes, I was told. Homs had been Syria's Stalingrad.

When I visited in May 2015, the fighting in those districts had ended, but the mountains of debris had not been cleared away. Aside from soldiers dutifully manning their checkpoints, not a soul walked the streets. Who could live in these ruins? In the brutal siege of Homs, thousands were killed. Civilians speak of experiencing "the fear of all fears" during the siege, a fear worse than any other.

Unfortunately, it wasn't just Homs. The first decade of the war cost 350,000 lives. With so many dead at the front, Syrian society now suffers from a shortage of men, which is reshaping social norms, and also leading to long-term food insecurity. Households headed by women are much more common, and because they are missing one income earner, such families are more likely to live in poverty. There were 5 million children born in Syria between

2011 and 2021; as of 2021, between a quarter and a third of them are malnourished. Even if the fighting ended today, Syria's families would continue struggling to feed themselves because of the war's profound demographic impacts.

The worst of the crisis has fallen on the *hadide*—"rebar" in Arabic, a nod to the group's spartan lifestyle. They are a class of people so poor they cannot afford to pay rent, and squat in half-finished buildings. They have little income, because the men have abandoned their families, or died during the war. They live their lives on slabs of bare concrete, with plastic tarps providing a measure of privacy. They are without running water or electricity, and cook on small stoves, when they can afford the propane. Unless they luck into an aid agency fuel voucher, the *hadide* face Syria's blustery winters without any heating. To feed themselves, they rely on charity and scavenging. And there is no clear end to the suffering.

Syria's protracted war has profoundly undermined the very structure of its society. The conflict has disrupted the country's farming, safety nets, and demographics in a way that makes generational hunger all but certain.

As conflict raged in Syria, neighboring Iraq was in the throes of a war with ISIS, which controlled a swath of territory that straddled both countries. By 2014 WFP was providing food to the displaced population in the camps of Iraqi Kurdistan, a government-held area. The displaced had mostly come from the city of Mosul and nearby Nineveh province. Iraq, like Syria, was engulfed by violence, with hundreds of thousands displaced as ISIS swept through Iraq's northern tier.

I went to Iraq to help WFP analyze the unfolding situation. The relief effort's headquarters were in Erbil, an ancient city at the foot of the snow-capped Zagros Mountains. Erbil, in those days, was a place of new, gleaming office towers, luxury hotels, chain restaurants, coffee shops, malls, and highways, all fueled by oil revenues. In previous years, migrant laborers had come en masse from South Asia to build these marvels. The hope was that Erbil would soon be the proud capital of an independent Kurdistan. But the front line with ISIS was coming uncomfortably close, and there had been bombings in town. For the leaders of Kurdistan, the priority was now security, and they were fighting to keep ISIS from advancing any farther.

For the humanitarian community in Iraqi Kurdistan, the focus was caring for the wave of displaced people. In an emergency, analysts like me are asked to help plan the response, including prioritizing assistance. Some of the data we were gathering was concerning to me—specific camps were much worse off than others, while getting the same level of assistance. I asked my colleagues what was going on. Why weren't we prioritizing the camps that were the most affected by hunger?

Marco, an Italian colleague, listened patiently, then sighed. "Those are the camps where the Yazidis are," he said. He explained that whenever he and his colleagues visited the camps, it was evident that the poorest families were almost always Yazidi. The community was ravaged by poverty and hunger, much more so than the Arabs or Kurds.

The Yazidi people are a Kurdish-speaking minority. Because of their unconventional beliefs, they are outcasts in northern Iraq. Centuries of ostracism and persecution had left the community socially isolated. When ISIS advanced in northern Iraq in 2014, it spelled disaster for the community. As the Yazidi are not Muslims, ISIS branded them infidels who were to convert or perish.

In August of that year, close to 100,000 Yazidis fleeing an ISIS assault were surrounded and trapped on Mount Sinjar, a windswept mile-long mountain crag, where they spent days without food or water. Kurdish troops finally broke through ISIS lines and opened a corridor to get the Yazidis to safety. Those who survived settled in the camps of Iraqi Kurdistan, but as many as seven thousand Yazidi girls and women had been sold as sex slaves and forced to marry ISIS fighters, with many taken to Syria. Chased from their ancestral home, the Yazidi community had lost whatever assets it had. Now they were stranded and hungry in Iraqi Kurdistan.

At the time, all camps received food rations from WFP, but what were humanitarians to do when funding inevitably dwindled? Should we only feed the Yazidis, and not others who had also fled ISIS? This would only aggravate tensions between already polarized groups. Besides, like Syria, before the war Iraq had a long tradition of providing food to all its citizens. This was done through a universal food program set up in 1990 in response to international sanctions the UN imposed after Iraq invaded Kuwait. Today, Iraq's public distribution system is still a generous, but unwieldy, program. After ISIS forced families from their home provinces, families needed to re-register for the program, a process that could leave them facing months without much-needed food. The Yazidis had no "cushion" to fall back on—no assets to sell, and no relatives to rely on for support. Emergency assistance was the only thing that could keep them from going hungry.

To the people I worked with in Iraq, the concept of prioritizing and targeting food assistance is a dangerous Western notion. In the West, public assistance is usually means-tested, and only the poorest get food stamps or free school meals. In places like Iraq, with a tradition of state-provided food, picking and choosing aid recipients is almost sacrilege. In that context, humanitarians were expected to feed all the people of the camps without distinction until the public distribution system food allocations resumed.

In Syria's breadbasket, war signaled the end of decades of state control over agriculture. It heralded the emergence of a "new normal" where farming was a lot less about feeding people, and a lot more about making money. While I was in Syria, I spent a few days in Qamishli, a large town on the border with Turkey, to talk to farmers and traders about how the war had changed farming in the area.

Qamishli had the feeling of a city embattled. Its dilapidated and fading art deco district, laid out in a grid pattern, was home to a long-established Assyrian community. Because they were Christian, they were ISIS targets. Kidnappings and bombings were common. The Assyrians were also wary of the Kurds, who had recently taken control of the area; many of them had claimed asylum in Germany, and it seemed that those who remained were eager to do the same. Northeast Syria was in flux: the encroaching front line with ISIS, shifting demographics, and, of course, abrupt changes in farming, the bedrock of the area's economy.

Politics in the region had been upended. While government forces were confined to the city's airport, Kurdish forces had taken over the rest of the town and a long strip of land along the Turkish border. The Kurds of Syria called their newly autonomous homeland Rojava. Rojava had two sources of wealth: oil and grain. Its new Kurdish leaders, now in control of the nation's most productive wheatlands, found themselves with a hefty bargaining chip.

My first evening in Qamishli's old town, I met a man who dealt in agricultural goods. He sat in a modest office on a side street; a bare bulb hung from the ceiling over a battered gray metal desk. A dark green barrel of pesticides sat in the corner. On the shelf was a dog-eared almanac from eons ago.

"I have *never* seen the Jazeera like this," he said, more than once. The *Jazeera*, the island, was a term used by locals to describe the fertile land between the Euphrates and the Tigris Rivers, the nation's northeastern breadbasket.

The dealer explained that his customers all over the Jazeera had pivoted to sell produce to the Turkish market. In Syria, the government no longer paid a good price for wheat, and the crop required costly irrigation that farmers couldn't afford. As a result, many farmers had switched some of their acreage from wheat to more lucrative—and less water-intensive—crops such as coriander, for which smugglers would pay handsomely. "Growing such crops would have been considered heresy in the old days!" the dealer said. Farmers were getting a taste of the free market, and it didn't take long for them to forget the quotas of a planned economy. In the rush to cash in on exports, less grain was grown in a country where millions starved.

That night, a squadron of U.S. Air Force jets flew low over the town, on a run to hit the ISIS lines near Hassake, some sixty miles to the south. A few weeks earlier, ISIS had taken the town of Palmyra, located halfway between the fertile wheatlands of the east and the heavily populated cities hundreds of miles west. ISIS had organized public executions in the town's spectacular, perfectly preserved temples, and the international press was working itself into a frenzy covering the turn of events. But the fall of Palmyra was significant for another reason: it had effectively split the country in two. Hundreds of thousands of tons of wheat were now stranded in the rural east, in Qamishli's towering grain silos, while millions of people in the war-ravaged urban and industrial government-held west suffered from bread shortages.

Aid agencies worried that the stranded grain would be left to rot. WFP called for a ceasefire, so that traders could transport the stranded newly harvested grain to the mills and cities of the west. There was no official reply from the warring parties, but they all somehow came to an informal understanding that they would let the wheat through. After all, both sides desperately needed flour to make bread. ISIS let the government move stranded wheat through their checkpoints—as long as it paid a hefty fee.

I met a group of traders in a wholesale market in Homs, as they were unloading crates of cucumbers and tomatoes, the staples of every meal in Syria. The men, middle-aged and in sharp black leather jackets, all sported a few days of stubble. Some had their hair slicked back. They looked like shrewd businessmen. They told us the market was just awakening from its slumber after being closed for years because of the war. In fact, the halls all around us were nearly empty. Traders had not operated here for some time because the population, their customers, had fled.

The men knew how to deal with ISIS in Palmyra and elsewhere, they said. The going rate to get food through ISIS-controlled areas was then the equivalent of $52 per ton, payable in cash or in grain. These payoffs added considerably to the cost of doing business, and whatever grain made it through to the west of Syria would be sold to millers at a corresponding markup. Wartime trade was lucrative for certain parties. Millions of consumers, meanwhile, were saddled with higher costs for their bread.

As I write this in 2023, the war continues, though on a smaller scale. The Syrian army has secured most of the nation's territory west of the Euphrates, but hunger in Syria remains extremely high. In 2021 a record 60 percent of Syrians were acutely food insecure—following ten years of war that had traumatized, displaced, and killed its people, and crippled the safety nets that had long kept them fed. Syria—once a food-exporting country with a decent standard of living—now ranks as one of the most serious food emergencies in the world.

The Syrian conflict has devastated lands that once were the cradle of wheat farming. Ten thousand years ago, humans domesticated the plants that were the ancestors of wheat in the mountains and plains that straddle the borders of modern-day Iraq, Turkey, Lebanon, and Syria—a swath of land historians call the Fertile Crescent, where some of the world's earliest settlements arose. The cultivation of wheat and barley slowly expanded to Egypt and then throughout the Mediterranean. It reached Britain around five thousand years ago and spread east to the Indus valley and then to China. Today, wheat is the world's most traded crop. Along with rice and corn, it is a pillar of the global food trade.

Wild grasses that are genetically related to wheat still grow in the mountains of Syria. Some farmers there raise hardy varieties that they bred themselves over generations. This makes the area a conservatory of genetic diversity that provides immeasurable value for humanity. Crop geneticists hope that by studying these wild grasses and varieties, they will be able to breed wheat varieties tolerant of the heat and the dry spells our changing climate makes more likely.

Syria's war put this possible treasure at risk of being lost forever. As Syria's agriculture became increasingly modernized in the 1970s and 1980s, high-yield crop varieties replaced hardy local ones. An international research organization had set up a gene bank to catalog and preserve the area's crops near Aleppo, in northern Syria. In 2014, as the Syrian conflict escalated, the scientists reluctantly abandoned their Syrian research station. But over the three previous years, little by little, they had managed to transfer its precious seeds out of the country and to the Global Seed Vault, an underground facility located on the remote arctic island of Svalbard in Norway. In 2015, scientists were able to resume their work on Syrian plant genetics in Morocco and Lebanon, using the seeds they had exfiltrated from Aleppo. It was the first-ever withdrawal from the world's doomsday seed vault—but will likely not be the last.

While some of Syria's wheat genetics have been preserved, the crop itself has been weaponized. In what has become a grim ritual, every May armed men set thousands of acres of wheat on fire, just as the harvest approaches. In May 2019, more than 110,000 acres of land burned in northwest Syria in just a few weeks—a third of all agricultural land in the area. While some of the fires were incidental, or a by-product of fighting, much of the burning was intentional. Incendiary weapons were used to torch the maturing crop in order to starve the people, or to undermine those who control it.

Such scorched-earth tactics have existed as long as warfare itself. They were used to devastating effect in America's Civil War. In the fall of 1864, Union forces used this tactic in the Shenandoah Valley, Virginia's breadbasket, an event locals call "The Burning."

Richmond, the Confederate capital, had been home to one of the world's largest flour mills, and the Shenandoah Valley was its main supply source. Before the war, the fertile valley had exported its wheat as far as Latin America and Europe. Wheat farms in the valley were hugely successful, helped by fertile limestone-rich soils, abundant water, and an enslaved workforce.

By 1864, after two years of war, the South showed no sign of buckling. The Union decided to harden its tactics. It adopted a policy that commanding general Ulysses S. Grant called "total war." There would be no reprieves for the Confederacy—henceforth, Union forces would fight year-round, and food supplies for civilians would be legitimate targets. The policy aimed to starve out the Confederate army and break the South's will to fight. Grant wrote ominously in July of that year that he wished to "eat out Virginia clear and clean . . . so that crows flying over it for the balance of the season will have to carry their provender with them."

That fall, Grant's plan was put into practice. In October 1864, the Union's General Sheridan organized thirteen days of destruction that sent the valley's agricultural bounty up in smoke. His men torched barns, mills, bakeries, and crops. They confiscated thousands of livestock and tore out rail lines. Sheridan's men burned a swath of farmland seventy miles long and thirty miles wide, between the towns of Staunton and Strasburg. The Burning involved thousands of cavalrymen and a brigade of foot soldiers.

The strategy was effective: weakened Confederate forces lost the ensuing battles against Sheridan. Starving soldiers began deserting the Army of Virginia. The Confederacy surrendered the following spring. In the aftermath of the Burning, a Confederate cavalry officer asked: "What is the worst in war, to burn a barn or kill a fellow man?"

General Sheridan knew that burning a barn was the sure way to bring an adversary to its knees. "Death is popularly considered the maximum of punishment in war, but it is not," he wrote. "Reduction to poverty brings prayers for peace more surely and more quickly than does the destruction of human life." Those waging war in twenty-first-century Syria and Iraq understand that burning vast acreages of food crops is a powerful instrument of warfare.

The forever wars of the Middle East might lead to forever famines. To end both, we will need more than empathy. The deaths of millions of innocents may inspire heartfelt outpourings of rage and concern, but we need leaders brave enough to make peace—or wise enough not to set their countries aflame.

Not War, Not Peace

Feeding a Nation After a Conflict

What do you think about this reconciliation business?

—Jacques Roumain, *Masters of the Dew*

I t was a confidential war. Almost no one outside Congo-Brazzaville had heard about it. In January 2018, after two years of fighting, a ceasefire between the Ninja insurgency and the government had just been signed, and all over the Pool district in Congo, groups were cautiously emerging from the forest. Entire families that had spent the better part of two years in hiding were turning up on roadsides and at markets, so thin and disheveled that they looked like ghosts even to those who still recognized them. Their clothes were threadbare, the colors faded from having been washed so many times. The men had full beards and their hair had matted into dreadlocks. Many had fled when the war started in 2016, surviving on wild leaves and rainwater. Many of their children were so malnourished that they needed immediate medical attention.

The Pool is where the Congo River spreads into a lake twenty-two miles long and fourteen miles wide. On its eastern shore lies the boisterous metropolis of Kinshasa, and opposite, the more subdued city of Brazzaville. The powerful waters of the Congo pause in the Pool before hurtling down a series of rocky cataracts and plunging into the South Atlantic Ocean, two hundred miles downstream. The Pool is also the name of a district on the western shore of the water. This district, home to the Lari ethnic group, is a stunning land of grassy hills, forested bottoms, and hidden waterfalls. Between 1997 and 2018, it was also, sadly, the theater of three wars, all of which caused massive population displacement.

During the last of these horrific wars, farming stopped after it became too dangerous for people to tend their crops. Many started gardens near their houses, but these plots didn't produce enough to live on. Armed men plundered homesteads and attacked traders. Food production in the area collapsed. Many civilians fled to the nearby bush, where they remained for the duration of the war; others walked for days seeking safety. Those who stayed in areas under insurgent control were at the whim of the Ninjas, a mysterious and hermetic ethnic and religious insurgency whose reclusive leader had been at odds with the country's president for years.

I had become the director of the WFP in Congo the year before. I'd spent years managing food aid programs, then nearly a decade working on food security analysis. Managing a country office was the natural next step for my career, and I looked forward to the challenge. Congo was a forgotten conflict, off the radar of even the international humanitarian community. Compared to other countries, it was a small-scale war—affecting perhaps 300,000 people, a far cry from the tens of millions killed or displaced in Syria or Yemen. But the degree of child malnutrition was just as bad.

Wars are the main driver of acute hunger in the world. But when hostilities end, food shortages inevitably persist. This was unfortunately the case in the Pool. Even after the guns fell silent in December 2017, bringing aid to civilians still meant dealing with hostile Ninja commanders. Rebuilding war-ravaged farms and the infrastructure that supports them takes years. And the humanitarians who were helping rebuild the Pool's shattered food system knew the former rebels could easily take up arms again.

The most seriously affected area was a western section of the Pool known as Mpangala country. The Ninja combatants had sealed off the area once fighting started, and the situation was dire. The government presence there was limited to a handful of tiny fortified landing zones where soldiers received their supplies via Mi-8 helicopters that flew in from Brazzaville.

The breakdown in authority here was complete: administrators had fled the area when the fighting started in 2016. The Ninjas looted government property. Trade stopped. The very essentials of life—food, soap, matches, batteries, fuel—were in short supply. A few lucky civilians were able to barter for salt or sugar with the soldiers. Women gave birth in the forests where they had fled, and many of them were raped.

A ceasefire at Christmas in 2017 brought hope that the darkest days were over. Four months later, we organized the first aid convoy from Brazzaville into Ninja-controlled Mpangala country. The team heading there would carry out the first food distribution in the country since the conflict began. We took extraordinary precautions to ensure this trip would go well. We had secured assurances from both sides—the Congolese military and Ninja leaders—that their commanders would let the convoy through. Our two white, indestructible Renault trucks were clearly marked with WFP's flags and emblems, to avoid any confusion with military vehicles. We loaded the rice, oil, and beans in shipping containers, rather than in an open bed, to avoid any risk of pilfering.

I picked Antoine to oversee the operation. A lively man of about forty, he had volunteered for difficult assignments during the war. Antoine was from the south of Congo and spoke Lari, the language of the Pool; I was certain that he would be able to gain the confidence of locals, whereas a Lingala-speaking northerner would have been met with outright hostility. No foreigners would travel in the convoy.

Antoine and the others headed off in a cloud of dust and diesel exhaust, hardly knowing what lay ahead. The convoy rattled along the only road in and out of Mpangala country, a muddy track that had been closed to traffic for the better part of two years.

The first contact between the convoy and Ninja fighters took place in Bangou forest, about a hundred miles west of Brazzaville. I've traveled all over the world and seen many places, but the forest really does feel like something right out of a fairy tale. Its dark, vine-covered trees block out sunlight. Thick stands of bamboo grow by fast-flowing, crystal-clear rivers. The forest itself is hilly, and the road through it winds past hollow after hillock. It had been a perfect hideout for the insurgents.

The wary Ninjas in Bangou forest had not seen trucks in a long time. Of course, they knew there had been a ceasefire, and they had gotten word from their superiors that an aid convoy was on the way. But after almost two years of war, they were suspicious of outsiders.

The Ninjas stopped the convoy at the checkpoint and their commander asked Antoine to open the containers.

"How do we know these rations are not poisoned?" he asked, wary, before abruptly announcing that the convoy would not be allowed to pass.

Antoine tried reasoning with him, but the Ninjas wouldn't budge. It looked as though the convoy would be stuck, or worse, might need to return to Brazzaville, leaving thousands of civilians stranded without much-needed food rations. Desperate, Antoine asked his colleagues to unload some of the food. He opened one of the polypropylene rice bags and a plastic four-liter container of cooking oil, before shoving a handful of dry rice into his mouth and making an impassioned plea to the militiamen.

"Do you really think this food is poisoned?" he asked, as he crunched the raw rice and swallowed. He drank deeply from the container of cooking oil, paused, and asked again, "Is this food poisoned? Look at me, I just ate the food, and I am still alive. Let us through."

The Ninjas conferred for what seemed an eternity, but finally decided to let the convoy through. Antoine's theatrics had done the trick: the trucks made it to the small town of Kindamba. After years of being cut off from the world, Kindamba was a shell of its former self. There was no electricity and no cell phone service. The district hospital had been thoroughly ransacked, and thieves had stolen the batteries in each of the solar streetlights in the town, leaving Kindamba pitch-black after sundown. Beleaguered civilians lined the streets, staring at the convoy in disbelief. Food distributions began the next day.

Before the war, WFP had a field office just outside Kindamba, but when the conflict started, law and order broke down and aid workers fled. A crowd broke into the office and made off with all the furniture. The day Antoine and his team arrived in Kindamba, they caught sight of a man on the side of the road, a Ninja. He was spinning around in one of the swiveling ergonomic chairs that had once been at our office.

"You all were really comfortable in there, weren't you!" he called to Antoine, laughing as he spun around in the stolen chair.

For the civilians who had weathered the war, the mere sight of the white UN trucks rolling into Kindamba brought hope that things might finally get better. But some of the Ninjas bristled at the loss of control that the arrival of outsiders represented. All the recent ceasefire did was consolidate a stalemate, with no winners or losers. Ninja leaders still called the shots in Mpangala country.

"We will get you in Bangou forest when you go back," one of them shouted to Antoine as he was leaving.

Nothing came of that threat, but it was a harbinger of the tensions that would persist over the next few years. Antoine's convoy was just the beginning of a broader humanitarian effort to help the people of Mpangala recover from the war. Most of the population had been left facing food shortages because of the conflict's devastating impacts on farming and trade, and because it had undermined the social trust between traders, farmers, political leaders, and administrative authorities so essential to a community's ability to feed itself.

Hunger does not evaporate once the shooting stops. As Antoine's experience shows, logistical complications and lingering tensions remain after a ceasefire. Investments in post-conflict food systems are vital, but also risky. In 2018 the Pool found itself at a fork in the road: either a genuine peace would hold and communities could rebuild, or an uncertain post-conflict situation would fester, creating a drawn-out food crisis.

As we began organizing convoys to Kindamba, colleagues asked about the risk the team was taking. Was it worth confronting an armed militia to bring aid? Why not wait until the situation improved? I told them that even though there were risks, we had an obligation to help. The level of suffering was such that it wasn't acceptable to do nothing. The discussion made me think about the motivations of the team going to Kindamba. Antoine and the others were not doing it for the money. Of course, they got generous stipends for the time they spent managing distributions in Mpangala country. But really, they were taking these risks because of a desire to right an old wrong.

Many of the Congolese humanitarians who went to Mpangala country in 2018 had been caught on the wrong side of the 1997 war. They were all southerners, and they remembered fleeing for their lives when the Cobras, a northern militia, took over Brazzaville, overthrowing a southern-led government. To this day, an invisible fault line splits the capital city in two. I met people from southern Brazzaville who wouldn't set foot in the north of town, and people from northern neighborhoods that regarded the southern part of town as a foreign country.

The southerners who would lead the Pool response had been excluded from the prestigious government jobs that the northerners had kept for themselves. Their kin had experienced displacement and hunger during the three wars in the Pool. Now they had found work with the UN and the NGOs, and they would use their positions to fix the damage the northern-dominated military had visited on their people.

It wasn't just the employees of international agencies that shone during the response. Emeline was the head nurse at a health center in Mayaba, a dusty hamlet about twenty miles south of Brazzaville. I met her not long after I arrived in Congo, on a day when she was organizing a distribution of ready-to-use food for malnourished children and mothers. These prepackaged foods are rich in energy, vitamins, and minerals that are designed to help children put on weight. The health center was a small, unassuming building with a badly corroded roof and walls that were gray and green with mold. While it was not much to look at, the center offered valuable services for the population, such as inoculations and prenatal consultations, and referred urgent cases to the district hospital in Brazzaville.

When the war broke out, Mabaya—like all neighboring towns—was sacked. When I drove through soon after the cease-fire, solar panels had been stolen, windows broken, and coops and yards emptied of chickens and goats—they had all been carried away by men in arms. As its people left for the relative security of Brazzaville or Kinkala, the regional capital, Mabaya became a ghost town. Weeds grew in the silent forecourts of abandoned houses. With no one left to pick the green and red mangoes, they ripened, fell to the sandy ground, and were left to rot.

For Emeline, the easy decision would have been to close the center and wait out the conflict in the safety of Brazzaville. But she was determined to help her people. She transported Mabaya's records and supplies to a safer location on a hilltop compound just outside Brazzaville, where a church had given her a space. The new, temporary Mabaya health center was even more basic than the old one, but it was enough. Emeline had collected a group of women, volunteers who wanted to help her. Soon enough, the displaced people of Mabaya who'd come to Brazzaville heard that their health center was open again, and they flocked to the site.

Emeline and her team provided essential nutrition to hundreds of children and their mothers. During one of my visits to the center, I met a young mother in her early twenties who had come for a distribution of therapeutic food, a peanut butter paste fortified with essential nutrients and fat. The paste comes packed in a foil pouch, ready to eat. As she waited her turn, her two-year-old boy on her lap, she told me that she had gone back to her hometown in the Pool after the ceasefire, only to find that conditions there were much too hard. There was no work, there were no crops being grown, and there was not enough food. Her child was weak and had been diagnosed with malnutrition. She decided to come back to Brazzaville, where she had heard she could get help for her son in the new Mabaya center. Emeline had enrolled the child in her nutrition program and now, two months later, he was doing much better.

Emeline did whatever it took to ensure her people would be fed, and she treated them with dignity. One day she called me at the office, and politely told me that she was low on food; if we didn't resupply her the very next day, hundreds of people would go hungry. And, she added, she needed a tent for shade, because too many of the women on distribution day waited in the sun. The next day, as requested, we delivered her food and the tent. Protocol and conventional hierarchies, of which there are many in the humanitarian community, were not going to stop her from doing her job; it's no wonder people traveled from miles away to see her.

In aid circles, there is a stereotype of the powerless and overly deferential local humanitarian worker. My colleagues often rolled their eyes when we'd have to do anything with the local health departments because decisions always seemed to take forever. Emeline shattered that myth for anyone who met her. She told us what she needed, and how to support her. She was the one in control. In the response to the emergency in the Pool, I met local people who stood out as brave, uncompromising humanitarians who found ways to get the job done.

As we continued to implement aid programs after the ceasefire, I became increasingly familiar with the Ninjas and their history. Reverend Ntumi, their leader, was born Frédéric Bintsamou. He is a Lari would-be messiah whose ministry began in the 1990s. Reverend Ntumi remains the uncontested political and religious leader of the enigmatic Ninja movement, whose practices seem designed to confuse. Its fighters wear purple scarves or armbands, the color of their movement but also that of the Catholic clergy and of the Congolese Republican Guard. Ninja fighters sport beards and dreadlocks, a choice made to shock the westernized, clean-cut elites of Brazzaville. Ntumi's church, almost exclusively Lari, imposes an elaborate set of rituals about dress, food, and farming on its members. But one rule stands above all: loyalty to Ntumi.

The Ninja movement emerged during the 1997 civil war in Congo—they were the ethnic militia that controlled the Lari-majority Bacongo neighborhood during the war. The name they adopted, and that of their mortal enemy, the Cobras from the north, were probably inspired by the kung fu movies that were popular at the time. Their choice of branding did not help me when I needed to explain to USAID, the Europeans, the Japanese, or WFP headquarters that armed "Ninjas" had caused a serious humanitarian crisis in a remote corner of central Africa.

Ntumi was one of the foot soldiers in the embattled Ninjas in 1998, when the militia was waging a rearguard action against the Cobras, who benefited from the support of French and Angolan forces. Legend has it that Ntumi, then a young Pentecostal preacher and healer, and a squad of sixteen Ninjas faced off against a detachment of 1,500 Cobra paratroopers near Mindouli in the Pool district. The Cobras were under the command of Colonel Obosso, whom Ntumi described as "a hulking monster bristling with fetishes." It was a David against a Goliath, and Ntumi later wrote a vainglorious account of the battle. His men, armed with only three rifles and sticks, were surrounded and out of ammunition. It seemed their fate was sealed. Suddenly "their sticks started firing like automatic rifles; pebbles thrown at the soldiers exploded like grenades. And death devoured the soldiers . . . None of the sixteen fighters fell, the enemy bullets rebounded off their bodies like rockets."

Ntumi's self-created notoriety as a magician and warrior helped him become the leader of the Ninjas, displacing those who had founded the militia. Drawing on biblical symbolism, he would claim to heal his followers of demonic possession with prayer, song, and symbolic foods that included wheat flour and olive oil. He came to see himself as the new Messiah. In 1998, after allegedly fasting for forty days, he had a vision of the Archangel Michael, who appeared to him shrouded in purple. The Reverend afterward began his ministry, announcing to his followers, "My reign is eternal, I am Yahweh's chosen one." He renamed himself Ntumi, the messenger.

Deep in Mpangala country, Ntumi built the beginnings of a holy city, with churches, a boarding school, and businesses. It was rumored all was funded by profits the Ninjas amassed from illegal logging. The Ninjas were an inward-looking movement, one that aimed to build a separate Lari society. They created a new flag by adding a broad stripe of Ninja purple to the green, yellow, and red national banner. Determined to play a leading role in Congo's politics, Ntumi maintained an army that he indoctrinated through mystical-martial training, the strict observance of rituals, and the avoidance of taboos. Ninja fighters, for instance, needed to pay for their pastor's permission to shave, which explains why they wore beards and dreadlocks. Ntumi would use the young men under his command to wreak havoc in Congolese politics for the next decades.

After a second war that began in 2002 and ended in 2003, Ntumi made peace with the government, and in 2009 he moved to Brazzaville and joined the Congolese cabinet. Frustrated by two failed attempts to run for elected office, he ultimately returned to his forest hideout and the separate society he had been cultivating. But within the ranks, suspicions grew that he was a turncoat who had been bought off by the authorities. Loyalty to Ntumi ebbed. He remained a hermit in Mpangala country, surrounded by a core of a few thousand loyal followers, keeping a close eye on national politics.

In April 2016, the Ninjas took up arms again after Denis Sassou Nguesso, the erstwhile leader of the Cobras, won another term as president. There was widespread suspicion the election was rigged. Fighting erupted in Brazzaville when the results were announced, and soon the Pool was in flames once again. The Ninjas blew up the bridges on the railway linking Brazzaville to its port, Pointe Noire, seriously threatening vital supplies of food and fuel to the capital.

The government dispatched waves of soldiers to the Pool to track down the Ninjas and their leader, deploying Mi-8 helicopter gunships whose low-altitude flights terrified the population. Holed up in Mpangala country, Ntumi and his remaining men more than held their own against the onslaught. The government's BTR-60 armored personnel carriers, juggernauts of steel and rubber, were useless on the Pool's sandy ground. Though the Ninjas were consummate underdogs, they managed to keep control of their base in Mpangala country and fought government forces to a stalemate. Eventually, representatives of the two sides signed a ceasefire on Christmas 2017.

As of 2023, Ntumi, a winner of sorts, remains in his holy city. He addresses his support outside Mpangala country through cryptic recorded statements he circulates through WhatsApp. His chaotic personal trajectory has taken him from the bush to the plush halls of power and back again. His "plan," Ntumi tells his followers, is currently known only to God himself, but will be slowly revealed to the faithful. As Ntumi ponders his next move, the population of the Pool continues to bear the consequences of his messianic aspirations.

As the months went by in 2018, humanitarian agencies were able to resume their programs in Mpangala country. With help from the UN, a laborious process began to initiate dialogue between national authorities, the rebels, and the community, so that differences could be discussed around a table. Projects to rebuild wells, schools, and hospitals began. Counselors came to support women who had been raped during the conflict. WFP provided food to people who worked to reconstruct the roads that had not been maintained for years, and invested to kick-start food production. Humanitarians reopened their offices in the area. But the important work of healing the wounds of conflict would be stifled by the fact that the Ninjas believed that they were entitled to a share of the resources that were finally trickling into the district.

Felix, a slim, intellectual Congolese man, became the head of the WFP office in Kindamba when it reopened in 2018. He would face the challenge of dealing with the Ninjas day-to-day. I got to know Felix through the years we worked together. He had been a quiet kid from the Lari-speaking Bacongo district of southern Brazzaville. A southerner in his thirties, he had grown up witnessing the Pool's troubles. When fighting broke out in 1997, he, like many others, was kidnapped by retreating Ninja forces as they fell back to the hills and forests of Mpangala country.

Separated from his parents, Felix had to adjust to life in the country. He stopped going to school and learned how to fish in the streams. Farming became a passion, which led him to study agronomy later in life. And he got to know the members of the Ninja movement, from leaders to foot soldiers. When I saw him interact with the Ninjas, he was always guarded and stern.

Early one morning in 2020, when I was at home in Brazzaville, I received an email from Felix with the subject line "security update"—a sign that he had something important to say. In this case, it was an understatement: Ninja fighters had threatened to rape Alphonsine and Grace, two of our local colleagues in Kindamba. The women had wisely halted a food distribution when a group of Ninjas turned up at the site; they knew that if the men stayed, they would steal the food from the civilians. Their actions aggravated the Ninjas, who were not used to being denied what they wanted and believed they could intimidate humanitarian workers with impunity. Rape was no idle threat; it was a fresh memory, common during the war. I asked Alphonsine and Grace to come to Brazzaville, and we stopped aid distributions until further notice.

I decided to travel to Kindamba to tell the militiamen to leave my staff alone. How could I expect them to work in Kindamba if I didn't have their back when they were in danger?

I set off with my driver. We went through the checkpoints where the Ninjas' red, green, yellow, and purple flag flew. Past Ntumi's churches. Through the dark Bangou forest. Over the bridges made of rough-hewn planks. In the Toyota, we forded the clear waters of the wide river at Tonato. I soon arrived in Kindamba.

The local authorities had offered to mediate the discussion. In such situations in rural Congo, men traditionally meet under a large shade tree, the *mbongui*, or "palaver tree," under which differences are discussed. A presiding elder, usually a patriarch from a powerful family, listens, mulls over the exchange, then delivers his opinion to resolve the dispute.

Here, we weren't under an actual palaver tree but the wide shady porch at the dilapidated district office, part of the old command post the French had built perhaps a hundred years ago. Its dusty lot, strewn with rusting vehicles, was where the helicopters from Brazzaville had landed to supply government troops when the Ninjas controlled the road. During the insurgency, bored government soldiers had carved dozens of messages and images into the mud walls; crude representations of a helicopter, gunships, and gun-toting soldiers decorated the walls surrounding us.

The district officer and the local Ninja commanders were seated around a table, along with other humanitarian workers from the UN and NGO community. In the second row was Ntumi's daughter, who sat silently, representing her father, who was in his village a few miles away. She never uttered a word, probably in deference to the patriarchal norms in Congolese society, but her presence was meaningful: she would be her father's eyes and ears.

The Ninja leaders were white-haired elders—they had fought their entire adult lives, taking orders from Ntumi for the past twenty-five years. The Ninja leader who sat across from me was thin and gray. His left eye was cloudy, probably from a cataract. He and his companions looked at me silently. Felix was seated behind me. The Ninjas had seen me before and our dealings had been cordial enough, but this time the tension between us was thick. They had gone too far.

The presiding elder—in this case a senior government official who had come from Brazzaville but was originally from the area—played the role of neutral arbiter. He called the meeting to order and asked the Ninjas to speak first.

The Ninja commander seated opposite me began to speak. In flawless French, without once looking at me, he explained to the presiding elder that they, the Ninjas, were not to blame for what had happened. He argued that the aid workers in Kindamba were too strict and should let the Ninjas take their fair share of the resources coming to the area.

When my turn came, I replied that nothing could justify a threat of rape. I told them we'd close the office in Kindamba and stop all distributions permanently if WFP staff were threatened again. The presiding elder listened in silence. Once everyone around the table had said their piece, the elder gathered his thoughts. He encouraged both sides to communicate and collaborate, using ponderous sentences meant to convey respect for everyone in attendance. The meeting was over. He hadn't offered a direct dressing-down of the Ninjas, but it was clear that he disapproved of their behavior.

Felix was with me as we walked away. His body language expressed relief. He was not one for words, but I understood from his demeanor that he was encouraged—the Ninjas knew there were consequences to their actions. I got into my car for the long drive back to Brazzaville. The Ninjas of Kindamba left my colleagues alone after that trip. We later heard that Ntumi, whose daughter had no doubt told him what was said, had disciplined the soldiers who'd threatened Alphonsine and Grace. After we aired our differences, and our red lines were known, we could continue working in Mpangala country.

Congo, like many states in the wake of conflict, tried to disarm the insurgency and facilitate a return to civilian life. The process is called Disarmament, Demobilization, and Reintegration

(DDR). It involves collecting combatants' weapons, disbanding their units, and supporting their life as civilians, typically through training and monetary grants, and often with counseling.

When the December 2017 ceasefire ended the war in the Pool, there was hope a DDR process would soon begin. In August 2018, the government organized a disarmament campaign and collected weapons. The weary Ninjas, who had been through such processes before, turned in many old hunting rifles, while keeping the most lethal weapons in their arsenal. Many of them, having spent years fighting in the jungle, grudgingly registered as ex-combatants, assuming it would entitle them to money: Ninja leaders told the rank and file they would receive a stipend and some training to return to civilian life, perhaps even capital to start a business.

Unfortunately, those promises were not kept. The Ninjas had spent close to two years fighting in the bush, only to be betrayed. The Congolese government was broke, and never funded the reintegration program, leaving Ninja leaders with nothing to offer their men. Tired of empty promises, some disgruntled Ninjas turned to highway robbery, attacking the rickety pickup trucks that ventured onto Route Nationale 1. Others robbed farms.

The ceasefire without real disarmament or reintegration meant that Mpangala country was stuck in a situation that was no longer war, but not quite peace. The Ninjas still controlled the roads, their purple flag flying from multiple checkpoints. At a checkpoint at the entry to Bangou forest, built from beaten-up oil drums and rope, Ntumi's younger brother sat in the shade of palm trees, monitoring who was coming and going, reporting any significant visitors to the Reverend. He and his men charged hefty fees to traders entering the area.

It was not war yet not quite peace because the teachers, nurses, and municipal workers who had fled when the war broke out only trickled back slowly, unsure of their safety. Like government workers, they were targets for the Ninjas. In March 2020, a high school principal in Mindouli had been beaten up by Ninjas, after he had dared discipline one of his unruly students, who happened to be a relative of Reverend Ntumi. The young man had ridden into the high school courtyard on his motorbike at high speed, disrupting classes. That even a principal could be attacked had shocked the other teachers. They had signed up to teach, not to live at the whim of armed men who acted with total impunity.

It was not war yet not quite peace because figures of authority were powerless to enforce the rule of law. The district officer in Kimba, north of Kindamba, needed to drive miles from his post and walk up a hill in search of a signal, in order to place a phone call. With such limited resources, keeping the peace was a whimsical proposition. The authorities could do nothing to stop the depredation of the Ninjas, not just because they lacked the money, but also because they were cautious to avoid incidents that would endanger the ceasefire.

It was not war yet not quite peace because the Ninjas were openly terrorizing the people. I visited a group of women who farmed fish near the town of Vinza, in Mpangala country. During the war the ponds had been abandoned and had silted up, and WFP was working to help the women restore them. The pond bottoms needed to be cured, their dykes raised, their sluice gates replaced. After a few months of painstaking work, the ponds looked just as they had before, but the women and their livelihoods were at the mercy of the Ninjas. "Go ahead, rebuild those ponds," a passing Ninja told the women at the cooperative. "We will come to loot the fish whenever we feel like it."

In 2019 half of all families didn't have enough to eat, as people struggled to rebuild.

Peacebuilding works best when ex-fighters can open businesses and earn an honest living. When the process occurs within a broad-based economic recovery, tensions between ex-fighters and the community are muted. None of these conditions existed in the Pool after the 2016–2017 war. The Ninja fighters who had threatened my colleagues and kept their community food insecure had followed an all-too-familiar pattern.

In Zimbabwe, veteran groups that fought a fifteen-year guerrilla war never disbanded after the country gained independence in 1980. They stoked political violence in the 1990s and 2000s, occupying white-owned farmland and undermining the country's food production. Failed DDR processes in the 2000s also contributed to the Central African Republic's protracted conflict, as frustrated fighters took up arms again, which contributed to one of the world's most serious food crises.

In Congo, the government's financial position was tenuous, and it could hardly afford a multimillion-dollar reintegration program. But it also knew the Ninjas were war-weary; their sympathizers seized the chance to make peace on the cheap, because they calculated that the insurgents would not take to the hills again anytime soon. This convenient shortcut to peace was a gamble that left the Pool's civilian population exposed to their disgruntled tormentors. The choice has made future conflict, and continued hunger, almost certain.

Going Viral

The Relationship Between Disease and Hunger

There are fevers that consume you without seeming to. We're like a piece of furniture that looks very solid, very strong, but the termites are already inside. And one fine day, we fall into dust.

—Jacques Roumain, *Masters of the Dew*

The Black Death that began in 1347 was one of the deadliest epidemics to hit medieval Europe. In waves that lasted until 1351, it killed about 25 million people, between one-half and one-third of Europe's population. The continent's population would only recover to pre-plague levels in the sixteenth century.

We commonly hear that the bacillus probably originated in Central Asia. A Mongol army had been laying siege to the Crimean city of Kaffa, on the shores of the Black Sea, when the plague tore through their camp. In an early exercise in biological warfare, the Mongols are said to have catapulted plague-ridden bodies over the city walls before they withdrew. The plague soon infested the population of Kaffa, and hitched a ride on a Genovese fleet that had been in the town's harbor. The ships never made it home. By the time they made it to southern Italy, the crews were dead or seriously ill. The scavengers who plundered the stricken ships then introduced the plague to the continent, where it proceeded to kill millions.

Why was the Black Death so devastating? Disease outbreaks

were not, after all, uncommon in the Middle Ages. We have recently learned there is more to the Black Death's grisly toll than a uniquely aggressive microorganism. Careful analysis of ice cores, tree rings, and written records has proven to historians that prior to the outbreak of the pandemic, a vast swath of northern Europe had gone through years of cool, wet weather that caused food production to plunge. The ensuing famines left the population much more susceptible to the plague. Hunger helped turn mass disease into a mass mortality event, as the plague preyed on the weakened immune systems of a malnourished population.

In our own time, the COVID-19 pandemic was a reminder that disease and hunger often go hand in hand. Hunger can be the soil in which illness thrives, but it can just as well be the consequence of mass disease outbreaks and our mistakes in handling them. As COVID spread, even wealthy societies struggled to respond to the effects of pandemic-induced food insecurity. Worldwide, the virus and our response—including severe lockdowns that shuttered businesses and markets—caused the number of those affected by acute hunger to double from 135 to 270 million people. The unintended effects of what were meant to be lifesaving measures force us to face uncomfortable questions. Were the public health benefits of lockdowns and quarantines worth it, considering their destructive impacts on people's ability to feed their families? Is there a way to contain a pandemic without sacrificing the poorest and most marginalized, or plunging well-off people into need? We need to look at these questions anew, and with a greater sense of urgency.

When I started working for WFP in the Sahel in 2001, an old-timer who was showing me the ropes told me that there were two variables that determine food security, *pluie* and *prix*, near homophones in French, which translate to "rainfall" and "prices." No mention of disease. When analysts like me were pulling together our monthly reports, we would, at most, take note of the usual seasonal surges in malaria or cholera that occurred during the rainy months. We would explain in our reports that these (sadly routine) diseases could make malnutrition worse and leave it at that.

But it wasn't long after the chat with my colleague in the Sahel that I heard the phrase "new variant famine." Alex de Waal, director of the World Peace Foundation and a professor at Tufts University, coined the phrase to describe famines caused by factors other than the familiar demon of drought. The term "new variant" acquired another sort of worrying connotation during the COVID pandemic. De Waal was using it to warn that the spread of the HIV/AIDS pandemic in southern Africa, where the disease affected one in five adults, would give rise to widespread food insecurity. He feared that with the most productive segment of the population—the young labor force—dying of AIDS, society would be less able to grow the food it needed, or to cope with episodes of scarcity.

In a seminal 2003 article, de Waal and Alan Whiteside outlined the mechanics of the new variant famine. Southern Africa had been facing a decline in food production that drought or policy measures alone could not explain. Agricultural statistics were clear: the maize farmers of Malawi, Zambia, and Zimbabwe were shifting to cassava, a nutrient-poor plant that was much less labor-intensive. It was a crop that the AIDS-depleted labor force could handle. De Waal and Whiteside saw this shift as part of the reversal of previous agricultural development gains.

While the decline in overall food production was concerning, the pandemic's impacts on how families earned a living were most alarming. De Waal and Whiteside argued that as HIV/AIDS killed young adults and breadwinners, surviving family members simply did not have the manpower to grow enough food, or to earn the money needed to feed themselves. By the early 2000s, 13 percent of all children in southern Africa were orphans, half of them because their parents had died of AIDS. The loss of a significant portion of a whole generation also meant that certain kinds of knowledge—such as the preparation of wild foods—were not being passed down to the next generation, who were losing important coping strategies that had sustained people through droughts and other hard times. Surviving adults had to care for sick relatives and AIDS orphans (many sent from cities to rural areas), thus diverting more labor away from farming.

De Waal and Whiteside also noted complex and dangerous interactions between hunger and disease: undernourished people are more susceptible to HIV/AIDS. Malnutrition abets mother-to-child transmission of the virus, while nutrition deficiencies in patients accelerate its progression. In English-speaking Africa, AIDS is called the "slims" because of the diarrhea and rapid weight loss associated with it.

"We must face the prospect," they concluded, "that this food emergency will become a structural feature of the southern African landscape for many years to come, unless innovative and generous interventions are made now." In the years since de Waal and Whiteside's article, HIV treatment has slowly become more widely available on the continent, in spite of obstacles linked to financing, supply chains, and the capacity of health systems. While accessing treatment can still be a challenge for many people with HIV/AIDS in Africa, a worst-case scenario was averted.

It wasn't long after I began as a humanitarian worker that the full force of the HIV/AIDS pandemic struck close to home. It was 2002, and I was chatting with a colleague who had popped into my office in Niamey, Niger. Djingarey had just come back from a week in Dakar.

"So, how did the trip go?" I asked.

Djingarey replied in a conspiratorial whisper that he thought the "snails" found in Senegalese cuisine were disgusting, slimy, pungent, and unappetizing. He was referring to shrimp. While seafood was abundant in Dakar, it was unknown in landlocked Niger, where he was from. "Hey, I brought you something from Senegal," he added. He reached into a plastic shopping bag and handed me a package of chocolate biscuits—a common snack around the world, but then a delicacy in Niger. Then he popped over to the next office, distributing chocolate biscuits to our coworkers.

Djingarey was the life of WFP's office in Niamey, an easygoing and energetic presence. His unmistakable enthusiastic chatter would echo through the ground-floor hallway. Nothing ever seemed to bother Djingarey. He was from the minority Gourmantche community of western Niger that happily accommodated Christianity, Islam, and traditional beliefs. Accordingly, Djingarey got along with everyone.

Djingarey had joined the organization as a young office helper during the famine of 1983–1984. When I first arrived on the team, he was making photocopies and pouring coffee—and also managing our email server and troubleshooting internet outages. Through smarts, ingenuity, and hard work, he became the person in charge of our radio and IT network. Visitors from abroad, often Anglo telecoms experts, were impressed with his work. He had taught himself English and would banter enthusiastically with these visitors. WFP decided to invest in his career and sent him to Dakar for training.

Not long after his return from Dakar, we heard that Djingarey was not well. He took some time off work, which was quite unusual for him. When he came back to the office weeks later, he was weak and thin, and more than once I saw him leaning against the wall for support. One morning I spotted him as he stood in the corridor, wearing a beige jacket instead of his usual well-worn powder blue uniform. There was a sad, drained look on his face, and I noticed beads of sweat on his brow. He gave me a weak hello, but I could tell his usual energy was gone; it seemed that it took all his strength to stay on his feet.

By then, people had started talking. "I hope he doesn't have AIDS," a colleague told me behind the closed door of his office.

That was the last day I would ever see Djingarey. The next news I heard of him came a few weeks later: he was dead.

I learned later that WFP had done its best to help him get care, but there were very limited options for treating AIDS in Niger at the time. In the late 1990s and early 2000s, HIV and AIDS tore through the continent, hitting healthy young adults. By the mid-2000s therapies developed in Western countries were finally being rolled out in sub-Saharan Africa. Affordable generic versions were available on the African market. While those came too late to save Djingarey and many others, the drugs would make a difference in slowing the pandemic.

A few years after Djingarey died from AIDS, I was placed in charge of WFP's programs in Guinea-Bissau. I realized there how food could play as big a role as medicine in treating disease. Located five hours west of Niger by plane, Guinea-Bissau is a West African nation once known as "Portugal's Vietnam." The nation won its independence in 1973 after a decade of fighting, its scrappy fighters pinning down an entire Portuguese army in the country's jungles and tidal creeks. By 2006, when I was assigned there, it was a place in decay, plagued by chronic infighting among the political elite. The nation had become notorious as an emerging hub of the narcotics trade, and for the grisly fate of its president, Nino Vieira, whose rivals hacked him to death with machetes in 2009. It was also a place where HIV/AIDS was stealthily taking a toll on society.

By 2006, antiretrovirals had become available in Africa, helping people with HIV live longer, healthier lives. The therapy involves swallowing a rotating set of pills every day. Patients taking the potent drug cocktail need to be well fed to withstand the treatment. The medication must be taken with food. In Guinea-Bissau, WFP provided food to people with HIV/AIDS and tuberculosis, the latter an opportunistic infection often associated with HIV. We didn't provide just any food: patients received a blend of corn and soya that packed just enough calories, protein, and fat into a single ration to help patients absorb the antiretrovirals and recover some of their weight.

One day at an HIV/AIDS treatment center located down a badly potholed road in Bissau, I met a woman in her twenties named Roselia. A local NGO ran the center out of a large, one-story pink house with a tiled roof and a wraparound porch. The place was packed with people coming for different types of care. Although it had no running water or electricity—almost none of the clinics in the country did—the center helped thousands of people with HIV and AIDS by giving them medication and support. Álvaro, the center's white-coated doctor, was leading me on a tour, and Roselia was tagging along. Álvaro led me to his office, opened a drawer, and pulled out a photo album.

"See this picture?" Álvaro pointed to a glossy color photo in the album. It featured a skeletal woman in a long green dress, nothing but skin and bones. "Do you recognize Roselia?" the doctor asked me, beaming, proud of his work. Roselia, who had been waiting for her moment, broke into a smile. I was floored: the picture, taken just a few months before, showed her at death's door. And now here she stood, next to me, the picture of glowing good health. The antiretrovirals and the food she received had revived her.

Roselia told me that she now felt strong enough to work. She had begun growing tomatoes with other HIV-positive people, on a nearby plot that the NGO had secured for them. The project was supposed to help people living with the virus find a way to provide for their families after they received treatment. Unfortunately, these patients faced stigma from others in the community—many buyers shunned the tomatoes that Roselia and her companions grew. The medicine and food had extended her life, but ensuring she could live with HIV in dignity was a more difficult problem to solve.

HIV/AIDS was a slow-onset pandemic that over several years grew into a juggernaut that threatened entire nations' food supply. But as we found out in 2020, sudden disease outbreaks can quickly drag unprepared societies, rich and poor, into a food crisis.

I was in Congo in late March 2020 when COVID-19 hit. Fear was sweeping through the streets of the capital. The government had announced that a nationwide lockdown would begin in seventy-two hours. The bus stations of Brazzaville were packed, as thousands fled the crowded capital for the countryside, where they planned to wait out the lockdown with relatives. My colleague Delphine said it felt like the war in 1997. Delphine was the elder stateswoman at the office, and she recalled how during the dark days of that war, columns of armed men streamed into the capital, dueling militias that fought each other to control Brazzaville. She was a UN nutritionist then, working to bring food assistance to thousands of displaced civilians. But this time, it was not men in arms that people were fleeing, it was a microscopic virus.

As the seventy-two hours ticked away, the tension became palpable. Despite being cash-strapped, the government had somehow managed to pay March wages on time, and civil servants flocked to the ATMs in front of the glass-fronted banks downtown. Under the tropical sun—and the watchful eyes of police officers—teachers, clerks, accountants, and nurses jostled to withdraw their wages ahead of the lockdown. There was a rush on food supplies as people bought in bulk. Crowds besieged the town's usually quiet supermarkets, and shelves were stripped bare. On the evening of March 31, the military and police set up impromptu roadblocks made of old planks, truck axles, and oil drums. At 8 p.m., the first nightly curfew started. Silence fell over the capital like a blanket.

Congo's COVID-19 lockdown was strict. Schools, churches, and restaurants closed, and "non-essential" businesses were shuttered. People were ordered to stay at home, except to buy food or medicine. Public transportation was halted: the city's fleet of bottle-green taxis and buses ceased to operate. Trucks stopped plying intercity routes. The town's ordinarily busy markets were open only on Mondays, Wednesdays, and Fridays. Armed military units enforced the curfew.

The food impacts of Congo's COVID-19 lockdown—*le confinement*—were immediate, as the measures meant to halt the virus strained the vital, fragile supply chains that kept the nation fed. Congo relies on food imports, and the restrictions on mobility meant that the country's only port operated at reduced hours. Longshoremen and stevedores had trouble getting to the port for lack of transportation, and left their shifts early to be home before curfew. Containers packed with imported food were stuck in the port, while local produce was stranded in farming areas, unable to reach urban markets. The vehicles that carried people from rural towns to Brazzaville, banned from operating under the lockdown, were the same ones that brought fresh produce to the market. Farmers who sold at Brazzaville market found themselves with mountains of produce they could not sell.

"The plantain is rotting in the forest," a colleague told me.

The scarcity caused food prices to creep up in urban areas. Shrewd bakers turned to "shrinkflation" to protect their profits. At the Marché Total, the large market in central Brazzaville, the 100-franc (20-U.S.-cent) baguette, the morning staple of the masses, usually slathered in mayo and washed down with a generous cup of sweet milky Nescafé, began looking more like a roll, as the bakers shortened its length to save on flour.

As serious as the impacts on the supply chain were, the consequences for the job market were devastating. In Brazzaville—as in many African cities—people depend on informal employment to earn a living. The lockdown was a death knell for the hairdressers, streetside food vendors, petty traders, hawkers, taxi drivers, and construction workers whose trade vanished overnight.

Desperation mounted as the confinement stretched into weeks. Kids tried anything to find the food they needed. I received a WhatsApp video from a colleague showing two skinny, bare-chested teenage boys, standing in the backyard of a house. They had caught and skinned a cat and were getting ready to roast it. They were grinning ear to ear because they'd finally found food. "It's the lockdown," one of them said to the other, proudly holding the cat's carcass to the phone's camera. "We'll start with this part right here," said the other, tapping the skinned cat's blackened hind legs with the side of a broad knife.

It reminded me of the stories I had heard about the starving population eating the animals at Brazzaville Zoo during the dark days of 1997. I'd never known whether those stories were true or not. But I could see now that many people were desperate. One morning in May, after six weeks (the lockdown in Brazzaville would last seven), I arrived at the office to find a crowd of a few dozen people waiting outside the gate. They had heard WFP was organizing cash distributions and were hoping to be enrolled in the program.

While the poorest districts of Brazzaville starved, the wheelbarrow boys at the market were busier than ever. With the banning of taxis, buses, and personal cars, the wheelbarrows normally used for hauling bulky items between shops and waiting vehicles had become the transportation of last resort. Market women who had once taken the bus now went home in the slow-moving wheelbarrows, pushed squeakily through the otherwise deserted streets.

A few weeks into the crisis, it was clear that social distancing, mask mandates, and an enforced lockdown would not be enough to make it through the pandemic. People needed food, as well as cash to pay for rent and utilities. In April 2020, the president announced that 200,000 families would receive a one-time emergency cash grant equivalent to $90. The announcement was welcome, but the disbursal of the assistance was excruciatingly slow. Drawing up a list of eligible families and then putting money into their hands was a sensitive, complex, and labor-intensive process. Congo did not have the expertise, or the databases and payment systems, to move any faster. So people waited.

Mercifully, the lockdown ended mid-May. Sights and sounds that had disappeared came back, although a nighttime curfew remained. It seemed like every bottle-green rust bucket taxi in town was back on the streets again, their drivers aggressively looking for fares, trying to make up for all the weeks they had been out of work. Still, the markets remained open only three days a week. Congo's recovery from the lockdown would be slow.

A June 2020 study, carried out right after the lockdown, showed that a third of the population of Brazzaville, or 700,000 people (including half the city's children), did not have enough to eat. This was triple the amount seen during a survey done in 2015. Of course, there had been some vulnerability before the lockdown, but the response to the pandemic had made it all so much worse. The areas most affected were the far-flung outlying districts of the city, where people already lived hand to mouth. The pandemic had brought mass hunger back to the cities.

By the end of 2020, there had only been one hundred or so official fatalities from COVID-19 in Congo. Granted, official statistics on the virus don't always reflect reality, especially in low-resource settings like Central Africa. But scientists struggle to explain why sub-Saharan Africa has had a lower COVID death rate than the United States. Perhaps it's because of higher immunity in central Africa, where coronaviruses are endemic. And while we know that hindsight is indeed 20/20, we have to ask, was it worth plunging a third of Congo's population into a food crisis when only a few thousand infections were reported?

"All this for a hundred deaths," sighed an exasperated Congolese official.

The food crisis COVID triggered in Congo was replicated, to varying degrees, in countries around the world. Even the United States, one of the world's wealthiest societies, was not immune to the pandemic's impacts on hunger, a fact that took Americans by surprise.

A comparable surge in mass hunger in the United States took place during the Depression. The era's breadlines, soup kitchens, and rail-riding hobos were photographed and filmed. These powerful images helped shape America's collective memory of hunger. Schoolchildren learn about families of starving "Okies" leaving their foreclosed-on farms behind, cramming into their Model-A Fords to head West, only to find themselves scraping by, confined to shacks of tin and tar paper.

Unemployment during the Great Depression jumped from 3 million in 1929 to more than 12 million in 1934. Household incomes plunged, and hunger reared its head. In 1931, there were 20 known cases of starvation in New York City; in 1934, 110 were reported. In suburban America, it's now fashionable to raise backyard chickens and bake bread at home. During the Depression, a time of frugality, doing so was a necessity. There was a boom in backyard gardening and in home cooking, as families strived to get by on reduced budgets. Succotash (a nutritious sweet corn and bean stew), Jell-O, and other thrifty recipes are the culinary legacy of that era.

Almost eighty years later, the Great Recession of 2007–2009

triggered another rise in the number of families struggling to feed themselves. Many Americans lost jobs and income, leaving 14.9 percent of households food insecure by 2011. It took eight years to return to the pre-recession range of 10–11 percent, equivalent to 38 million people.

The COVID-19 pandemic threatened to undo decades of progress against hunger in the United States. In the weeks that followed the start of the pandemic, the country's food security suddenly stood on a knife edge. Anyone who engaged in panic buying in the spring of 2020, or attempted to do so and found the grocery store shelves empty, suddenly understood that there was a relationship between health, human psychology, and hunger; that even a brief spike in demand could undermine supply chains. The workforce in our slaughterhouses fell ill, forcing the government to invoke its emergency powers to keep supermarkets stocked with meat. Ripe vegetables that could not be picked for lack of farmworkers were plowed back into fields.

Meanwhile, the pandemic was crushing labor markets: a record 7 million new jobless claims were filed the week ending March 28, 2020, and unemployment reached 14.7 percent, a post–World War II high. In the spring of 2020, we all saw long lines of cars at food banks. Experts feared the worst, that the labor market's springtime implosion could cause hunger levels in the United States to triple.

Thankfully, a massive response took place: the $2.3 trillion CARES relief plan was passed in March 2020. That act was followed by a $900 billion package in December, passed in extremis (due to partisan brinkmanship) before CARES benefits expired. In March 2021, Congress adopted the $1.9 trillion American Rescue Plan. These relief measures cushioned the blow; there was a moratorium on evictions, forbearance on mortgages, extended unemployment insurance, funding for school meals, an increase in SNAP benefits, and, importantly, generous stimulus checks for everyone—the 2020 "stimmies."

Although the infusion of money was far from an ideal solution, the trillions of dollars did stave off the worst-case scenario. The level of food insecurity in late 2020, estimated at 10.5 percent of households, was unchanged from the year before, in spite of the pandemic's disruptions. But, as ever, there was more to the story than the numbers revealed. While the situation improved for most demographic groups, indicators worsened for African American households (increasing from 19.1 percent in 2019 to 21.7 percent in 2020), and for families with children (6.5 percent to 7.6 percent). Despite all the resources marshaled by our leaders, the most vulnerable in society slipped through our hastily reconfigured safety net. That even a trillion dollars couldn't protect these families from hunger says a lot about the flaws of our system. Policymakers did not design the interventions with the neediest in mind. It's easier to help an unemployed white-collar worker than someone one paycheck away from the breadline.

The staggering figures must be put into perspective. The nearly 40 million "food insecure" in America in 2020 are in no way comparable in their level of vulnerability to the tens of millions struggling to feed themselves in Syria, Yemen, or Afghanistan. The U.S. Department of Agriculture (USDA) defines household food security by measuring the quality, variety, and desirability of a family's diet, and disruptions to their eating patterns, including reductions in food intake. The 10.5 percent of American families that are food insecure in 2021 are eating cheaper foods because they can't afford preferred items, or are switching to less nutritious, lower-quality foods because they're on a budget. They often aren't certain where their next meal is coming from. This is a different version of hunger, not one that kills, but still a harrowing experience that involves deprivation and stress.

The pandemic also teaches us a broader lesson: it was only during a once-in-a-century outbreak of mass disease that American leaders found the political wherewithal to put up the money needed to avert a national food crisis. It is telling of our society's attitudes toward hunger: we tolerate the phenomenon when it affects the poor and minorities, and when it remains at a consistent level that we have somehow deemed tolerable. But the imminent threat of widespread middle-class hunger, the shocking sight of SUVs in breadlines, is what finally made our leaders take hunger seriously.

Nobody starved to death in the United States during the COVID pandemic. But averting starvation is setting the bar low. America's pandemic response showed that it's too late to stitch together a food safety net after millions have lost their jobs and are already in line for food parcels. To be effective, our social protection systems must be both permanent and flexible—not managed on a crisis-to-crisis basis or held hostage to political gamesmanship. This is true in relation to mass disease, and to any other "black swan" event that could disrupt food systems, such as natural disasters, market failure, or war.

For most of my adult life, I have worked to help manage food crises abroad. It was a startling experience to see one play out in my own country. In Jefferson County, West Virginia, where my family lives, Washington, D.C.'s exurbs overlap with the edge of Appalachia. It's a place where subdivisions, strip malls, and highways pop up amid centuries-old homesteads, orchards, and country lanes. Transplants from Virginia and Maryland (such as myself) mix in with a population of born-and-bred locals whose families have been there for generations. Social workers estimate that food insecurity here has a baseline level of perhaps 1,200 people in a county of about 55,000. When the pandemic hit in early 2020, a lot more people in the county suddenly needed food.

The racetrack and casino at Charles Town, a sprawling, gaudy complex, is easily the busiest place in the county. It's impossible to miss: at night, you can see its bright lights from miles away. The smell of the racetrack's horses and stables waft through town when the wind blows just right. The casino's customers are a welcome source of business for the hotels, shops, and restaurants on Main Street. In April 2020, at the onset of the pandemic, the complex suddenly closed its doors and the lights went out. A few months later, more than five hundred men and women who once worked there became unemployed. Food insecurity suddenly threatened a group of people who never imagined they'd be in need.

Many of these people turned to the food pantry at Jefferson County Community Ministries, a charity run by a consortium of area churches. The pantry—complete with shelving and super-market caddies—operates out of an unobtrusive one-story brick building on Main Street, where the JCPenney department store used to be. "When COVID-19 started, we suddenly went from serving 2 families a day to 12," said Robert Walsh, who worked at the food pantry throughout the pandemic.

I first met Robert when I volunteered at the pantry. Robert lives with his grandson now, but when he first moved to the area in the mid-1990s he struggled to make ends meet. The free food he got from the pantry was a lifesaver. He resolved to support it for the rest of his life. Now retired, Robert stocks the pantry's shelves. When the pandemic hit, many volunteers stopped turning up, not wanting to risk being exposed to COVID-19. Robert, on the other hand, increased his shifts.

I asked Robert about the early days of the pandemic. He explained that even though needs in the community surged during the first wave, the food pantry never ran out. The USDA delivered food to local charities, and Robert met their truck in the Home Depot parking lot every week. Two local supermarkets, Martin's and Food Lion, provided food donations and store credit. And donations from individuals increased. Referring to recipients of food aid as "clients," Robert added that the food pantry needed to carry items that require little or no preparation to cater to those who struggle with long-term poverty. "Most clients don't have a cooking stove or even a microwave. Some eat in their cars."

The charity's executive director, Keith Lowry, met me in his office to go over the pandemic's impacts on hunger in the county. He told me that he had seen a relationship between the stimulus checks people received from the government and the traffic at the food pantry; as soon as the funds dwindled, people came back to the pantry. At the same time, more aid became available in the county: not only did the pantry increase its assistance, but many other organizations began providing free food. "Those days, anyone could drive to a local church and get their car filled up with food, no questions asked," recalled Keith. And, in these exceptional times, individuals also became more generous. Keith noted that the cold-weather shelter had fewer visitors than usual, a fact that was initially hard to explain. "I believe people were couch surfing," said Keith, indicating that, unexpectedly, the unhoused were taken in by relatives and friends, moved to generosity by the pandemic.

I later talked to George Rutherford, head of the Jefferson County NAACP, at his home in Ranson. George also leads the Black History Preservation Society and is an authority on the past and present of the community. He is old enough to remember the hobos passing through town on the Winchester and Potomac Railroad in the late 1930s. They were all white. "I never saw a Black hobo," he recalled. Jefferson County's Black families would feed the white hobos at their dinner tables. Black families back then were poor, but they always had something to eat: they had vegetable gardens; they raised chickens, cows, and pigs; and they trapped rabbits, groundhogs, and even blackbirds. The owners of nearby orchards let them gather apples, pears, and peaches that had fallen to the ground—fruit they canned or turned into sauce.

On winter Sundays, Black families gathered fieldcress, a thick, nutritious green that grew in cornfields before the era of Roundup and other herbicides. They prepared the peppery green at home or sold it raw to white people for 10 cents a bucket—equivalent to $2 today. People also picked and cooked dandelions and lambs-quarters, a spinach-like green. Black families bought flour and other staples at the store, but for the rest, they were self-sufficient. Many kept preserves for years, and what they did not need was stored in a food closet, on hand for a church meal or another family in need.

Contrary to statistics at the national level, and contrary to what happened in nearby urban areas like Washington, D.C., and Baltimore, the Black communities in Charles Town and Ranson weathered COVID-19 food insecurity reasonably well. George was startled when, in the spring of 2020, he saw a line of about a hundred cars in line at Wright Denny elementary school, where USDA food parcels were being provided. "The people waiting for food were almost all white," he remembered. It was like an echo of the 1930s. In Jefferson County, the newly food insecure were professionals who had lost their white-collar jobs. There they waited, parked in a breadline, in need of free food.

"Why weren't there more Blacks waiting for food parcels?" I asked.

George said that he believes the African American community in a "country town" like his is better able to cope with hard times. Of course, some Black families in the area fall on hard times and need food aid as a result. But overall, the community is resilient. Home food processing know-how is passed down from generation to generation. It used to be that at a young age, members of the Black community learned to can fruit, vegetables, and even meat, and many families still keep vegetable gardens. To this day, some residents readily cook up the groundhogs they trap in their backyards. Whether the new generation will be interested in acquiring these skills is another matter. During the pandemic, though, many Black families fell back on this know-how.

Moreover, Black men weren't shy about taking odd jobs, such as cutting grass or painting—anything to keep their families fed. In the early days of the pandemic, "some of them came around to ask 'do you have a job for me?'" said George. But above all, members of the community looked out for each other. Grandparents looked after grandchildren, uncles and aunts after nieces and nephews. And the church provided meals. Knowledge about small-scale food production, hard work, and community kept hunger at bay.

COVID's massive impact on hunger should not have been a surprise. Unbeknownst to many, we'd had a preview of what was to come with the Ebola outbreaks in west and central Africa. In late 2013, somewhere on the border between Guinea, Liberia, and Sierra Leone, Ebola passed from bats to human beings, triggering the West Africa Ebola outbreak that lasted through 2015. Procedures that would become familiar during COVID were put in place throughout West Africa: thermal imaging cameras at airports, contact tracing for travelers, closed borders, and quarantines.

The Ebola pandemic infected 28,000 people and killed more than 11,000 between 2014 and 2015. This outbreak was unprecedented in its scale. Until then, Ebola had been known to surface in isolated communities in dense, sparsely populated central African rainforests, where it would rapidly burn itself out. But West Africa is more densely populated and has a network of roads, allowing the virus to quickly reach the three capital cities of Monrovia, Conakry, and Freetown.

The West Africa Ebola outbreak rattled the cross-border trade routes that the region's farmers use to sell their produce. The forests of Guinea, Sierra Leone, and Liberia form the hub of a long-distance trade in red palm oil (shipped in glistening 42-gallon oil drums), black pepper, dark honey, and green coffee. These delicacies are transported north to the cities of faraway Senegal, where they fetch high prices.

In 2014, Ebola brought all this to a halt. Borders were closed and affected areas "cordoned off"—with few exceptions, no one was allowed into or out of these zones. Some observers were quick to call Ebola quarantines "medieval," "barbaric," or "draconian" because of their dramatic impacts. Something had to be done to limit the spread of Ebola, but the quarantines had a dramatic impact on the poorest families. In 2014, there were no stimmies in Guinea, Liberia, or Sierra Leone to soften the blow.

The measures adopted, which banned gatherings—even those meant to grow crops—devastated the family farms that account for the bulk of food production in Guinea, Liberia, and Sierra Leone. Because the farms are not mechanized, small farmers must pool their family labor for critical, labor-intensive tasks such as transplanting rice, weeding, harvesting, or maintaining irrigation systems. As Jacques Roumain wrote in *Masters of the Dew,* "Today I work your field, tomorrow you work mine. Co-operation is the friendship of the poor." But now this labor-sharing practice was outlawed. Relatively few farmers got sick, but they were all affected by the Ebola quarantines.

The impact on the harvest was serious: in the worst affected districts within Liberia and Sierra Leone, the rice harvest dropped by as much as 20 percent. By mid-2015, 2.2 million people had been dragged into a food crisis while millions more were able to feed themselves only by selling their belongings or cutting back on essentials. As food indicators plunged in Ebola-affected areas, people began to ask if the consequences of the restrictions would be worse than the disease itself.

During the panic generated by Ebola, policymakers in Guinea, Liberia, and Sierra Leone leaned in favor of public health, even if the cost of certain measures damaged farming and undermined the food supply. Maybe they chose to focus on public health because the invisible virus could strike anyone, whereas the intractable hunger that was a reality of rural Africa was concentrated among the poor—not people who tend to make policy.

Community resistance to quarantines soon became a major barrier to the Ebola response, abetted in part by people's justified fears of not having enough to eat. Public health officials in affected countries recommended that those who had been in contact with an Ebola case were to observe a strict, twenty-one-day home quarantine—an unrealistic order that was nearly impossible for people to abide by. In places like Conakry, Freetown, or Monrovia, many people earn a living every day and couldn't stay at home for three full weeks—if they did, they would starve. Calling for quarantines in the absence of accompanying financial support, public health officials all but ensured community resistance. Authorities also banned traditional funeral practices without explaining that they represented a substantial risk of Ebola transmission, leading to mistrust in the community. Frustration turned to hostility. Health workers responding to the outbreak were assaulted or killed.

In Guinea, the response was more successful. Public health and humanitarian professionals were able to articulate a strategy to contain the outbreak that combined voluntary movement restrictions, door-to-door medical checks, and the distribution of food. Health workers focused on case finding and contact tracing, while humanitarians distributed cash or food to soften the blow of the quarantines. This hybrid model, where food support bolstered public health interventions, was also put into place during the Ebola outbreak that occurred in the Democratic Republic of Congo in 2018.

But the lessons were slow to travel. When COVID-19 broke out, authorities worldwide initially had trouble grasping the link between pandemic response, including lockdowns, and the increase in food needs that would result. Policymaking first focused largely or entirely on medical issues. While this omission was corrected later, it showed that a gulf still separates the health and food communities. When mass disease threatens, hunger cannot be an afterthought.

No sane decision maker ever purposefully sets out to cause a food crisis. But in the flight to safety during COVID-19's emergence, that is exactly what happened. The lockdowns and other restrictions that were hastily put in place undoubtedly helped to save thousands of lives, but they also had wide-ranging impacts on food access, even in the wealthiest societies. When the next pandemic hits—and it's a question of when, not if—we will need to manage it without plunging millions into hunger. We will need to ensure that people stay home, stay safe, and stay fed.

Because of the way mass sickness disrupts every aspect of our economies and social systems, disease and hunger are fellow travelers. We need to include access to food in pandemic preparedness strategies and ensure that the food and public health communities work together as the natural allies they should be.

8

"P" Is for Pygmy

Indigenous Peoples and the Right to Food

We ordinary folks are like a pot. It's the pot that cooks the food, that suffers the pain of sitting on the fire. But when the food is ready, the pot is told, "You can't come to the table, you'd dirty up the cloth."

—Jacques Roumain, *Masters of the Dew*

In the town of Gamboma, a few hours north of Brazzaville, there is an unremarkable open-air café under a giant shade tree. Located near the market, the café is where truck drivers, teachers, laborers—those who get up early and who can't or don't cook at home—grab a made-to-order omelet and a cup of sweet Nescafé before heading to work. A single overturned red plastic cup sits on the cafe's countertop. A capital letter "P" is written on it in black marker. This is a warning. "P" is for Pygmy, and the marking means that the cup is to be used only by the café's Indigenous customers, for them to drink out of and put back. No self-respecting member of the majority Bantu group would ever drink their rehydrated soluble coffee out of the red cup.

I saw this for the first time when I was in Congo in 2017, and I wondered what the Indigenous people thought about this. The Indigenous people I knew there considered "Pygmy" a slur. They prefer "Baka," their tribal name. Or the word *autochtone*, which means "indigenous" in French.

The Baka and the majority Bantu group are on a collision

course, and the conflict is unfolding in real time in the remote virgin forest of northern Congo. An independent minority of hunter-gatherers, the Baka are being dehumanized, criminalized, and starved out of existence. More and more of the Baka are falling into hunger and malnutrition, problems unheard of before the Bantu expansion into the Baka's forest homeland.

The Baka are of shorter stature than the Bantu and are traditionally hunter-gatherers. They are semi-nomadic and move from place to place to forage or hunt. They are custodians of ancient knowledge about the forest and animals and plants within it. Because Baka weapons and tools are Stone Age, they can't resist the Bantu encroachments.

No one knows how many of them are in the country. A census in 2007 estimated that they accounted for 1.2 percent of the population, but the government acknowledges the number could be as high as 10 percent. There are many reasons why counting the Baka is difficult. For one thing, their camps are hard to locate. It is also possible that the Bantu do not consider the Baka, the underclass, to be worth counting. To further complicate things, there have been rumors that Bantu politicians from the north overstate the numbers of Baka in their districts, to exaggerate the strength of their electoral base.

I first met a group of Baka after a two-day drive from Brazzaville, following a track that snakes north all the way to the Central African Republic. After long hours bumping along on dirt roads in the forest, my driver, Francis, a Bantu, stopped our Toyota in the town of Thanry. Its lone street was an orange mud track with rough clapboard shacks on either side. Francis had parked in front of a shop owned by a friend he knew from his years working in the north of Congo long ago, and we hopped out to stretch our legs.

Edouard, the owner, came out, and Francis introduced me. Edouard was a Rwandan trader who'd lived in the town for years.

Inside his shop there were sundries that had been hauled from Brazzaville—matches, batteries, candy, scratch cards, notebooks. I opened the chest fridge, long disconnected from a power source, and pulled out two lukewarm plastic soda bottles whose labels read, in red and white cursive lettering, "American Cola." If I had wanted something stronger, the shop advertised the giant blue, red, and gold Primus logo on the wall. Primus is a popular beer; the place catered to the thirsty Bantu workers from the nearby lumber camp.

Edouard lived modestly in Thanry, but he told us that business was good. He added, with a smile, that he also dealt in diamonds. He was one of the entrepreneurs who'd come to this frontier where the Baka had lived for generations.

The three of us chatted for a few minutes, then Francis and I got back in the car. We weren't far down the road when we saw, to the left, a Baka camp, a cluster of low huts. I asked Francis to stop so we could talk to the family standing outside—a mother with her two sons. Francis nodded, but before we got out of the car, he looked at my unfinished soda and said, "Are you done with that?" I said that I was. We got out of the car, and Francis handed my half-empty bottle of warm cola to the mother, who smiled instantly.

"They like the sugar," Francis told me, a little overly satisfied with his knowledge of Baka tastes.

The warm soda broke the ice, though; the Baka family was staring at us with unconcealed curiosity. It was mutual: I had never seen a Baka camp before. The inhabitants lived in round huts made of leaves—they were perfectly waterproof and held up even in the most torrential downpours. The Baka family went barefoot and wore rags. They told us they had recently set up near Thanry because their men worked in the lumber camp.

As Francis chatted with the family in Lingala, a feeling of unease came over me. If a bottle of warm soda was enough to gain the Baka's goodwill, then how easy might it be for the unscrupulous characters of northern Congo's rough-and-tumble frontier to abuse or take advantage of them? I had heard horrific stories about Bantu employers paying the Baka for their labor in alcohol. About the physical violence the community was exposed to, and about how Baka women were forced into prostitution. I had heard that some Bantu bought and sold the Baka, whom they enslaved for work.

An anthropologist who lived with the Baka for months later told me that when they are in their element, the rainforest, they see us Westerners as the vulnerable ones. Once on their own turf, the nimble Baka, so lost outside the forest, had teased the anthropologist mercilessly. They laughed at her clumsiness in the thick undergrowth, which they navigated with ease. But that day, from where I stood, the Baka appeared naive and extremely vulnerable.

The Baka are far from the only Indigenous group facing the grim threat of hunger. Worldwide, there are between 370 and 500 million Indigenous people, defined as those with a distinct language and a strong link to a specific territory, who have been present on the land since before the arrival of other ethnic groups. Indigenous communities commonly face discrimination and are being violently dispossessed of their land by commercial farming and by mining and logging interests. As a result, they make up a disproportionate number of the world's poor: although they are only 5 percent of the global population, Indigenous people account for 15 percent of the world's extreme poor. They are being pushed out of their homes and into towns and cities, where they starve in silence, casualties of progress. The Baka's situation illustrates certain distinct causes of hunger: the Indigenous community's lower status, along with denial of their very personhood, leads to the invasion and destruction of their homeland and food sources by profiteering outsiders.

There is very little data on food security in the Baka community. What does exist suggests that Baka families who remain in the forest are largely able to feed themselves, while those living near towns struggle. But the Bantu are pushing the Baka out of the forest into lumber towns like Thanry, where they earn meager pay and rely on the Bantu for food. This once self-sufficient community—who survived by hunting game, fishing, and gathering honey, mushrooms, nuts, and fruit—has seen its diverse diet devolve into one heavy in cassava starch. Their new economic dependence on Bantus has brought food insecurity and malnutrition.

Modern Congo has a legal arsenal that robs the Baka of the ancestral lands that have kept them fed for millennia. One of these is the allocation of long-term logging concessions to companies that export precious hardwoods to Asian, European, and North American markets—an arrangement disquietingly close to the colonial-era concessions described in chapter 4. CIB-OLAM, registered in Singapore and one of the larger companies in Congo, holds rights to log hardwoods on a swath of 2.1 million hectares, an area the size of New Jersey or Israel. Not surprisingly, the commercial logging interests of companies such as CIB-OLAM are clashing with Indigenous livelihoods.

Logging companies in Congo harvest sapele mahogany trees, a kind of wood that is in high demand on the international market. Sapele are the kings of the forest, their long bright trunks shooting straight up to the canopy; they can grow to 150 feet, and even higher in some cases. To loggers, a sapele tree is a prime resource to be exploited for money. To a Western consumer, it is the source of the rich, red-brown wood in a stylish chair or musical instrument or luxury flooring. But to the Baka, a sapele is above all a home for caterpillars: one of their primary foods.

Forest butterflies lay their eggs on the sapele's leaflets. The eggs mature into caterpillars that the Baka harvest and use in countless recipes. Some caterpillars are fat and sizzle like bacon on the griddle. Smoked caterpillars make a crunchy snack. I've been told they are good with beer. Caterpillars, which are more than 50 percent protein, are essential to nutrition throughout central Africa. To communities of the forest, a sapele, with its caterpillar colonies, is a carefully guarded food-producing asset, much like a dairy cow, a henhouse, or an orchard. For some Baka communities, caterpillars are a source of income, one that people will defend with their lives: in Tanganyika Province in the eastern Democratic Republic of Congo, Batwa Pygmies took up arms in 2016 after the Bantu tried to tax their caterpillar sales.

But the logging companies specifically cut down the sapele trees. And when the sapele disappear, the caterpillars do too. A few logging companies have made bona fide attempts to be responsible stewards of the forest and good neighbors to the Baka. CIB-OLAM's operation in Congo is now 100 percent Forest Stewardship Council certified; their customers pay a premium for sustainably managed "good wood." The company's machines pluck only the hardwoods from the forest, leaving everything else intact. CIB-OLAM will not remove from its concession more than a single tree per hectare (4 acres) over the course of twenty-five to thirty years. A large swath of the land under CIB-OLAM's control has been set aside and will never be logged. The company has hired and deployed community liaison officers and, to avoid open conflict with the Baka, they have promised never to cut down the sapele trees that produce the most caterpillars.

But this "responsible" approach is far from universal. For the many uncertified or unlicensed logging businesses, Congo's frontier feels more like the Wild West. They export sapele lumber to Asia, where buyers are less sensitive to sustainable forest management principles—and to the hunger the industry is causing in the Baka community.

When we think of the forces taking away land from Indigenous communities, extractive industries or farming interests first come to mind. But the creation of natural parks has also dispossessed the Baka of their land and food sources. Since the 1990s, four new national parks and three nature reserves have been established in Congo, and more are planned. The trend reflects an effort to protect the forest and save endangered animals—it's a response to the devastating toll the illegal wildlife trade has taken on the country's unique fauna. And the national parks don't just separate the Baka from their food sources; those who run them have criminalized the Baka's customary hunting and foraging lifestyle.

Congo's parks are Edenic destinations, landscapes straight out of *National Geographic*. Odzala Kokoua national park, located in the north of the country, spans an area the size of Puerto Rico and has become a draw for the global elite. The park's website touts it as one of the "wildest, most isolated, most remote places on the planet" that's "barely touched by humanity." On Facebook and Google visitors rave about this "magical rainforest" with western lowland gorillas and forest elephants. Packages start at $9,670 for a four-night stay at the park's luxury lodge—a fortune in a country where most laborers earn $5 a day.

In all the park's promotional material, there is no mention of the Baka, the people of the forest, who have lived on the land for millennia. Neither is there mention of their dispossession or their subsequent struggle to feed themselves. Why would there be? Tourists come to the park to experience a myth—the untouched African Eden. They don't want to think about the exploitation— and the starvation—underlying the park's existence.

Western entities such as Africa Parks, the World Wildlife Fund (WWF), and the World Conservation Society (WCS) manage the parks. They sign multimillion-dollar, multiyear contracts with the

Congolese government and international donors. The agreements feel similar to the country's logging concessions, except that the commodity is conservation, not hardwood timber. To create the expansive parks, the government pushes the Baka out, depriving them of access to their hunting and foraging grounds, triggering tensions like those caused by the incursions of the logging industry.

Park rangers, called "eco-guards," are employed by the government to protect the flora and fauna from poachers, but they are essentially paramilitaries, who receive training, stipends, equipment, and vehicles from Western conservation organizations. They do not hesitate to brutally unleash their force against the Baka.

In our collective imagination, poachers are gangs of heavily armed men killing elephants by the dozen and selling piles of ivory to Asia. But all too often, the "poachers" apprehended by the heavily armed eco-guards are none other than humble Indigenous men hunting game to feed their families. Unable to go to the forest for game or honey, the Baka are left with no alternative but to work in the lumber camps—or as guides for illegal commercial poachers.

In the 2010s, conservation interests began advocating for the creation of a new park in Messok Dja, an area of Congo on the border with Cameroon. It would be a $21.4 million project involving the two countries, the UN Development Programme (UNDP), the European Union, the United States, the WWF, and logging and palm oil companies. The new Messok Dja park would cover 1,456 square kilometers, an area the size of the city of Houston, Texas, or Greater London. It would serve as an essential cross-border wildlife corridor, protecting elephants, gorillas, and chimpanzees.

In 2018, a group of Baka living near the proposed park sent the UNDP a complaint denouncing abuse from the eco-guards and the starvation their actions were causing. They reported that the eco-guards were preventing them from going into the forest, that they burn down their camps, that Baka children are getting thinner, and that the WWF was not listening.

The UNDP investigated and confirmed that the eco-guards had indeed prevented the Baka from going to the forest for the food and medicine they needed to survive. What was worse, UNDP found that the eco-guards protecting the Messok Dja subjected hundreds of Baka to harassment, extrajudicial beatings, and arrests. Women were made to strip naked. One Baka man was forced, at gunpoint, to beat another. Eco-guards once detained a Baka man for six months on poaching charges; he was tortured and repeatedly raped by other inmates, and died shortly after being released. The man's daughter, in an interview for British television, said of the eco-guards, "They think of the Baka as animals."

The Messok Dja investigation caused an uproar in the human rights community. The NGO Survival International accused the WWF and WCS of practicing "colonial conservation" in central Africa. It might just as well be called starvation conservation, considering the devastating impacts on food security in Indigenous communities. For decades, WWF has acknowledged the importance of working with, and even protecting, local populations. But in practice, in Congo, conservation NGOs operate in environments rife with corruption and discrimination.

Anthropologist Jerome Lewis, who has worked with Congo's Baka community for decades, reports that the eco-guards collude with poachers involved in the illegal wildlife trade. Lewis described WWF staff as being unequipped to deal with the complex political and economic situations they face. "They're trained in biodiversity research and ecological monitoring, and so they're in way over their head."

Safeguards were built into the process of creating Messok Dja park, including the requirement that the Baka community be involved. But discrimination from the Baka's oppressors is so entrenched that these safeguards utterly failed to protect the community. In order for the Baka community to survive, it's key that they retain control of their resources. Free, prior, and informed consent (FPIC), a consultative, bottom-up planning method, is meant to ensure that projects aren't implemented against the wishes of local populations like the Baka. FPIC is considered best practice in Congo, and an FPIC process was launched for the Messok Dja park project.

Community consultations with the Baka had indeed been organized. But the investigation found that these "consultations" had consisted of Bantu outsiders arriving in villages and summarily warning the affected Baka communities that swaths of the forest were now strictly off-limits to them. The Baka never agreed to the Messok Dja project, and they were terrified, fearing retribution if they voiced any objections. One of the few Baka able to write had found the courage to complain when they sent their message to the UNDP.

It is indisputable that we need to protect what's left of our forests and the treasures and ecosystems they contain. But conservation can't happen at the expense of the Indigenous populations who have effectively been the stewards of these forests for millennia, and who rely on the land for their food.

Unless conservation policies include a robust system to identify and tackle risks at the community level, the dispossession and abuse that are driving the Baka from their ancestral forests into hunger-ridden roadside camps will continue unchecked. The fundamental asymmetry that exists needs to be addressed. The Baka are a voiceless community of outcasts, while the conservation lobby, which promotes multimillion-dollar projects, wields considerable political influence.

In February 2020, after the UNDP investigation was published, the European Union canceled its support for the project, which sent an important signal that Baka voices need to be heard. The project is now on pause. More principled action of this type will be needed, not only from international agencies, but from governments as well.

When I was appointed WFP's director in Congo in 2017, it was a career opportunity I embraced. But my spouse and I soon came to realize our teenage children needed some time at home in the United States. Our children were growing up in a bubble of privilege in a foreign society; the experience was often jarring. After two years in Congo, my wife and kids moved to Charles Town, in West Virginia's eastern panhandle. The place has a relaxed, small-town feel that was right for a family of returning expats.

The Shenandoah Valley, where my family had just settled, has a tortured history with eerie parallels to the places where we had lived. It isn't just in Congo, of course, where long-established, food-secure populations have been summarily removed to make way for parks. The forced displacement of voiceless inhabitants to create playgrounds for the elite happened to the mountain farmers of Appalachia in the twentieth century.

In the 1930s, the U.S. government decided to create Shenandoah National Park, in Virginia's Blue Ridge, the easternmost range of the Appalachian Mountains. At the time, the area was home to a thriving farming community. Much of the mountaintop area was pasture for cows. The rich soil produced staples such as beets, beans, and potatoes; huckleberries were plentiful on the mountainside.

A national park would soon replace the mountain farmsteads.

There were discussions among federal officials about letting the locals stay on after the creation of the park, but they went nowhere. The authorities wanted to create the illusion of an untouched natural environment, a park that would be the Yellowstone or Yosemite of the East, and such an Eden could hardly include farmers. This is in keeping with America's familiar history of declaring entire groups of people obstacles to progress and replacing them with others.

In the eighteenth century, European settlers pushed west and seized the Shenandoah Valley and the Blue Ridge, hunting grounds of the Iroquois and the Shawnee nations. Native Americans, who had inhabited the areas for thousands of years, were forced off their land to make way for farmers and their homesteads. Two hundred years later, it was the mountain farmers' turn to go. In all, at least five hundred families were dispossessed.

At the time, some elites in D.C. considered the removal of the farmers to be a "humanitarian act." George Freeman Pollock, a developer and something of a showman, was a driving force behind the creation of the park and the eviction of the mountaineers. He owned a ranch on the Blue Ridge, where he played host to tourists and organized parties for Washington high society. He had great bonfires built for his visitors, where he would appear dressed as a Native American chief or a Mexican mariachi. But Pollock was deep in debt, and he stood to gain handsomely from the creation of the park.

Over the years, Pollock had exploited his neighbors. He framed their apparent poverty as quirkiness to visiting outsiders, and he brought in anthropologists to document their "backward" lifestyle—to better make the case for their eviction. In 1933, at Pollock's invitation, Mandel Sherman, a sociologist, and Thomas Henry, a journalist, visited Corbin Hollow, which would become part of the park. *Hollow Folk,* their sensationalized account of mountain life, described "families of unlettered folk, of almost pure Anglo-Saxon stock, sheltered in tiny, mud-plastered log cabins and supported by a primitive agriculture." The people of the Blue Ridge, they said, had "no community government, no organized religion, little social organization wider than that of the family and clan, and only traces of organized industry." Quite simply, they were "not of the 20th century." The book's dehumanizing tropes about southern mountaineers persist to this day.

Pollock's campaign paid off: the farmers of the Blue Ridge would be evicted from their land. The Commonwealth of Virginia offered compensation for the homesteads. Some families were resettled in the valley below and had to rely on Depression-era food-aid programs. Others resisted, writing desperate letters to their elected representatives, begging to stay, to be allowed to plant just one more garden. But their pleas had no effect. A court order was issued to evict recalcitrant families, by force if needed. In some cases, farmhouses were burned in front of their owners. A painting of the evictions, by a grandchild of the displaced, depicts, in naïf style, a family packed into the bed of an army truck, surrounded by men in arms. Their homestead's doors and the farmyard gates are left open. An abandoned teddy bear lies on the ground.

Even with the eviction orders, some of the Blue Ridge mountaineers wouldn't go quietly. In October 1935, H. M. Cliser refused to vacate his forty-six-acre homestead and barricaded himself in his home. As the authorities closed in, the elderly man sang "The Star-Spangled Banner." It took four sheriff's deputies to remove the man from his property.

Heartbroken and bitter, the last of the mountaineers retreated. For some, displacement was not the only misery inflicted: at least thirty of them, probably more, were sterilized at the hands of the government.

Shenandoah National Park is an hour's drive from Washington, D.C., at least when the traffic on I-66 cooperates. Cars zoom to and fro on Skyline Drive as hikers angle for Instagram-worthy pictures of the foliage. But to the old-timers who remember the dairy farms of yore, there's nothing worth seeing up there anymore. Where meadows, gardens, and homesteads once stood, a mature artificial forest, planted after the eviction of the mountaineers, turns orange and yellow each autumn, as if on command, for the day-tripping motorists.

What is now happening to the Baka in the forests of central Africa echoes what befell the farmers of the Blue Ridge. The families never expected that one day, they, too, would be uprooted. These are stories of people who stood in the way of "progress," who were dehumanized and deemed expendable, and whose food security collapsed as they lost their land to powerful outside interests.

None of this is an invitation to lapse into nostalgia. Mountain farming is an extremely difficult way of life, and many farmers outside park boundaries chose to move from their mountain homesteads as the economics of Appalachia changed in the twentieth century. Family farming was doomed when policies and economies of scale favored large farms over small ones. Similarly, the nomadic Baka way of life, practiced for millennia, might not last, and some Baka communities have taken to growing food crops. But governments need to ease these transitions by providing a cushion for the most vulnerable, and a plan for what they might do next, rather than accelerating the disruption through state-sanctioned evictions.

The world's 500 million Indigenous people face a choice: integrating with the dominant culture, or holding on to the old ways. One way of assuring survival is enabling Indigenous people to exercise their rights to the land that feeds them. And it starts with education.

Melaine Ngokia leads an NGO in northern Congo's Sangha region. She is a Baka, and she sees up close how the Bantu expansion is devastating her community. First, the logging companies roll in. Then, villages are built. The Indigenous population sets up camp nearby, where many contract malaria, an illness unknown in the deep forest (the mosquito that carries the malaria parasite is not able to reproduce in the forest). Some begin abusing liquor, a substance the Baka don't consume traditionally. Malnutrition follows. Before long, their new neighbors have taken over. When the forest disappears, the Baka people disappear too.

For Melaine, the answer to all of this is education: "We can't defend ourselves from a society whose language we do not speak, and whose ways we ignore."

Melaine has taken on an immense challenge: creating an education system from scratch, one that caters particularly (though not exclusively) to Baka children. While there are some public schools in Sangha, they are located far from Baka camps, and Baka children who attend them suffer from prejudice; aside from being different, they are also very poor, unable to afford supplies, shoes, and uniforms. As a result of these obstacles, two-thirds of Baka children are not in school.

Baka parents know very well that their children must learn how to read and write if they are to have a future in modern-day Congo. Some of them, desperate to see their children educated, began building rudimentary schools themselves, out of palm fronds and thatch, and retained volunteer teachers. Melaine, one of the few Baka women with formal schooling, decided to work with the parents.

Melaine opened the first ORA school in Sangha in 2008. The schools are best thought of as a stepping stone to formal public school education. ORA is the French acronym for "Observe, Think, Act," a pedagogical approach adapted to cross-cultural learning. At an ORA school, children are exposed to the rudiments of French and math. After two years, they are ready to enter the first grade in the public school system. Melaine now manages nineteen ORA schools. As of 2021, she had given nearly six thousand Baka children the chance for an education.

Perhaps the greatest benefit of attending the ORA schools is not the knowledge the children absorb. It is the self-esteem they acquire. I once visited an ORA classroom near Enyelle, which we reached after driving through a miles-long green tunnel in the forest. The Baka children, in rags, were learning in a rectangular wood frame hut with a low thatched roof. The day's date had been written in neat cursive on the blackboard, which was otherwise blank. I looked at one of the children's notebooks; although classes had been in session for weeks, there was not much there.

But then the thirty or so children began singing along with their teacher, a song that helped introduce them to basic French vocabulary. As they sang and responded to their teacher's cues, the children's eyes gleamed, and the modest hut resonated with energy and confidence. For Baka children, the very act of heading out to school every morning with their notebooks —just like the Bantus—helps them internalize the message that they too matter.

Helping Baka children become self-confident learners has come with a slew of challenges, not least the Baka's nomadic lifestyle and material poverty. In Baka families, the children need to earn their keep; they also need to eat. In 2017, Melaine began working with WFP to offer hot meals at the ORA schools. Now, in each ORA school in Sangha, volunteer cooks prepare a large pot of rice, beans, and fish for the children to eat. If the children are fed at school, parents don't worry as much about the lost labor.

But a hot meal doesn't ensure that the children are learning what they'll need to survive. Teachers are often unskilled "volunteers," paid in game, fish, honey, sometimes cash—whatever Baka parents can spare from their foraging. The children are taught in French, a language they hardly understand. School also interferes with the transmission of traditional knowledge. During daylight hours, Baka children need to be with their parents to learn the Baka way of life: how to fish, hunt, and learn the nutritional and medicinal properties of thousands of plants in the forest. Also, the

ORA schools lack official status. Some education experts worry that they are a separate education system that will keep the Baka community in a state of permanent marginalization.

Melaine is aware of all these issues. For all its limitations, a rudimentary and separate educational system for Baka children was better than none at all. After years of effort and advocacy, Melaine and other activists convinced the Congolese government to recognize some of the ORA schools as official public schools. The Ministry of Education has now sent certified teachers to Baka communities. This is only a first step in the right direction, but it signals that the government now considers Baka children worthy of formal education.

Humanitarian agencies, with their million-dollar footprints and ambitious agendas, have been increasing their presence in northern Congo—just as the logging companies and conservation NGOs have. If humanitarians in places such as the Congolese frontier are to better support the Baka, we will need an especially keen sense of the inequality in our relationship with them. All donor-recipient relationships are inherently unequal, but in the case of the Baka the dynamic is even more pronounced because of the community's otherness and extreme vulnerability.

Carine is a Baka woman from the south of the Congo, where the relationship between the Bantus and her people is better than in the north. Bantu and Indigenous children in the more densely populated south routinely sit in the same classroom. Carine was the first member of the Baka community in Congo to work for the UN—or perhaps the first to identify as such. Because of the stigma against them, Baka often keep their ethnic identities private.

When I met Carine in 2018, she had been an activist for Indigenous rights for years. She was young and petite, but boldly took on the established advocacy organizations that she saw as having betrayed the cause. At the WFP office, she would question our assumptions and counteract our biases. If we were to address the issue of hunger in the Indigenous community, she said, we didn't need to bring them bags of rice or farming tools and seeds, or to organize classes about nutrition.

"First of all," she said, "we need to tell Indigenous people that they too count." She suggested that we make posters clearly stating that the Baka had the right to education and health care, and that we display these in schools and health centers in areas where they lived.

"I can tell you right now," she said, "it will make a big difference."

Providers of humanitarian aid tend to focus on delivering tangible benefits to the communities we support. Goods and services that can be seen, weighed, or counted. By contrast, many people working to support the Baka community focus on ensuring recognition of the Baka's legal personhood—for instance, that everyone receives a birth certificate. Their approach begins at a more fundamental level. Carine was telling us that ideas matter, even more than the food we brought, perhaps because centuries of discrimination had conditioned the community to see themselves as people not worthy of adequate food, nutrition, health care, or education.

Although groups like the Baka account for a relatively small share of the millions suffering from hunger in the world, their situation is emblematic of the challenges facing many food-insecure populations. Their struggles with encroachment and starvation illustrate how dominant groups can undermine the food security of weaker ones. The Baka's story is also about the impact of forces that have been at work for millennia.

Until about 10,000 years ago, all human beings were hunter-gatherers. The shift to agriculture, when our distant ancestors made a fateful choice to become farmers, revolutionized how we feed ourselves, and how society itself is organized. The process of marginalizing hunter-gatherers and moving them off their land through violence and starvation is still under way in some of the world's most remote areas: in Congo, as we have seen, but also in the Amazon and New Guinea.

In a tongue-in-cheek essay published in 1987, anthropologist Jared Diamond argued that adopting settled agriculture was "the worst mistake in the history of the human race." Pushing back against the notion of hunter-gatherer life as nasty, brutish, and short, Diamond contended that nomadic humans were in reality better fed and healthier and had more free time than their farmer counterparts. He noted that at a critical juncture millennia ago, bands of early humans had a choice: either continue hunting and gathering or take up the practice of agriculture. Those who opted to grow crops experienced malnutrition, zoonotic disease, and tyranny due to the complex social hierarchies that took shape in a farming society.

Diamond pointed out that in the late twentieth century, the Kalahari's bushmen, who spent only twelve to nineteen hours a week looking for food, enjoyed a diet that provided to each person an average 2,140 kilocalories (kcals) and 93 grams of protein per day—more than the minimum requirement for people their size, and much more than what people eat in starving farming communities in Africa. The bushman diet was based on seventy-five plants, and therefore unlikely to be significantly affected by a single crop failure—the sort of catastrophe that unfolded in nineteenth-century Ireland, when famine followed the blight and failure of the potato crop.

It may have been agriculture, as Diamond writes, "that enabled us to build the Parthenon and compose the B-minor Mass," but its adoption was a nutritional disaster for early farmers. Skeletons from Greece and Turkey have shown that the average height of humans crashed after the adoption of agriculture, dropping from five foot nine for men to five foot three, and five foot three to five feet for women. Diamond argues that the adoption of corn-based agriculture among Native American communities in present-day Illinois caused serious nutritional deficiencies: farmers had 50 percent more tooth-enamel defects and were four times more likely to have anemia than their hunting-gathering predecessors. With the advent of agriculture, life expectancy fell from twenty-six to nineteen years.

So why did farming societies prevail if their members were nutritionally worse off? Strength in numbers, for one thing. Farming supports one hundred people per square kilometer, whereas the same area supports only a single hunter-gatherer. Because one hundred malnourished farmers can easily overwhelm one hunter-gatherer, farmers quickly displaced their rivals. They also became immune to the infectious germs introduced by livestock, which they then spread to hunter-gatherer communities with lethal effect.

Diamond's essay prompts us to challenge our assumptions about the trajectory of progress. As our society hurtles toward possible self-destruction through a process of environmental degradation and climate change launched by our embrace of agriculture, it appears that early humans may have made a fatal choice when they opted to settle down and grow food crops. The fragile, artificial systems we've built to feed ourselves are buckling under the strain—perhaps we're heading for a world where recurrent shortages and widespread malnutrition are the norm, not the exception. Anyone who looks at the excesses of factory farming, overfishing, widespread unsustainable water use, and overextended global food supply chains might be entitled to conclude that we've been trapped by the choices our ancestors made. It's not just the Indigenous people of the world who are in danger, it's all of us.

Digital Food

The Ambiguous Promise of Technology and
Innovation

Trust is almost a mystery.

—Jacques Roumain, *Masters of the Dew*

The Pouncer was designed to be the world's first edible drone. The drone would fly one-way into dangerous, conflict-affected communities, where starving civilians would take it apart, and then cook and eat its components. The snub-nosed, delta-shaped aircraft with a wingspan of nine feet was designed to deliver a payload of 50 kilograms of food—enough to feed one hundred people for a day. Each would cost $300.

Designed in 2014, the Pouncer was the brainchild of Nigel Gifford, a British entrepreneur and adventurer who resolved to use drones to fly aid to dangerous places. In a 2017 interview with the *Financial Times,* Gifford explained that he was considering using honeycomb, a structurally robust material, to build the Pouncer. He mused that the landing gear could be made of salami, which, after all, has excellent tensile strength (but might not be part of the diets of some of those the drone was meant to feed). The Pouncer's plywood frame could be used for kindling. "Our food technologist guys [are] thinking of wrapping the electronics in bouillon cubes," he added.

I first heard about the Pouncer at a gathering of humanitarian innovation experts in Italy. A drone expert told us the Pouncer could be the solution to the challenge posed by the need for food deliveries to war-torn northern Syria. Immediately, hands shot up. We knew the area was bristling with air defenses that had already made airdrops of food all but impossible, and that would be sure to fire at the drones. How would flight authorizations be obtained? How would civilians tell the difference between a military drone that could kill, of which there were many in the skies of Syria, and its edible humanitarian counterpart? There were no obvious answers to these important questions, and the Pouncer left us all decidedly skeptical.

As of 2023, the Pouncer hadn't taken off (no pun intended). It seems destined for the graveyard of well-intentioned but stillborn humanitarian innovation projects. Gifford's invention was, to say the least, controversial. In fact, many in the broader community were openly hostile to the Pouncer. Kevin Watkins, then chief executive officer for Save the Children UK, said in an interview, "This is someone who's come up with a crackpot idea based on the assumption that technology can solve all problems." Drones are "good at killing people and blowing things up. They are absolutely irrelevant for resolving acute hunger."

While the potential of new technology in humanitarian settings is undeniable, its role in highly complex and fragile situations is never simple and is always fraught—not so much for the promoters of tech taking on financial risk, but for the people on the receiving end of the innovation, whose very lives may be put at risk. Humanitarians work with some of the world's most vulnerable populations. As technological innovation changes the lives of people around the world, those of us working with these communities need to ask ourselves how we can make use of new tech while upholding our foundational principle to "do no harm." How are we to separate the wheat, the innovations that actually help, from the chaff, such as the Pouncer? And how can we design technology *with* the communities we aim to serve rather than pushing ready-made Silicon Valley tech that's wildly out of touch?

Technology is changing how the world is fed and how the fight against global hunger is being waged. In 2016, German economist Klaus Schwab, founder of the World Economic Forum, wrote of a "Fourth Industrial Revolution" that was set to transform society. (The previous three involved steam power, electricity, and computing.) According to Schwab, the Fourth Industrial Revolution will involve advances in biology and computer hardware and software and combine them with connectivity to the internet. There will be breakthroughs in robotics (including drones), artificial intelligence, nanotechnology, and many other fields. The Fourth Industrial Revolution, which is transforming the manufacturing and service economies, is already changing the way food is produced, processed, and sold, and the way humanitarian aid is provided.

Technology is reconfiguring food supply chains across the world. In the past two decades, cell phone towers have popped up all over the world, connecting billions of people. When cell phone towers were built in Niger, the market for millet was transformed—wholesalers, such as the one we met in chapter 2, had often played on information asymmetries to sell millet for a high price. With cell phones, anyone could call a friend or relative and learn what millet prices were in the next town, instead of taking a wholesaler's word for it.

Voice and text were just the beginning. Now that internet access is widespread, e-commerce platforms are allowing family farmers and food processors everywhere to sell their produce directly to consumers, bypassing layers of middlemen. This is the case with a host of new online services that allow people to order food from farmers to be delivered to their doorstep: these include Farm to Home in Pakistan, Twiga Foods in Kenya, and Waruwa in Latin America. Twiga serves 10,000 customers a day. Its Nigerian counterpart, FarmCrowdy, collects food from 25,000 individual farmers to sell in Lagos.

By making digital payments instantaneous, mobile money—a currency that's managed by cell phone operators, not traditional banks—has enabled the rise of agricultural e-commerce and access to financial services for billions of people without bank accounts. Mobile money is now in widespread use in East Africa, where opening a mobile money account is as straightforward as buying a SIM card, and paying for a cab or a meal is as simple as sending a text message. The mobile industry estimates that in 2020 more than 1.2 billion people worldwide had access to mobile money services. Mobile money is often available where access to traditional financial services is low, and its use is rising sharply in sub-Saharan Africa and South Asia.

Mobile money is a first step. Many other digitally enabled payment systems are still emerging. Blockchains are open, decentralized digital ledgers that combine the reach of the internet and the power of cryptography. They could—in theory, at least—democratize banking and trade. Blockchain technology promises to bring transparency to opaque food supply chains, whose workings tend to be obscured by backroom deals.

As the Fourth Industrial Revolution takes root in the world's most hunger-prone and vulnerable communities, a generation of digital natives is finding increasing benefits from life online. Many of the refugees or displaced people I have met use Facebook, WhatsApp, and other digital apps to stay in touch with loved ones, make money, find the assistance they need, or express their opinions. Savvy social media users, they also value the anonymity the internet offers. A Syrian refugee in Jordan's sprawling Zaatri camp asked me with a wry smile, "Do you want my Facebook name, or my real name?" Access to Wi-Fi is such an essential service that humanitarian agencies now provide connectivity for affected populations. In fact, Syrian refugees arriving in Greece have been known to ask for the Wi-Fi hotspot before food or water.

These changes brought on by technology have meant that humanitarian agencies have had to adapt our operating models to keep up with the digital world. In the 2010s, the aid sector was facing what seemed to be insurmountable funding deficits, and donors pushed humanitarian organizations to unleash technology and innovate. Striving for efficiency in an era of tight budgets is common sense. But money alone is an insufficient metric when the goal is to protect and save lives. Before we jump headlong into the dream of a humanitarian techno-utopia, we must remember who it is we're serving and what is at stake.

For all the enthusiasm of experts like Klaus Schwab, the means of bringing the Fourth Industrial Revolution to the humanitarian front line are anything but obvious. I saw this firsthand when WFP tried to set up a digital payment system in central Africa, where refugees rely on humanitarian assistance to survive.

Bétou is a forlorn frontier town deep in the rainforest in Congo's north, only thirty miles from the border of the troubled Central African Republic. The ramshackle settlement sprang up around an Italian-owned lumber mill on the Ubangi River; timber is barged on the river down to Brazzaville. The town's main drag, a wide, dark, muddy track, leads straight to the mill. The population around Bétou is so sparse that people from all over West Africa came to work at the facility. On the riverfront, a few Mauritanian Arabs sell food out of shabby storefronts. A decrepit Catholic mission, its concrete walls stained dark green by the humidity, stands next to the river.

When I first visited Bétou, a few thousand refugees had been living in a camp that had been around for years. Many of them were Muslims who had fled Bangui's violence in 2013 and had built shacks on an undeveloped patch of land. Since refugees were not allowed to acquire land where they could grow their own crops, the refugees relied on food from WFP. I recall that one in ten refugee children were acutely malnourished, a rate that never seemed to drop. And it seemed that every time UNHCR, the UN Refugee Agency, planned to help the refugees go back home, another round of fighting would break out in Bangui, postponing yet again their longed-for return.

For more than three years, WFP had been providing the refugee community with food rations, but we had recently started mobile money transfers instead. We moved from providing bags of food to giving "digital food"—in the form of a mobile money transfer people could use to buy food. WFP's introduction of cash transfers in this remote area was part of a global trend in the humanitarian community to provide more assistance through cash or vouchers. The hope was that people would have more choice in the items they buy with cash, and that local economies would benefit from the cash injection. Humanitarian cash transfers were virtually nonexistent in the early 2000s, but reached $5.6 billion in 2019.

Bétou was one of many places going through a transition in assistance from in-kind food to cash. The refugees were given a mobile phone chip. Once a month, they would receive a mobile money payment equivalent to $20 per person, which they could use to buy food at the Mauritanian shops in town. The digital payment system also brought a level of transparency that helped keep our donors on board, because it allowed them to see the money going directly to food purchases.

So what did the refugees think of the new system? One day, four leaders of the community came to the WFP meeting room to talk to my colleagues and me. The men, clean-shaven and in their best clothes, entered rather shyly and sat down. We exchanged prolonged greetings. When it was time to talk about substantive matters, they looked uneasy, shifting in their chairs, their eyes cast down. Abdou, a slim man of perhaps forty in a threadbare yellow shirt, took the bull by the horns and explained what was on their minds.

"For years, you gave us bags of rice," he began. "But a few months ago you began giving us mobile money to pay for our food." There was an awkward pause. Abdou inhaled, and then continued: "Do you think we could go back to the old system, where we used to get the rice?"

This is what a humanitarian never wants to hear—that a new, creative program isn't working. I knew there had been issues with the first mobile money distributions, but I wasn't expecting outright rejection from the people who were receiving them. After all, we had been cautious and had only introduced the technology after months of debate, studies, and consultations.

Abdou explained that for his community, mobile money payments had been a headache. The chips we had provided were too easily blocked; after three failed PIN attempts, the chip needed to be reset, leaving its owner unable to buy food. Sometimes chips were lost, or there were errors in the amount of credit transferred. When these inevitable problems arose, they took too long to resolve with the cell phone company. To make matters worse, there had recently been a prolonged network outage, rendering all mobile money transactions temporarily impossible.

"Could we not go back to the old way of doing things?" he repeated.

Abdou and the others had a point. But the old way of bringing food aid to their isolated community also had problems and could be extraordinarily slow. First, food grown in the U.S. Midwest was barged down the Mississippi River to a port on the Gulf. From there, a vessel loaded it up to cross the Atlantic, delivering the containers to Pointe Noire, Congo's deepwater port. After clearing customs, the food was hoisted onto trucks for a three-hundred-mile road journey to Brazzaville. At Brazzaville, the containers were lifted onto river barges that a diesel-powered pusher boat slowly nudged up the Congo and Ubangi Rivers until they reached the camp in Bétou, a week or two later. All going well, the entire process took at least five months. If we missed the high-water season on the Ubangi, we'd have to wait until the river rose again. Of course, the food was a lifeline for the refugees, but the process was complex and time-consuming.

And it wasn't just in Congo: all over the world, food aid programs have traditionally relied on transcontinental shipments of bulk commodities. This is because purchasing food in a donor country is good politics: it helps support farmers, a powerful voting bloc.

With mobile money, we could load cash onto the refugees' phones within days of it arriving in our own account. We could instruct the mobile money operator to "push" credit to their numbers; as soon as the credit hit their phones, refugees could pick out and buy the foods they needed from local retailers. But something had gone wrong, and now we risked losing the trust of the community.

The person managing the mobile money transfers for WFP was a man named Nasser, an aid worker from Niger in West Africa. In Congo, people like Nasser were a group set apart because of their Muslim religion and their willingness to work as traders and farmers—occupations that the local elite considered low status. This prejudice didn't rattle Nasser, who'd seen it all before. He had studied in Tunisia, where some local Arabs treated Black African students like him as curiosities. He had spent years working with Oxfam and Catholic Relief Services in Africa's toughest humanitarian crises, including Mali, Niger, and the Central African Republic. He joined WFP soon after my discussion with the leaders of the Central African community in Bétou about the mobile money project. He was the person who could get the project back on track.

Fueled by gallons of lukewarm drip coffee, Nasser spent many days and sleepless nights at work, figuring out how the tech could work better for the refugees. He'd be on the phone for hours with our partners to check that every detail was in order before the mobile money was credited to accounts. He routinely called me on weekends or late at night to ask me to approve payments, so that people would not wait a minute more than necessary for their food. Nasser was known to write furious emails upbraiding his colleagues for not working fast enough and holding up the distributions: *You're sitting in the comfort of your air-conditioned office while the beneficiaries are waiting in the sun!* Nasser could be pushy, but always for the right reasons.

We made important modifications to our system: if people had technical issues with SIM cards, they could call in to a hotline. WFP required the mobile company to deploy a team to Bétou so the host of problems that occurred on distribution days could be resolved on the spot. And the refugees themselves became more familiar with the technology. Though it took more time and effort than we had anticipated, the mobile money transfers began to work, and the refugees from the CAR in Bétou changed their minds about the program. We'd fallen prey to the comforting illusion that shiny new technology would solve everything. But technology does not work on its own; it needs attendants, people like Abdou, Nasser, and all those who worked to get things right for the refugees in Bétou.

Ultimately, mobile money transfers proved to be an effective solution to a humanitarian supply-chain issue. Still, there was a larger problem left unsolved: the community was still unable to feed itself without aid. Working with UNHCR, WFP advocated with authorities to allow the Central Africans to obtain the land they needed to farm. The Congolese had given the refugees protected status, but they still refused to let them acquire farmland. Ultimately, an agreement was reached that allowed refugees to lease farmland from locals for three to five years—enough time to give them some security, and to plant food crops for themselves and sell the surplus. Soon enough, the Central Africans began growing cabbage and tomatoes, which they sold at Bétou's riverside market. Technology had streamlined one aspect of food delivery, but the larger issue of access to land and a sustainable future for the refugees could only be resolved through negotiations between human beings.

The Old Testament tells us that in ancient Egypt, Pharaoh once dreamed of standing by the river Nile, where he saw seven fat cows. But then seven lean cows appeared, and ate the fat ones. The dream startled Pharaoh awake. When he fell back to sleep, he dreamed of seven full heads of grain on a single stalk. But then seven other heads of grain, withered by the east wind, swallowed up the full ones. The following morning, Pharaoh called a meeting to make sense of the disturbing dreams. His magicians and wise men had no answers. Flustered, they called in Joseph, a Hebrew slave, who had a reputation for dream interpretation.

Joseph did not disappoint: he announced that Pharaoh's dream was a warning that Egypt would experience seven years of bumper crops, followed by seven years of drought. He recommended that Pharaoh build stores of grain all over Egypt and set aside a fifth of the crop each bumper year. Delighted with the plan, Pharaoh made Joseph the governor of all of Egypt. Surplus grain was set aside each year for seven years. There was so much accumulated grain it was like "the sand of the sea"—estimating what was in the stores was impossible. When the drought hit seven years later, Egypt was ready. Joseph opened the storehouses and sold the grain to the population, as well as to emissaries from desperate drought-stricken neighboring nations.

When trying to avert a food crisis, it is essential to act as early as possible. Humanitarians must react immediately to a signal or warning of danger to compensate for the lengthy delays involved in organizing a substantive relief operation. Generations of analysts have dreamed of being able to predict famines, so that humanitarian agencies have a chance to act before a crisis even occurs.

Today, those of us who respond to food crises do not need Joseph's psychic abilities to predict famine. We have the next best thing, an array of data models that allow us to forecast droughts and floods, as well as their impacts, with uncanny accuracy. Advanced hunger analytics have transformed how food assistance is triggered and targeted. We've come a long way since my first posting in the early 2000s. At that time, food security analysis was the preserve of old-school agronomists. Once a year, after the main rainy season, they would assess crop yields and estimate the size of the grain deficits that the markets or aid agencies might need to fill. Information systems focused on analysis of rainfall totals, measured in millimeters in analog rain gauges that field staff looked after. Analysts compared totals to a carefully curated series of data points from previous years. They would do the same thing with food prices. Data from remote locations would take weeks, sometimes more, to make it to capital cities, where it would be entered by hand into a spreadsheet.

Many of us believed there must be a better way, and we were right. Expanding mobile and satellite coverage has driven down the cost of data, and a new generation of specialists has been able to tap into a plethora of information about the weather, agriculture, supply chains, migration, food prices, and markets, along with a dizzying array of household indicators. The problem I saw when I entered the field was soon turned on its head: the data drought turned into a data deluge.

When I worked at WFP headquarters, I kicked off a project called "mobile vulnerability assessment and mapping," which marked the coming of age of humanitarian phone surveys. It started with helping people who were living in camps near the city of Goma in the eastern Democratic Republic of Congo to communicate with WFP. We provided them with basic mobile handsets, and because there was no electricity in the camp, we built a solar charging station that they could use for free. The people in the camp took periodic phone surveys from WFP about what they ate, and what they were paying for food. They would also call us to express concerns, or sometimes just to thank us for the food we'd given them. The data helped ensure WFP was more responsive to changing needs. But by providing phones—the first one many of these people had owned—we also helped people connect in other ways. We learned that a family that had been separated when they were displaced had found one another and been reunited, thanks to inquiries they made with the phone we'd provided.

The project was taken to scale during the West Africa Ebola response in 2014, when we ran tens of thousands of surveys each month through automated text messaging or automated voice calls. We managed to connect with places that were under quarantine during the outbreak, which gave us real-time insights into food supply in Ebola-affected areas. The approach was soon replicated in many other emergencies, including those in Iraq, Syria, and Yemen. It helped the agency understand what was going on in no-go areas.

The science of Earth observation has also undergone a revolution, and we now have access to much more satellite imagery than ever before. It used to cost a fortune to send a satellite into low Earth orbit. Now, a small satellite can be built in a day, and companies manage "constellations" of hundreds of low-cost satellites that beam back granular imagery of Earth in real time. Today's humanitarian analysts have at their fingertips high-resolution maps of crops, rangelands, and floods, and of the settlements where displaced people live.

After his nightmare, the Pharaoh was wise enough to call on Joseph, who made sense of the dream and took specific actions to avert famine. For all of Joseph's talent at dream interpretation, what was most admirable was the way he translated his vision into a clear plan of action that he then implemented, saving Egypt from famine.

We're in the age of the data-fied famine, where a stream of information about hunger is captured, cleaned, calibrated, sliced and diced, and archived. The question is whether humanitarians in the field are equipped to fully digest all this data and use it to adapt their programs quickly enough to make a difference.

Of the different technologies humanitarians are now engaging with, artificial intelligence (AI)—powerful data models that "learn" like a human—may offer both the greatest promise and the highest risk. AI could well be the most momentous advance in technology since the invention of the movable-type printing press in the fifteenth century, one that could fundamentally reshape our social and political structures. Artificial intelligence is operating everywhere, often unbeknownst to us. Its algorithms guide what appears in our social media feeds, and what advertising we see when we're online. Existing "business" AI already helps many companies optimize supply chains or streamline countless labor-intensive back-office tasks such as accounting or payroll.

For humanitarians, AI's potential to end hunger goes much further than stretching aid dollars. Machine-learning algorithms are now being used to estimate hunger in real time, processing oceans of data and producing estimates in the blink of an eye. AI is also performing one of the essential tasks that has frustrated generations of aid workers, that of identifying individuals who need food assistance.

In 2020, the U.S. NGO Give Directly used an AI algorithm to identify cell phone subscribers who qualified for an emergency COVID cash grant in Togo. The process—which when conducted through traditional door-to-door household surveys can take weeks or even months—was completed in minutes when the NGO's algorithms were unleashed on troves of mobile call data records. (The records, which include information about subscribers' airtime top-ups and credit, are a good proxy for their ability to feed themselves because people without money to buy food also tend to top up their phones less often.) Once that information was collected, all Togolese citizens had to do was text a government number and, if eligible, they got a mobile money transfer almost instantly on their phone.

This project points to a future in which some of the humanitarian community's most important processes and decisions—who gets food when, right down to the individual—will be in the hands of algorithms. This change could well improve service provision: research shows that the AI-assisted targeting used in Togo outperformed alternatives.

For all its promise, some experts worry that AI could also open the door to a more dystopian future. Aid workers will need to learn how to use a profoundly new tool in ways that achieve humanitarian objectives rather than undermine them. According to its foundational principles, humanitarian action is meant to be neutral, impartial, and independent. But AI operates according to criteria defined by its (necessarily flawed) human programmers. AI is less reliable when dealing with individuals, such as members of minority groups, who are underrepresented by the data used to train algorithms. What's more, much of the data needed to train and improve AI is locked up by large data companies, who charge a fortune for access.

Because of these limitations, humanitarians will need to keep human beings in the loop as AI gains traction in the sector. We need to monitor what the algorithms are doing: hopefully, helping people feed themselves and not just reinforcing their creators' biases. To ensure humanitarians retain agency over the AI we use, we should work with the open-source AI movement, which makes research, patents, and data free for anyone to use. We must also have a seat at the table as governments of the world begin regulating AI, such as at the Global Partnership for AI, which the G7 launched in 2020.

The Fourth Industrial Revolution's implications for the fight against hunger are not all about emerging tech. It's also about an important shift in the types of foods we grow and eat. In 1973, *Soylent Green* hit the screens, a dystopian sci-fi movie set in 2022 in an overpopulated New York City. The planet has suffered an unspecified cataclysm, and there are serious food shortages. The starving population riots to get their hands on "soylent green," an unappetizing plankton-based wafer.

A strapping square-jawed Charlton Heston plays a policeman investigating the murder of a board member of the Soylent Corporation. As he works the case, we come to understand that a profoundly unequal society has taken shape in the aftermath of the catastrophe, one in which fresh food and clean water are reserved for the elite. Heston eventually discovers that soylent green is not made out of plankton but manufactured from the bodies of dead people. He knows too much, and the police turn against him. As they carry him away after a shootout, Heston screams out the truth (and the movie's concluding line) to the crowd: "Soylent Green is people!" I cringed when I learned that there is now a successful company called Soylent whose product, inspired by the movie, is drunk by people who are "too busy" to eat.

While food supplies in our world are getting tighter— rising food prices, competition over arable land, and supply-chain strains are clear indicators—no one is suggesting we recycle dead bodies for their protein. Yet. All the same, it's well known that the planet can't support a population of 9 billion people if everyone adopts the average American diet, which is high in animal protein. The UN estimates that food production would need to increase by 60 percent by 2050 if we are to feed everyone, and simply put, we are running out of planet. We'll have to eat foods that require less land, pasture, and water.

An ecosystem of companies is appearing to innovate and change the foods we eat. Billion-dollar investments are being made to produce cultured foods. For instance, the U.S.-based Eat Just produces lab-grown chicken. The process involves taking fat or muscle stem cells from a live animal and feeding them nutrients under precisely controlled conditions in stainless steel bioreactors. After two weeks a cut of chicken is ready to be harvested. No conveyor belts, no slaughter, and ten times fewer resources than are used in raising the real thing. The product has obtained regulatory approval in Singapore and Israel, where it is marketed to the ecologically conscious consumer, and as "no-kill" meat to those who object to the slaughter of animals. However, there's a long way to go before lab-grown meat becomes an affordable mass-market product. In Singapore, a portion of "Good Chicken" goes for $17 a serving.

Eat Just has been attracting hundreds of millions of dollars in funding. Its CEO, Josh Tetrick, wants to expand from chicken to beef, pork, and seafood, ultimately producing tens of millions of pounds of cultured meat. He sees two obstacles: regulatory approval and social acceptance. Tetrick is bullish about both. Consumers worry first and foremost about genetic modification, and he thinks they are ready to embrace cultured meat, which is not genetically modified. And tastes evolve: many novel foods that were once considered artificial have entered the mainstream. He has a point: a lot of the "food" in our refrigerators would hardly be recognized as such by our great-grandparents.

It isn't just meat that's being grown in a lab. Fearful of the impact of climate change on the world's coffee crop, researchers have grown "coffee" in a bioreactor, merely by culturing coffee cells and nourishing them with oxygen and nutrients. The resulting product is identical to natural coffee at the molecular level. Its flavor changes with different degrees of roasting, just like the real thing. Yet even if cultured coffee tastes good and provides us with our morning caffeine fix, it will never sustain millions of independent growers, or the social fabric that keeps coffee-growing communities together. Those essential features of our food system are lost when food production is centralized in a line of humming bioreactors.

The implications of these technologies on how the world is fed will be profound. It's no coincidence that Israel and Singapore are at the forefront of the synthetic meat industry: these rich countries import much of their food, and they see lab-grown meat as a way to secure their nations' food sources at a time of climate change and stretched supply chains. Their embrace of cultured meat is more than a luxury or an attempt to corner a lucrative emerging industry. It's a national security imperative.

Ongoing experiments with lab-grown food suggest that the technology may help keep food scarcity at bay. But this may be true only for the portion of humanity that can afford synthetic foods; for this population, an increasing amount of what is consumed will come from shiny stainless steel vats—where dissolved oxygen and precisely controlled pH and temperature optimize cell growth—instead of from rolling fields and meadows. It is difficult to say whether these capital-intensive and costly technological solutions will deliver desperately needed nutritious food to people starving in the Sahel, the Horn of Africa, or the refugee camps of the Middle East, where bioreactors and the delicacies they produce will remain little more than a rumor.

In addition to putting money into synthetic foods, companies are also moving into the production of insect protein that is "culturally acceptable" to Western consumers. (Already, outside of the West, billions of people worldwide regularly eat insects, including the Baka we met in chapter 8.) Insects are very efficient at turning their feed into high-quality lean protein, making them a food uniquely suited to a world of limited resources. In January 2021, the European Food Safety Agency declared yellow mealworms (an unappetizing inch-long creature) fit for human consumption. The French startup Ynsect is building a $372 million factory that will produce 100,000 tons of mealworms each year. Yellow mealworm burgers are already available in Swiss supermarkets. Expect more of these developments as time goes on. And to those who cringe at the thought of eating maggots, remember that in the 1980s sushi caused the same reaction in consumers in the West, where it's now considered a delicacy. Attitudes change.

These new foods fit into a long-term pattern, in which food production has become more capital-intensive over the centuries. Today's farmers hold millions of dollars in assets—machinery and warehouses—and in lines of credit to grow the grain and soy crops that are the foundation of our agriculture. (Many of their counterparts in the Global South are family farmers, of course, who make do with their own labor.) The capital-intensive system has boosted food production and benefited large farmers but has harmed family farming communities worldwide.

The movement to new foods like cultured meat and insect protein could herald a bold new future; instead, I'm often reminded of *Soylent Green* and the deeply troubled society that the film described—an uncanny, warped account of the inequalities in our own midst. Measures such as open licensing of cultured foods may help to ensure that the technology needed to produce these new foods will become available to the nearly 1 billion people who are undernourished. But as of now, no such moves seem to be planned. Unless that changes, power over the global food supply will be even more concentrated in the hands of a few companies with the capital to make billion-dollar investments in R&D and to acquire and maintain the equipment needed to produce tens of millions of pounds of what industry insiders now call "alternative protein."

Eat Just stands to profit from the growth of the cultured meat industry in rich countries. To balance the scales, CEO Josh Tetrick also launched a social enterprise in Liberia. In 2015, in the waning months of the Ebola outbreak, Josh sent Taylor Quinn, a twenty-two-year-old food anthropologist, to scope out what this new project might be. Taylor met with Dr. Jude Senkungu, who worked at Redemption Hospital in Monrovia. Acutely malnourished children came to Doctor Jude's ward from all over Monrovia. He treated the children with therapeutic foods such as F75 and F100, which he received from UNICEF or the Red Cross. F75 and F100 are made of powdered milk, oil, and nutrients. Thanks to their high energy content, protein, and fat, the milk products help malnourished children recover lost weight. Mothers were also given courses in nutrition in the hope the children would do better after treatment.

But Doctor Jude had learned that after being sent home from the hospital, back to the deprived environment where they'd become malnourished, the children would begin losing weight again. Many of the same children were coming back again and again to Doctor Jude's ward for second and third rounds of therapeutic milk. Doctor Jude became convinced that what was needed was a cheap, nutritious product that families from all walks of life could afford to buy at the market.

After meeting the doctor, Taylor saw that there was an opportunity to challenge dominant approaches to fighting malnutrition. He decided then and there to call his colleagues at Eat Just to create the food product Doctor Jude had described. Taylor's philosophy was to look at what foods were available in the local market that people already ate, and then to improve on those. He determined that to be affordable, the product would need to cost less than six U.S. cents a serving, and that to be sustainable, it would need to be mass-produced by a local business.

For the next year, Taylor flew each month from Monrovia to California, returning home with suitcases heavy with samples of cassava, a Liberian staple. He worked with the cooks, engineers, and food technologists at the Eat Just lab in San Francisco, trying to produce a food that was local, cheap, tasty, and nutritious. There was a lot of trial and error; they tried cookies and then bouillon cubes. Finally, they settled on a porridge they called "Power Gari," which could be made exclusively from local ingredients, including cassava, and flavored with oil from wild palms, sesame, or coconut. They added protein, vitamins, and minerals.

Recipe in hand, Taylor's next challenge was finding a Liberian company that would produce Power Gari. There were local Liberian food processors, but it seemed to Taylor that their operating models were more about attracting grants from international donors than running profitable businesses. These processors often relied on expensive, off-grid generators that burned gallons of diesel to process modest amounts of food. To Taylor, it was obvious that those "businesses" would fail as soon as their grant money dried up. He was determined to do things differently with Power Gari.

Then, in 2018, Taylor met with a group of people from Kawadah Farm, local agro-entrepreneurs from Nimba County. They were businessmen looking for new markets, and were willing to produce Power Gari. To save money, they decided to set up a new business in an abandoned hotel room. After thoroughly cleaning it up and sealing its cracked walls to create a sanitary environment, they put together a basic production line with $850 worth of equipment, mostly motorcycle parts. The system was entirely hand-powered and -operated; it did not require a drop of expensive diesel fuel and didn't rely on any equipment that would take months to repair if it broke. The modest production line could crank out 30 tons of Power Gari a month—equivalent to 600,000 meals. "As it scales," Taylor wrote in a blog post, "this approach can ensure that everyone, everywhere has access to nutritious, delicious, affordable food. It may not be high-tech, but it's high-impact."

Nutrition and business communities viewed Power Gari—a socially minded, for-profit product—with a lot of suspicion. Nutritionists tend to see fortified foods as a medical product that requires very strict quality control, not something small local food processors should venture to produce. The business community thought there was no way to turn a profit selling nutritious food products like Power Gari. A 2018 *Washington Post* article about Power Gari quoted critics calling the product "nothing new" and "not a magic bullet," and unsuited to those under two years of age, who make up the bulk of severely malnourished children. Critics also pointed to the fact that Africa has been a graveyard of initiatives to produce fortified foods for low-income consumers, and that big name companies like DuPont, Danone, and Pepsi had tried before and failed.

The skepticism is understandable. But in 2023, as I write, Kawadah Farm is still going strong. The company moved out of the abandoned hotel to a dedicated facility, where they have made and sold Power Gari for the last four years. The company employs a dozen women in Nimba County, and more than twenty sales-people in Monrovia. Thanks to a USDA grant, Kawadah Farm is gearing up to build a new production facility, set up cassava-processing centers in southeast Liberia, and supply hundreds of schools with Power Gari each week.

I met Taylor in 2019, by which time he had worked on a number of food projects. He is not your typical humanitarian. Taylor is a foodie at heart, and his idea of fun is to taste his way through loud and busy local markets, sampling the aromas and textures of everything on offer, from fried donuts at roadside stalls to rice and meat stews. When on the road, Taylor eats everything, including, he confesses with a chuckle, "bats and rats."

In 2021, Taylor traveled to Tanzania, where he learned there were plans to build three factories to produce fortified porridge for children, based on corn flour, artificial flavors, and vitamin mix. The government was establishing an official standard for this porridge, which only these new factories would meet. At first glance, the project looked like a step in the right direction in a country where childhood malnutrition remains a problem. But after visiting the market in Dar es Salaam, Taylor realized that most mothers in Tanzania bought their infant porridge from one of the thousands of women who produced it by hand using wholesome local products such as pumpkin seeds. The trade was based on trust between new mothers and the women who made the porridge.

"Why would you destroy that?" Taylor asked.

It's only natural that, in trying to solve food insecurity, governments attempt to reshape local supply chains in the image of those that their Western advisors promote. But if we want markets to work for the poorest of the poor, we need to be conscious of the systems we're reshaping. Do people in the Global South want their food to come from heavily mechanized industrial food supply chains, which will leave them open to repeating mistakes made in the West?

Innovation, for humanitarians, is all about the choices we're making and the spirit in which we approach those we assist. The

Silicon Valley ethos of innovation strikes me and many others as bloodless, perhaps even brutal and militaristic. It's about "disrupting" entire sectors of society. In its early years, Facebook's motto was "Move fast and break things." Granted, Silicon Valley has brought us tools that are very relevant to the fight against hunger. But there is a big disconnect between new tech and the values of the humanitarian community.

I believe there are different and perhaps better ways to innovate. Aid isn't another industry to be disrupted; it serves extremely vulnerable people in high-risk situations. We can't simply invite Silicon Valley in to unleash their latest tech on people whose lives are often dependent on support that is consistent, reliable, and safe to access. We need to be careful we aren't letting the wolves into the barn.

The Black Humanitarian

Race and the Aid System

"You damned Haitian! You black hunk of dung!" the police howled in Spanish.

—Jacques Roumain, *Masters of the Dew*

I don't want to see another Black man for as long as I live," said a French aid worker to a group of expatriates, including me, at a WFP office in West Africa.

Our colleague had just been notified that he would soon be relocating to the agency's European headquarters, after a years-long assignment in the country. He sounded upbeat and relieved.

Others around the table chuckled. They looked delighted at the joke; I certainly wasn't. Underneath what he thought was a light-hearted comment were decades of racial tension that still exist in humanitarian agencies. It is also revealing of a structural flaw in the aid sector, whose history of inequality between those who give and those who receive aid has led to deep misunderstandings and gross imbalances in power.

Although much has changed since the 1950s and 1960s, racial dynamics continue to influence the way the aid system works, from workplace politics to the way assistance is delivered on the ground. Underrepresentation of Blacks and other minorities in leadership roles means aid agencies struggle to relate to the societies they're meant to be helping. The system's inability to come to grips with race means that even well-intentioned assistance can undermine, rather than heal, the communities that receive it.

In principle, humanitarian assistance is colorblind. In practice, race remains a pervasive and often unacknowledged force in how aid is provided. This book explains how hunger is caused by inequalities and tensions specific to each society that suffers from it. But the aid sector itself needs to acknowledge, and confront, its own history and its own biases if it is to truly alleviate hunger. This chapter focuses on the specific experience of Black communities because they face glaring inequalities from the very institutions that are meant to help them feed themselves. I offer my own insight as a biracial man who has worked in Africa and Haiti for the majority of my career.

The history of food aid is rife with racial inequities. Racist policies instated during the colonial era have led to the worst famines in human history. Mike Davis, in his magisterial work *Late Victorian Holocausts,* describes how British authorities, during the terrible 1876–1878 Indian Famine (which killed between 5.6 and 9.4 million people), not only failed to help the population but actively denied aid to those who needed it most. Authorities initially refused to mount any serious attempts at relief, instead cheering on the Great Famine as a "a salutary cure for overpopulation." Viewing India primarily as a revenue source, the British balked at spending anything on food programs, and administrators who dared to do so were upbraided for their extravagance.

A belated and miserly relief effort took shape under the leadership of the lieutenant governor, Sir Richard Temple, who organized camps where starving people could do hard labor on canals or railroads to earn meager food rations. Workers in these disease-ridden camps received the "Temple wage," a daily ration of only a pound of rice, no legumes or protein, which offered less than half the calories that a man needs to survive. Horrifyingly, even those held at the infamous concentration camp of Buchenwald would receive more sustenance.

Mike Davis called the approach "punitive relief," because Temple thought the starving laborers were receiving their just deserts. "Nor will many be inclined to grieve much for the fate which they brought upon themselves," Temple declared, "and which terminated lives of idleness and too often of crime." Temple's dehumanization and criminalization of the recipients of colonial food aid was a way to justify the unjustifiable.

The cynical and racialized response to the subcontinent's Great Famine is a case study in unequal power relations applied to a nation's food security: India continued to export grain to Britain while millions of its people starved. The famine had been triggered by drought, but it became a mass mortality event because of the colonial era's racist ideology.

France used similar tactics, engaging forced labor to build the infrastructure of its African colonies. Just as in British India, tropes of the time were trotted out: Blacks were "lazy" and "indolent" and needed to be forced to work. Colonial authorities rounded up men and turned them over to the companies that built the colonies' bridges, dams, roads, and canals. In many cases, workers were fed meager rations or left to fend for themselves. Forced labor was cheaper than bringing in machines; the gigantic port of Abidjan was largely excavated by hand.

The historic memory of being forced to carry out hard manual labor while subsisting on meager rations explains why contemporary, well-intentioned humanitarian food-for-work schemes— where people receive food rations in exchange for planting trees or building dams—easily conjure up echoes of colonial abuse.

Today's aid workers aren't always aware of this painful history, and they wonder why projects providing workers with a food ration aren't welcome. But for many of the Africans I worked with, the abuses are part of the collective memory, while some white humanitarians don't know, or don't dare to ask, about this past.

Today, racial inequalities are more subtle than in the immediate postcolonial period. Many aid agency offices in Africa are diverse, with senior management coming from Africa and all over the world. The heads of field offices I have worked in were from Burkina Faso, France, Mali, Angola, Japan, and Cameroon; to be an expatriate today does not mean to be white.

Still, racial imbalances endure, at the workplace and with the communities we serve. Headquarters tend to be less diverse than field offices, and very few head office executives are Black or African. Although statistics are hard to come by, it's obvious that Europeans and North Americans are overrepresented in high-ranking posts and in plum postings, such as Rome or Nairobi. At WFP, only about a third of senior executives are from "developing nations." And racial tensions are all too common: in 2023, the UN reported that one in five among its staff experienced racial discrimination or harassment at work.

In field locations, old habits persist. Many white aid workers in Nairobi or Dakar live alongside rich locals in exclusive districts, insulated from the society they're meant to help. When white privilege becomes ostentation, it invites hostility. I remember that in 2003, locals in Zinder, Niger's second town, called its French cultural center "Club Rhodesia" because its clientele of aid workers was so white. In 2015 rioters burned the place down, after it became a lightning rod for anti-Western protests.

I saw the tensions firsthand when I was once hurriedly sent to a small, troubled, French-speaking country in Africa to help humanitarian agencies cobble together a response plan to an emerging crisis that involved sudden population displacement after a conflict broke out. It was immediately clear that relations between the UN and the NGOs in the country were strained, and that race was part of the problem.

I attended a series of coordination meetings where I heard a group of cocky white French NGO directors in blue jeans and untucked shirts speak impertinently to their UN counterparts, all formally dressed Africans many years their senior. "Here we go again," I thought as I sat in the back of the room as the all-too-familiar scene unfolded. The NGO directors spoke with the insolence of high school kids talking back to their parents or teachers. The NGO workers sneered that the UN was inept and unfit to lead the response; the UN accused the NGOs of undermining their work. In the mildewed, over-air-conditioned rooms where we would meet, disagreements about the humanitarian community's response to the emergency broke neatly along racial lines. I saw the whites huddle together on their side of the conference table, the Africans on the other.

The NGO workers could afford to be arrogant with their African peers because they had the financial support of Western donors in the country, who were white like them. They would be the ones with the money to implement the response to the crisis, while the (African-led) UN agencies would be left underfunded, and irrelevant at the critical first stage of the response. The NGOs would be calling the shots.

Let's be clear: People don't attend humanitarian coordination meetings to sit around a campfire and sing "Kumbaya." Disagreements can be profound, especially in a crisis. The NGO staff in the room probably felt that their behavior was legitimate. But when the dynamics regularly pit whites against Black Africans, there's reason for pause.

The nexus between food programs and race is evident in the United States too. In the civil rights era, self-organized community food assistance projects helped support the African American community. Perhaps most famously, the Black Panther Party, founded in the 1960s on ideals of socialism and Black liberation, regarded hunger as one of the greatest forms of oppression. Unsatisfied with paltry government aid, the Panthers started their own food program. They focused on breakfast, a meal that many poor Black children then went without. In January 1969, the Panthers began providing breakfast to schoolchildren at St. Augustine's Church in Oakland, California. The grits, eggs, toast, and milk were donated by sympathetic individuals, or by groceries and supermarkets.

Starting a program to provide food to the poor—historically a responsibility of the state—was extraordinarily helpful. It was also an astute move. The Panthers' cofounders, Bobby Seale and Huey Newton, who once bravely sold copies of Mao Tse-tung's *Little Red Book* out of the back of their car, knew that the free breakfasts would advance their broader goals. In addition to helping thousands of African Americans, their food program would highlight the federal government's indifference to hunger in Black communities, and show that the Panthers were far more than gun-toting socialists with afros.

The Panthers' free breakfast program became one of the party's most visible initiatives. It proved so popular that it expanded to forty-five schools around the country, feeding twenty thousand kids between 1969 and 1970. The benefits for children were immediate: teachers reported that their once-lethargic pupils were now alert and did better in the classroom. And there was consensus that the program made sense. "I mean, nobody can argue against free grits," said actor, writer, and filmmaker Roger Guenveur Smith, who would go on to portray Huey Newton in a 2001 movie.

J. Edgar Hoover, then head of the FBI, saw things differently. Hoover called the breakfast program "potentially the greatest threat to efforts by authorities to neutralize the Black Panther Party and destroy what it stands for." Hoover understood that the program was dangerous precisely because it legitimized the Panthers by burnishing their image with Black moderates and whites. The FBI launched a campaign of disinformation and intimidation to discredit and destroy the program. Federal agents told white parents that Black kids were learning to be racists while they ate their breakfast. They spread rumors that the food was contaminated with venereal disease. They raided program sites in Richmond and Baltimore. In Chicago, agents destroyed and then urinated on the food supplies intended for the children. The FBI's harassment ultimately disrupted the party and caused the food program to end in the early 1970s.

But the Panthers were on the right side of history. The USDA scaled up its own free breakfast program in the 1970s. Opinions vary, but many people believe the Panthers' program was a catalyst behind the development of similar federal programs. As of 2018, 14.5 million American children were receiving breakfast for free at school, exactly as the children in Oakland and other cities did during the Panthers' program.

In the past couple of decades, the relationship between race and food aid has been less contentious than it was in the 1960s. But there has always been a degrading assumption that Black communities should gratefully accept whatever is on offer. This has been the case in the United States, where, according to Cornell University's Andrew Novakovic, "almost all of the major food assistance programs were ideas that came from agriculture because we had too much of something." In other words, aid was only provided when the government needed to get rid of farmers' leftovers, rather than being driven by the needs of Black families.

An example of this is the emblematic government cheese program that began in the Reagan era. In 1981, there was a glut in the U.S. dairy market. To help midwestern dairy farmers, the federal government bought excess dairy and began distributing 30 million pounds of free "American cheese" to the poor, including many inner-city Black people. The orange cheese came in five-pound, highly processed, shelf-stable bars.

The Black community's relationship to the cheap government cheese was ambivalent. The bars were unappetizing—sometimes covered in a strange sheen, and sometimes rock hard. Lactose intolerance, a digestive disorder that's more prevalent among Black people than among whites, meant that many recipients simply couldn't stomach the stuff. Still, eating the food became a common experience in the community, one that the rapper Kendrick Lamar celebrated in his 2012 hit "Money Trees," about growing up amid poverty, drugs, and orange government cheese.

In my years in West Africa's Sahel, I often heard that "the hand that gives is better than the one that receives." It's a *hadith* (teaching) in the Islamic tradition. It's also a quote attributed to Napoleon. Whatever its origin, the saying captures the inherently unequal relationship between givers and receivers of aid. While the phrase is meant to encourage generosity, I also understood it to mean that the person who can afford to give is better than the person who needs help—a crude and stigmatizing mindset. And when the "givers" are white and the "beneficiaries" are frequently Black—whether dark-skinned colonial subjects, recipients of food assistance in Africa, or those who got bars of government cheese in America's inner cities—it's easy to see how aid programs mirror or reinforce broader, race-based inequalities in power.

As a young aid worker, I remember struggling to understand why the food rations we provided in Africa were so paltry. Soon

after starting at WFP in Niger in 2001, I met an American colleague who had worked in the Kosovo emergency a few years earlier. I understood from her stories that the population of Kosovo
was getting much better rations than that of Niger. She told me
how a highlight of her assignment was setting up a refrigerated
supply chain to bring dairy and other fresh foods into Albania for
the refugees. As I listened to her, I made a mental note that at
that time in Niger, we were providing a meager ration of millet to
people who had just experienced a drought. That grain would fill
stomachs but would not provide the nutrition the body requires.

When I naively asked others why we treated people so differently, I was told that living standards were lower in Africa than
elsewhere, and that our cost-conscious donors would not be willing to pay to provide high-quality foods in the world's poorest
nations. While this has changed somewhat with the introduction
of cash transfers in some African settings—a welcome change
that means people choose what foods they buy with the assistance
they receive—a double standard lives on. There is a tacit sense
that Black communities should be grateful for whatever assistance
they get.

Susan Sebatindira didn't grow up wanting to become a humanitarian. She's from Nairobi, a place swarming with NGOs. Like
many other Kenyans, Susan once dismissed humanitarian workers as "people in Jesus sandals trying to tell us what to do." That
would soon change. She looked up to her mother, who worked
at the African Development Bank. The agency funded health and
education programs that allowed Africans to support one another,
Susan decided she wanted to work in international development.

As she studied for her master's at the London School of Economics in 2013–2014, she and the other students were all too aware
of the irony of a largely white faculty lecturing a diverse student

body about the political economy of Africa. London is one of the world's true global cities, with residents from all over the world. And yet, here at one of the city's most prestigious universities, her professors didn't reflect that diversity. Thankfully, Susan's advisor was Professor Thandika Mkandawire, the one Black African member of the department of international development. His guidance helped Susan thrive at the LSE.

After graduation, Susan became an intern at the UN office in Denmark. When she got there, she was stunned by the lack of diversity in the workplace. "Why are we so few?" she asked herself. There happened to be one other Kenyan intern, also a woman, at the Copenhagen office, and the largely white staff kept confusing the two. "We didn't look anything alike," she remembers. It seemed that in the eyes of their white coworkers, their blackness erased all other individual characteristics. Even though Susan's white colleagues were experts who traveled the world to work on development projects, they couldn't tell one Black coworker from another. The implications for how they might approach the African communities they worked with weren't encouraging.

After feeling that sense of alienation in a largely white office, she moved to Bangkok, where her experience was different. She found community with other Africans, who were better represented there. She remembers the knowing nods to other Africans in the hallway, and sitting together in the cafeteria. Their camaraderie showed her how important it was that young Africans starting out at the UN have access to safe, inclusive spaces.

Years later, as the COVID-19 pandemic hit and the Black Lives Matter movement swept the world, Susan thought back on the community she had found in Bangkok and decided to act. She single-handedly created The Black Humanitarian, an Instagram-based platform for aid workers from Africa and of African descent. Susan explained to me it was meant to amplify and connect Black voices and inspire those seeking to start a career as an aid worker.

The Black Humanitarian has since become part of a broader movement to promote diversity and inclusion in the sector.

Thanks to the platform, people who are as isolated as Susan had once been are able to find support. Now an established network of professionals, The Black Humanitarian organizes mentoring sessions and talks. Its thousand members come from all over the world, and volunteers in Germany, Canada, and the United States manage the network. Many of its members are in their twenties and thirties, giving the group a refreshingly youthful vibe. Susan's posts focus on the Black experience in the aid sector, but also on thematic issues of the day, such as technology and innovation. On The Black Humanitarian, Susan also helps young Black aid workers deal with the hurdles they face as they try to break into the industry. Susan knows that while The Black Humanitarian has lent a voice to a long-silent community, it only offers so much—dominant, widely accepted mindsets and structures will have to change to become more inclusive.

Susan and the network she created are emblematic of a new generation of humanitarians of African descent who aren't shy about speaking out. If we don't talk about race, nothing will change. Of course, speaking out doesn't ensure that real change will happen.

Racial bias can also shape how aid is delivered in communities in need. Aid worker Sandra Uwantege Hart, the daughter of a white American diplomat father and a Rwandan mother, explained to me how racial stereotypes shaped the response to the devastating January 2010 earthquake in Haiti. Sandra then worked on humanitarian coordination in Haiti—helping the UN agencies and NGOs work together.

Wearing the cheap Chinese-made clothes she'd bought at the market in Port-au-Prince, her hair in braids, Sandra looked so much like a local that the agency she worked for mistakenly used her image on the front page of one of its publications—as though she were a local aid recipient. Sandra believed that the thinking behind it was this: her coworkers had found her picture in an archive and assumed that because Sandra was Black, she could only have been a beneficiary. And that because she had light skin, her picture would make an appealing front cover illustration. Sandra and the white colleague who made the faux pas laughed about it later, but the incident shows how easily Black people fall victim to mistaken identity and are fetishized by others.

Sandra's misgivings about the earthquake response itself were not as easily laughed off. Using public taxis, she crisscrossed Port-au-Prince, a city in ruins, and began peeling back the layers of the relief effort. She was dismayed to see that the international response had been built on questionable stereotypes. For one thing, relief agencies provided food to women only, a group they saw as passive victims, confined to their role as providers of food to their families. Sandra knew this was wrong. She had met many Haitian men who had lost their spouses in the earthquake, men who were now single fathers struggling to feed their families. Susan saw that Haitian men were viewed as violent, selfish, unreliable individuals not to be trusted with rations. Somehow, damaging stereotypes about Black men had been turned into policy.

Sandra tried using her position as an aid worker to explain to the agencies and NGOs that their strategy was misguided, built on myths about Black men. She argued that survivors deserved a more thoughtful response. "You need to calm down," she was told by her manager.

The system needs to get things done fast to save lives. This might be why it never quite finds the time to question itself. Interrogating built-in, systemic racial bias might seem secondary in the midst of an emergency, when the priority is to save lives. But at some point, these questions must be addressed.

During my years in central Africa, I was constantly reminded that appearance matters enormously. In the Lingala language, being called "poorly dressed" is a scathing insult. This is why the dandies of Brazzaville and Kinshasa are considered a national treasure: they wear sharp suits, white shoes, red suspenders, and horn-rimmed sunglasses. Some sport broad-brimmed hats, smoke long pipes, and accessorize with a cane or an umbrella. On Friday nights, all decked out, they strut and swagger, to the cheers and applause of revelers outside nightclubs. It's not just men that dress up extravagantly: some women are dandies too. Their over-the-top attire, inspired by the European style of dress in colonial days, has become a form of self-expression and freedom.

In the streets, the dandies rule, superbly subverting the Western dress code. But in professional circles in central Africa, a neat Western appearance is a must, and anyone aspiring to be taken seriously dresses conservatively or runs the risk of being asked to leave the building and come back in proper attire. This strict adherence to Western dress codes means that officials in the region like their aid workers clean-cut and buttoned up—just one example of how Western codes continue to pervade the environment humanitarians operate in.

The fact that twenty-first-century central Africa still clings to European social conventions reminds me of French activist and philosopher Frantz Fanon. In 1952, Fanon (himself a Black man from Martinique) wrote about colonized Blacks wearing "white masks," by which he meant that Africans and other colonized people were so profoundly alienated from their own identity that they mimicked Western culture, a self-denial that only undermined their own self-interest. The "white mask" is Fanon's term for internalized racism. Fanon wrote of how African officials wearing the white mask donned tailored suits, spoke flowery French, and drank the finest imported liquors—all while ignoring the needs and aspirations of their own people. In my time in Africa, I saw that the white mask is still with us. But where it appears in society is changing, which has profound, concerning implications for the future of humanitarianism.

Aside from dress, perhaps the most apparent proof of the white mask's enduring influence is the fashion of skin whitening all over Africa. As one of my Congolese friends joked, "There are so many light-skinned people in town you'd think we're in the Caribbean!" People using creams with bleach to lighten their complexion are not only attempting to deny their blackness but are seriously harming their skin. When overused, these aggressive chemicals do permanent damage. As people age, telltale purple-red marks appear on their faces.

I have seen Black Africans give white aid workers the benefit of the doubt because of the color of their skin. Compared to locals, it's comparatively easy for white aid workers to get past security and into the premises of a UN agency, a ministry, or an embassy and speak to executives. It's not that their ideas are better or more deserving of a hearing, it's just that access is easier than it is for locals, because their skin is white.

The white mask also lives on in the currency of many African countries. To this day, fourteen countries in west and central Africa use the CFA franc, a currency created in 1945 and long pegged to the French franc. (The French themselves stopped using the franc in 2002, when the euro replaced it.) This arrangement is one of many grating reminders that independence in these countries remains, in some ways, nominal. In its former colonies, food aid provided by France or through French NGOs is easily perceived as an unwelcome instrument of postcolonial domination. It can go as far as communities rejecting much-needed aid outright: "Keep your food," the representatives of a poor conservative settlement told my local WFP colleagues in Mauritania in 2004.

The white mask extends to the foods people eat and what they choose to drink. From Dakar to Djibouti, bakers everywhere sell a version of the French baguette, made from imported wheat. And such copious quantities of Champagne and Cognac are imported into central Africa that economists have worried since the 1960s that the pattern could compromise the region's ability to afford imports of the technology they need to industrialize.

Urban elites shop at supermarkets where the shelves are stocked with imported Western brands, and they have developed a taste for fast food. This desire for European and American foods has stunted agriculture in the region. As long as Western tastes dominate, no campaign to "eat what you grow, and grow what you eat," as I have often heard officials proclaim, stands a chance.

We see the mask embedded in relationships to political and administrative history. In the local language, Brazzaville's name is Mfoa. But to this day the city is officially named after Pierre Savorgnan de Brazza, an Italian-born French explorer whose treaty with King Makoko formalized France's control over the area in the 1880s. In 2006 the Congolese state spent millions on a mausoleum of gleaming marble to house his remains. A larger-than-life statue of the explorer stands on a pedestal in front of the monument, towering over the busy streets of the city named after him. The memorial is visited by uniformed schoolchildren who pay their respects to the white man who drew the borders of their country. City names and monuments are only symbols. Still, I often wondered if Congo's people would be better off if it had cast off its colonial heritage and embraced its own identity.

In many forlorn district offices all over the Sahel or in central Africa, I have seen large, hand-painted, prominently displayed *tableaux de commandement*. The *tableaux* are boards that list, in chronological order, the names of all the administrators who have been in charge of that area, and their dates of service. The lists, which start in the late nineteenth or early twentieth century, begin with the names of French colonial commanders. After 1960, African names follow French ones. By adding their names to an unbroken line that began with their white predecessors, local administrators align themselves with a history of governance that harmed their people. In many local languages, the word *commandant,* the military rank the colonial French commanders held long ago, is still used to refer to a district officer or prefect. Even after decades of independence, it's sometimes as though locals remain under foreign occupiers. Wearing yet another white mask.

"He wears a mask, and his face grows to fit it," wrote George Orwell in *Shooting an Elephant,* pointing out how easy it is for an individual to lose their identity. The individual wearing the mask thinks they can take it off as they please, only to find they've become the mask they wear. Fanon's white mask is everywhere in central Africa, but it is not just the clothes, foods, currency, languages, history, and modes of governance. The mask seeps into humanitarian work as well. Even though many humanitarians are now African, the values, methodologies, mechanisms, and (most important) the funding are Western. An example is the fact that most Western aid agencies insist on providing aid to individuals and households directly, with stringent measures in place to identify recipients (including requiring official ID and sometimes biometrics to receive aid). Such individual-based approaches are difficult to reconcile with Africa's tradition of community solidarity, which is essential to people's well-being.

Thankfully, winds of change are blowing. The new generation of Africans is less accepting of the old arrangements that kept their countries closely tied to former colonies after independence. There has been a rebellion against the CFA franc: Young activists have burned banknotes live on TV, which led to African leaders announcing that they would revisit the currency peg to France. More African youth are studying in South Africa, China, or the Middle East now, signaling a future of diversified cultural references and economic ties. Brazil, India, and China are now emerging as humanitarian donors. The governments of the Global South have more partners today than ever before. As incomes rise, some governments have become leading funders of UN projects in their countries. This gives them more leverage in negotiating humanitarian assistance, leveling the playing field between the proverbial white savior and the Black beneficiary. As the aid sector changes, seeing unequal humanitarianism as a matter of Black and white is passé.

As Africans increasingly question the baggage they've inherited from Europe, they also demand much more from the humanitarian community. This forces agencies to review long-held assumptions and up their game. Rising standards of living mean today's leaders expect something more than bulk shipments of free rice—they expect sophisticated assistance, including analytics on humanitarian needs, digital platforms to manage benefits, and bridges to longer-term solutions and their own government-run systems. On this new, more level playing field, humanitarians are being pushed to design their programs to support government priorities, rather than donor agendas. In practice, this means much greater emphasis on purchasing food supplies from local farmers, building financial ecosystems, collaborating with local NGOs, and building national capacities that last.

My dark skin has led to misunderstandings with white people my entire life. Probably ever since that day when I was a child and my white paternal grandparents tried to rub the black off my older sister's knees and elbows when they gave us a bath. It wasn't mean; it was just ignorance. But my run-ins with race became less innocent as I got older. As a student in Europe, I was frequently accosted by white boys looking for drugs who assumed I was a dealer, or older white men who wanted directions to the whorehouse, and who seemed disappointed when they found out I wasn't a pimp.

And then there were the police, whose crude approach to race has had deadly consequences for so many young Black men. On a fall day in 2016, I was in eastern France and decided to visit my white grandparents' grave—the ones who had tried to scrub the black off my sister. The road to the town of Saverne, where the cemetery is, winds through rolling hills, cherry orchards, and vineyards. That fall day the hills were alive with yellow and red, and I was marveling at how lovely it all was. Soon after pulling my Fiat onto the highway into town, I saw a police van behind me, blue lights flashing. My heart skipped a beat. I signaled right and pulled onto the shoulder. An officer came out and instructed me to move the car farther up the road. I was so jittery the vehicle stalled when I tried to comply.

In a slow, calm voice, a tall officer with brown hair asked me to turn off the engine and step out of the car. He escorted me twenty yards up the road. The squad of a half dozen had formed a semi-circle around me, as if to cut off any attempt on my part to escape through the shrubs and into the fields below. Each wore a Day-Glo yellow vest over their uniform, and each had a submachine gun hanging from their neck, resting on their chest. The blue lights on the van kept flashing. When they failed to ask for my ID or driver's license, I realized that these officers weren't standard policemen. They were from the narcotics agency. The traffic on the busy highway slowed to a crawl, and I felt hundreds of eyes on me as I stood on the roadside surrounded by narcos armed to the teeth.

The officer asked me where I was headed. I told him I was on my way to visit my grandparents' grave in the next town.

By the way, he asked, were there drugs in the car?

I said no.

"Are you *sure* there are no drugs in the car?" he asked again. He was giving me a last chance. The calm, even voice he had first used was now gone.

I told him again: "No, there are no drugs in the car." Then I added that what I did have in the car, on the passenger seat, were chrysanthemums. I was taking these to my grandparents' grave.

On the officer's signal, a small sniffer dog came out of their van and hopped into my Fiat. Front seat, back seat, nothing. The officer who'd searched the car along with the dog reported back to the others, confirming the presence of chrysanthemums and nothing else. I exhaled. The commanding officers' jaws tightened. Without a word, the narcos took their dog and their guns and got back in their van. I was free to go.

There was no way they could guess I was a UN aid worker, but there were no signs I was a drug dealer either. And there was no way the thousands of cars rubbernecking on the highway could've known they were looking at a crude exercise in racial profiling, and not a bona fide drug bust.

I got back into the Fiat, tried to calm down, and continued to Saverne. The visit to the cemetery was a blur. I have not been to my grandparents' grave since.

Years earlier, I had realized my race was affecting my work. The opportunities I had were not the same as those of my white colleagues. When I was being reassigned after my first post in Niger, I had heard there was a vacancy in a neighboring country. I turned for advice to a senior European colleague. "No," he told me, "that's not for you. We want a white man in that post—to show the government we mean business."

I did not question what I had just been told: that my skin color placed me on a lower rung of the pecking order, in a lower caste of humanitarian workers. It didn't sink in at the moment, and I moved on. When I think about it now, I am ashamed I didn't speak up and say such thinking had no place in a UN agency. My colleague had also unwittingly pointed to the horrible reality of internalized racism in the places where we work: in this case, that an African country would need a white official assigned to it to be convinced the UN was taking it seriously.

The color of my skin has been a blessing and a curse, an asset and a burden, depending on the situation. "Aren't you Cape Verdean?" I have been asked many times in Boston, Guinea-Bissau, and in Senegal by total strangers hoping to forge a connection. My skin color has resulted in people confiding in me because I look like them, which helped me be a better humanitarian worker.

I happen to look a lot like the Moors of Mauritania, and many people would assume I spoke the local Hassaniya dialect when they met me. The misunderstanding helped to break the ice and allowed me to get to know people. The Mauritanian civil servants I worked with invited me to their houses (or their low square tents) for tea and would open up to me. They once told me about how they would hoodwink their bosses into thinking they had gone halfway across the country to supervise government projects when they were really hanging out at home, playing cards. They'd hide the government cars they were meant to be traveling in. They would even answer radio calls by saying they were in locations far upcountry when they were really lying low in the capital. I listened in, uncomfortable, and had a hard time imagining them telling the same stories to my white colleagues.

While being biracial helped forge connections, my Western sensibilities often jarred my local colleagues in Africa. I had heavy conversations with my incredulous, largely male staff about the issue of sexual exploitation and abuse, an absolute red line in the humanitarian community, which has unfortunately had its share of sex scandals. I once explained to them that paying for sex was strictly forbidden under the code of conduct, and that they could be fired for it. My explanation prompted questions, commentary, and perplexed looks from the men, even after the meeting was over. What was a red line to me was just not a big deal to them.

Like many other African Americans, I have never felt as American as I did in Africa. When I first arrived in Africa, I felt like I had found a new home. There is something about the flair with which people dress on Friday night, the flavors of the food, the sound of the music. I recognized words that survived the middle passage centuries ago. It all makes the continent feel tantalizingly familiar to me. But after centuries and generations apart, it's not that simple.

In America I am Black; in Africa, I am not quite Black and not quite white. An angry man in Dakar called me *sale metis*—you dirty halfling—when I refused to give him some change. Years ago in a remote part of Haiti, a child no older than three contemplated my brown skin and curly hair before pointing his chubby finger at me and blurting out *"blan."* Haitian Creole has its subtleties, and *blan* means the color white, but also "foreigner." It felt almost like an insult.

Being biracial, someone who is at once an insider and an outsider, means I have access to the inner workings of the humanitarian system, while being keenly aware of some of its absurdities. At headquarters, important decisions are made in meetings that involve a slew of different divisions or agencies, but where those in attendance are almost all white. I remember a UN meeting in Geneva that was about responding to emergencies, where I was the only nonwhite person in attendance. All those discussions about this or that crisis in Africa, and not a single African in the room. Was I the only one who noticed this? Had others seen, and, like me, kept their silence? Or had they become so accustomed to it that it didn't register anymore? If we as humanitarians are to become more effective at delivering assistance and supporting local communities, we need to become more inclusive, to ask ourselves who *isn't* at the table.

The first step to resolving a problem is recognizing that there is one, and the humanitarian community needs to acknowledge that no one is immune to racism. We need better data on race in the aid sector to inform action plans and improve the representation of minorities. Hiring more Black people, especially in executive roles, will help make governing structures more sensitive to the aspirations and needs of communities on the ground. We need leaders to step up and say that racism has no place in the workplace. Change won't be easy or immediate: overturning racism is not something a single agency can ever hope to achieve on its own. But that shouldn't discourage us from trying to make change.

Real Food

Grassroots Solutions to Feed Us All

Then one morning you see your ripe fields spread out before you under the dew and you say—whoever you are—Me—I'm master of the dew, and your heart fills with pride.

—Jacques Roumain, *Masters of the Dew*

When the French king Henry IV was crowned at the end of the sixteenth century, during the closing years of the Wars of Religion, France's once fertile fields lay fallow. After two generations of fighting, at least 2 million of his subjects had died from famine and disease. A true statesman, Henry IV had converted to Catholicism to end the bloodshed, bringing peace and order to his devastated realm. He restored agriculture. He built roads, bridges, and canals to relaunch the economy.

The "Good King" understood that his people were desperate for reassurance that there would be enough to eat, and once declared, "I want every laborer in my Kingdom to have a chicken to put in the pot on Sundays." The *Poule au Pot*—a whole chicken stewed in a beef broth with herbs and vegetables, a specialty of the king's native Béarn—became an iconic French dish, and an enduring symbol of the promises the monarchy had made.

King Henry met a bloody end in 1610 when a religious fanatic stabbed him to death in his carriage. Henry's promises would not be kept by his successors, and for most of the French monarchy's subjects, pots remained empty. The kings of Henry's line persecuted and expelled the Protestants, waged protracted wars of conquest, and built the gilded Palace of Versailles. Feeding the people was not the priority. There was a satirical song that made the rounds in Paris as the 1789 Revolution brewed:

> *Finally the chicken will be in the pot*
> *At least we can presume*
> *Because it's been promised to us for 200 years*
> *And it's still being plucked.*

All over the world, kings and rulers, however benevolent, have too often struggled to feed their people. There have been unkept promises, like the *Poule au Pot*. There have been lost opportunities. In a January 1865 wartime order, Union general William T. Sherman confiscated a swath of plantation land and redistributed it to freedmen. But after Lincoln's assassination, President Andrew Johnson overturned the order, and Sherman's radical promise to the nation's freedmen was never delivered on, leaving millions of African Americans landless and food insecure. There have been new approaches that look like solutions, such as the Green Revolution, which boosted food production through mechanization, improved seeds, and chemical inputs—a system that worked for big business but left small farmers deep in debt. There have also been flashes in the pan, like Brazil's Zero Hunger initiative in the early 2000s—an innovative program that led to impressive reductions in hunger, but that stalled after a change in leadership.

But not all efforts to reduce hunger have been failures. Quite the contrary. While it might seem counterintuitive to anyone watching the evening news (or reading this book), in the twenty-first century fewer people than ever starve, thanks to technological progress and the creation of systems to bring aid to people in need. Hunger crises today are not as bad as they were during, for example, the Wars of Religion in the sixteenth century. Even so, implementing solutions to hunger in our day and age calls for fresh approaches. What should food security programs look like going forward, and how should they differ from those of the past? How can we apply emerging lessons to humanitarian aid for societies in both the Global North and the Global South? And what can we do at the local level to ensure everyone is well fed?

Different schools of thought have informed approaches to food policy, and understanding this history helps put today's challenges in context. We have traveled a path from food nationalism and aspirational self-sufficiency to a more holistic view that puts local participation at the center of food policy.

In the early twentieth century, the world's powers aimed to produce enough food to avoid being starved out in wartime. Becoming a self-sufficient food fortress was a matter of both national security and national pride. An extreme application of this autarkic approach was Fascist Italy's "Battle for Grain," an attempt to achieve self-sufficiency through brute force. From 1925, the regime began to restrict grain imports, reclaim swamps for agriculture, and promote mechanization. Italian farmers were encouraged to grow as much wheat as possible. A crop of wheat was even symbolically planted in Milan's Piazza del Duomo (Cathedral Square). Production climbed by 40 percent, and the campaign ensured that the country could weather a wartime trade embargo. Aspirational autarky was not merely a fascist foible—it has been a hallmark of communist agrarian regimes such as the Khmer Rouge in Cambodia in the 1970s and contemporary North Korea.

Food nationalism remains alive and well in the twenty-first century: it was an important factor in the 2008 global food price crisis, which was triggered when countries with surpluses announced export bans to keep domestic prices low. In my years in the Sahel, I heard many officials worry about traders from neighboring countries "siphoning off" their country's millet, as if it were their own blood, conveniently ignoring the fact that when needed, the traders also brought in grain from abroad. It's been the force behind the land grabs described in chapter 3, and also explains why countries in the Middle East have attempted to grow wheat in the desert, at great financial and environmental cost.

The version of agriculture we now have in the West—extractive, mechanized, chemical, and subsidized—emerged after World War II. It's been self-sufficiency on steroids; the system churns out huge surpluses that exporting countries use to consolidate their economic influence. As Raj Patel explains in *Stuffed and Starved*, the downsides of the model include overproduction, depressed prices, and environmental damage. It's led to a global, monopolistic food system that ruins small producers, while fueling overconsumption and obesity.

Thanks to Amartya Sen's work in the 1980s, policymakers have known that food security is about more than the quantity of grain a nation produces. It is also about access: it's about people being able to buy enough healthy food. This approach shifts the focus from farming to understanding the complexity of people's incomes and the markets they rely on. As governments began to value individual and family-level dynamics, they established impactful safety net programs—school lunches, as well as food and cash transfers for low-income families, such as the Supplementary Nutrition Assistance Program (SNAP) in the United States (formerly known as food stamps, the benefits it provides are now provided through an electronic card). Versions of these programs exist all over the world. Providing access is only the first step, though—grassroots movements are adamant that these programs still don't address the root causes of hunger, which revolve around larger issues of systemic inequality.

In the 1990s, the "food sovereignty" movement began as a reaction against the excesses of global, commercialized agriculture. La Via Campesina, an activist movement representing 200 million farmers worldwide, was the first to define food sovereignty. The movement calls for "the right of peoples to healthy and culturally appropriate food produced through ecologically sound and sustainable methods and their right to define their food and agriculture systems." The food sovereignty movement advocates for land reform and for "peasant driven" food production that respects the environment.

José Bové, a mustachioed farmer and militant who was once La Via Campesina's spokesperson, has argued that food sovereignty is a basic human right, and that each *terroir* or "foodshed" should feed the people around it with quality local food—pushing back against our globalized food supply chains. To make the point, he and a group of tractor-riding farmers dismantled a McDonald's restaurant in southern France in 1999, taking down a universal symbol of cheap, mass-produced, unhealthy food.

While the wisdom of food sovereignty might seem self-evident, there is still much to do to change international food trade policies that undermine family farming. Such policies have invariably led to the dislocation of family farmers, as Mexico's corn producers found to their detriment when cheap U.S. corn began pouring into their country after NAFTA was adopted in 1993. Two million Mexican farmers lost their land during the NAFTA era. And the impact of NAFTA went beyond food markets—when Mexican farmers' livelihoods collapsed, there was a sharp increase in migration to the United States.

I saw these dynamics play out in Guinea-Bissau, where I served as a young aid worker. It was a country with a rich rice-growing tradition. Like other coastal West African societies, Guineans had perfected mangrove rice farming, a highly productive system that involved backbreaking work—carving fields from tidal marshes, excavating a network of canals and embankments—and mastery of the complex alchemy of seawater and freshwater. (Enslaved men and women from this part of the West African coast brought their rice farming know-how to the Carolina Lowcountry in the seventeenth century.) As the country's population has moved to the cities, Guinea-Bissau's old, labor-intensive rice farms are fading away. The new generation of farmers prefers to grow cashews—a tree crop that doesn't require as much work, and for which exporters will pay cash. As the mangrove rice farms have begun to disappear, the local rice varieties that have nourished the country for centuries have come under threat.

When I was working there, the food sovereignty movement in Guinea-Bissau was trying to revive a forgotten variety of rice—a flavorful heirloom grain with a purple hue that had been largely displaced by the flood of stale, cheap imports. A local NGO worked with farmers to sell the rice in the capital, and convinced the city's only supermarket at the time to stock it. The idea was to help small farmers get a better price for their heirloom rice, and give consumers access to a healthier, local alternative. And indeed, the purple mangrove rice variety was unlike any rice I'd ever had—fresh, fragrant, and tasty. Still, it had no chance in the market because the group of urban elites that could afford it was tiny. Most people in Guinea-Bissau were so poor they really had no choice but to buy the cheapest rice available, the white, stale, brittle product that came by the container from Asia.

The country's farmers were up against powerful forces and had almost no support from their cash-strapped government, which, in any case, regarded cheap rice imports as a safety net for its restive urban population. Guinea-Bissau's food sovereignty movement was waging a worthy but hopeless battle against an international market that was rigged against small farmers. Much in the same way that Haiti began relying on Miami rice after the 1990s, Guinea-Bissau—a verdant, fertile country—became addicted to low-cost rice from overseas. The purple rice remains a costly treat for a few initiates.

The unequal trade patterns that undermine small farmers all over the world is a symptom of the deep-rooted power imbalances that sustain hunger. In recent years, a loose movement calling for food justice has materialized in the United States. In *The Omnivore's Dilemma,* food writer Michael Pollan presented a compelling critique of our dominant agrifood systems, but he left out the thorny issue of discrimination that has crushed minority farmers for generations. In America, many Black farmers never got the USDA-backed loans their white counterparts did, and as a result lost 90 percent of their land in the last century, the equivalent of $250 billion to $350 billion in lost income and wealth. Black farmers accounted for 14 percent of all U.S. farmers in 1917, but by 2017 that number had dropped to 2 percent. The long-unacknowledged discrimination Black farmers suffered, and the generational loss of wealth that resulted, is a big reason why food insecurity among African American families is double that of their white counterparts.

The food justice movement acknowledges this history and calls for restorative approaches in the present and opportunities for all in the future—for instance, the reform of property laws so that minority landowners aren't dispossessed of their property or excluded from government programs. Recognizing the need to level the playing field, the USDA is now providing financial support that specifically targets disadvantaged farmers, and is helping bring infrastructure and services to minority farming communities. Food justice also aims to eliminate food deserts in inner cities through planting urban gardens and supporting minority-owned food businesses. The common thread in these varying approaches is the emphasis on giving individuals agency over their food choices.

The food sovereignty and food justice movements remind us that food insecurity is linked to economic, social, and environmental issues. They push us to ask *how* people are being fed, and *why* some people suffer from food shortages. The answer often lies in the fundamental power imbalances that are present in every society. Fighting hunger, therefore, must be about redressing these imbalances and tackling root causes in a way that is holistic.

In addition to food availability and access, this view of food security also stresses the importance of sustainability. It's not enough to grow mountains of food and make it affordable to the masses—we need to make sure that the food is healthy, that it's produced and distributed in a way that is not harming the environment, and that it is culturally appropriate to those who would consume it. This school of thought also argues that farmers and consumers must have agency in shaping food policies.

Cecilia Rocha, who teaches at Ryerson University, has developed the 5As framework, a holistic view of food security. The 5As acknowledges that Availability and Access are key considerations, but they also include three additional dimensions—Adequacy, Acceptability, and Agency. Adequacy is about food being healthy, diverse, and produced in an environmentally sustainable way. Acceptability is about food systems being culturally appropriate, dignified, and respectful of human rights. Agency refers to people's ability to influence food policies and processes.

This wider and more inclusive perspective—far removed from the production-centric approaches of old—is helpful in all contexts, from the acute hunger crises of the Global South to the food deserts of the West. Programs that embrace this approach have produced compelling results. In 1993, Belo Horizonte, a city of 2.5 million people in Brazil, established a food program that included twenty interconnected initiatives and involved the food industry, consumer groups, churches, and civil society. Among them was a subsidized meal program in which restaurants and cafés served millions of healthy low-cost meals. The city planted 185 vegetable gardens, including in prisons, welfare centers, and nursing homes. Lunches were provided for children in 126 schools. The program helped small farmers who practice responsible agriculture sell their produce in underserved inner cities at low prices. It included courses in food preparation and provided enriched flour to expectant mothers and low-income families, leading to a 72 percent drop in child mortality. What sets this program apart from others is the large number of initiatives it included, its emphasis on the dignity of those being assisted, and its focus on the inclusion of marginalized groups.

In 2003, the program was scaled up across the entire country as part of Brazil's *Fome Zero,* or Zero Hunger, spearheaded by President Lula da Silva. This national version also included *Bolsa Familia* ("family grant") cash transfers, and a mechanism to purchase food from small family farmers. Thanks to its implementation at scale, the initiative has now reached 48 million people. The results are evident: undernourishment among Brazilians fell by more than half in its first four years.

Many have wondered if Brazil's model could be exported to other countries. Interestingly, New York City once had its own cash transfer program modeled on Brazil's *Bolsa Familia,* and something similar was rolled out with more success in Mexico. Ideas *can* travel from south to north. But there are limits on how replicable such programs are: the political will, financial space, and capacities that were in place in Brazil are simply not in place in the most hunger-prone countries of the world. *Fome Zero* showed that reducing hunger is possible, but that it's a complex, long-term commitment. And sadly, Brazil's food security gains went into reverse due to a lack of interest from the Bolsonaro administration. In Brazil, as in sixteenth-century France, the promises of a benevolent ruler are being left unfulfilled by his successors. Lula launched a revamped version of the *Fome Zero* program soon after he returned to power in 2023.

The movement to comprehensively rethink food policy, with its emphasis on sustainability and agency, has also informed the way aid groups respond during a crisis. In 2010 José Andrés, a chef and humanitarian, founded World Central Kitchen, a nonprofit that deploys volunteer cooks to disaster areas. José Andrés partners with local restaurants to help them feed their communities. The World Central Kitchen pays these restaurants to serve free or low-cost hot meals to those who need them, including both first responders and people affected by disasters, helping to dismantle the dichotomy between those receiving aid and those providing it.

World Central Kitchen came to global attention during the response to Hurricane Maria, which devastated Puerto Rico in October 2017. They sent food trucks and cooking crews across the island, and at the height of their operation were serving 130,000 meals a day. Most of the food was purchased from the island's family farmers, pumping much-needed dollars into the economy. Andrés helped church and community groups provide beloved local dishes such as *arroz con pollo* or *carne guisada*. World Central Kitchen, a nimble organization, shone by responding quickly to the disaster, and then scaling its programs, while the U.S. government response was criticized for being too little too late. In an interview with the *The New York Times,* Andrés himself sounded surprised by what they'd been able to do. "We only came here to try to help a few thousand because nobody had a plan to feed Puerto Rico, and we opened the biggest restaurant in the world in a week. That's how crazy this is."

In Maria's aftermath, Andrés clashed with the Federal Emergency Management Agency (FEMA), which he saw as overly bureaucratic. "I am doing it [feeding the island] without red tape and 100 meetings," he said. In turn, some in the aid establishment saw World Central Kitchen as uppity amateurs. But there is no doubt they made an impact in Puerto Rico. They also fed people in Washington, D.C., where they provided meals out of RFK Stadium for months to people who'd lost their jobs during the pandemic. Andrés's teams served food bought from partner restaurants, helping them to stay afloat during the lockdowns.

World Central Kitchen's approach exemplifies a broader trend of aid organizations partnering with local businesses. Other relief groups are increasingly working through businesses such as restaurants, caterers, food trucks, and delivery services. The approach is emerging as a scalable way to respond to disasters. Of course, serving a cooked meal is more expensive than providing a dry ration. But it also has an impact beyond simple nutrition. Andrés is emphatic about providing people with "real food, not emergency rations that might just underline how desperate their situation is." When it comes to dignity (not to mention taste and satisfaction), a military MRE cannot beat a hot plate of *arroz con pollo*.

One of Andrés's inspirations is Jean Anthelme Brillat-Savarin, a nineteenth-century lawyer and epicure who is now remembered as the founder of French gastronomy. Brillat-Savarin's 1825 treatise *The Physiology of Taste* is an unabashed paean to the pleasures of food. Brillat-Savarin opens the treatise with aphorisms that emphasize food's cultural and aesthetic quality. "Animals feed themselves, men eat, and only enlightened men know how to eat," he wrote. "The discovery of a new dish does more for humankind's happiness than the discovery of a star." Andrés and Brillat-Savarin remind us that the value of food is not measured simply in calories and grams—its meaning also comes from cultural, emotional, and experiential associations. Andrés's approach to feeding people considers the psychological comfort a good meal provides, and the importance of food to the social fabric. He is challenging humanitarians to incorporate more lateral, more integrated—and, frankly, more human—approaches to assisting people.

When I read Andrés's description of World Central Kitchen's response to Hurricane Dorian in the Bahamas, it was clear to me he had tasted the excitement of being on the front line, the satisfaction of helping people in desperate need, the thrill of putting together a solution on the fly. "When we couldn't safely establish a kitchen in Abaco," he wrote, "we went with plan B—and then to plan C. With few navigable roads, we made deliveries by helicopter and seaplane, and we rebuilt a washed-out dock to land our fleet of boats." His way of working is reminiscent of an era when humanitarian aid was less formalized and coordinated than it is today, when a group of buddies could sail off to a disaster-affected country to save lives—as the French doctors did when they created Médecins Sans Frontières in the 1970s.

Andrés doesn't hesitate to speak truth to power, pushing for bold, systemic food policy change. He was one of the voices that called on President Biden to organize the 2022 conference on food security. He also advocated for the appointment of a "food czar" who would sit on the National Security Council. These ideas would have been fringe just ten years ago. But given the latest threats to our food supply presented by climate change and the pandemic, they are now highly relevant.

When Kabul fell to the Taliban in August 2021, chaos reigned in Afghanistan. A flood of people, many affiliated with the previous U.S.-backed government, besieged Hamid Karzai International Airport. They wanted to flee their country and reach safety abroad, some so desperate that they clung to the hulls of departing U.S. Air Force cargo planes. More than 80,000 Afghans would arrive in the airlift the U.S. government had hastily organized. When the evacuees began to land at Washington, D.C.'s Dulles Airport, one of the designated points of entry, World Central Kitchen was there to serve them hot meals. The organization had made arrangements with a dozen halal restaurants in Northern Virginia to cook for the new arrivals, so that they would be welcomed to the United States by a warm meal that tasted like home.

I spent a night at Dulles helping out, serving food that came from Kabobi, an Afghan restaurant in Herndon, a stone's throw from Dulles. Kabobi's dishes take inspiration from cuisine served in Helmand—a province where fighting between NATO forces and the Taliban had been particularly brutal.

Around 9 p.m., I went out with two others to meet Kabobi's owner, who arrived in a beige Honda Odyssey that was idling at the Arrivals level. In the back were hundreds of individual meals, packed into large brown paper bags. As soon as he opened the tailgate, we were engulfed by the appetizing smell of hot, fragrant Kabuli rice. The owner had come to the United States from Afghanistan years earlier, and he was bursting with pride that his meals would be feeding other Afghans on their first night on American soil.

The World Central Kitchen brigade had set up in a waiting area along with the Red Cross, where there was seating for a few hundred people. We'd been told to expect four planes that night. None of us spoke any Dari or Pashtun, but Amanullah, an Afghan volunteer who had lived in the United States for years and whose day job was working for the federal government, was on hand to help.

"I hope you have enough tea!" he told us. "Tea is essential for us. At any construction site in Afghanistan, it's one man's job to keep a big pot of tea going and make sure there's always enough for the entire crew. I can assure you that some of them will drink gallons in one sitting."

Amanullah was exaggerating, but I started to wonder about our tea supply. All we had on hand that night were a few two-quart pump thermoses.

The first plane landed and the rush began. Hundreds of tired feet shuffled into the room, eager for a meal. Some of the Afghans were proud soldiers who still wore the uniforms and combat boots of their freshly defeated national army. But most looked like ordinary civilians—all wearing leather sandals, the men in their *shalwar kameez*, the women in abayas. There were entire families, including infants and elders. They had had no time to prepare before fleeing, and many carried what few belongings they had in white drawstring garbage bags. They were jet-lagged and weary from the flight. After greeting us with a hand to the heart, they asked for *naan*, bread. And, as we'd been warned, for tea.

One of the women, I'll call her Wahida, asked for her tea in a British accent. We filled her twelve-ounce paper cup, and she closed her eyes, took a few sips of the beverage, and exhaled deeply. Wahida explained that she, along with the others, had spent two weeks in transit between Kabul and Dulles, and that they had not had any hot food that entire time. Conditions at the airbases in Qatar and Germany, where the Afghans stayed before being sent on to the United States, had been spartan. Now, she was sipping liquid relief. A volunteer spent a good part of that night sprinting back and forth between our serving area and the kitchen of a nearby airport restaurant to keep the thermoses full of hot water for tea.

At the end of that late night, I sent an email to World Central Kitchen to let them know that a lot of people had asked for naan and we had none to give them. I got a friendly reply, which mentioned that others had told them the same. By the following day, they had started serving naan to the new arrivals.

What I saw at Dulles, and what World Central Kitchen has been doing all over the world, was an illustration of where the humanitarian community as a whole should be going. We're headed toward a world where aid workers will engage directly with food businesses in affected communities, and help them provide meals. The next generation of humanitarians will be providing grants, loans, equipment, and systems for bakeries, mills, markets, retailers, community kitchens and restaurants, and food processors, feeding people in need while also injecting cash into and creating jobs in local communities. Humanitarians should provide foods that people love, that are locally made, and that taste great. Jose Andrés saw it coming when he wrote that "food relief shouldn't just be measured in calories; it can be a catalyst of rebuilding a community."

This decentralized and localized approach won't be possible everywhere, of course. Airdrops and trucks will remain the only option in many conflict-affected or remote areas. But working with businesses in such settings is not impossible: aid agencies are increasingly doing so, sowing the seeds of sustainability, even in the middle of wars.

Less than a month after that night at Dulles airport, WFP sent me to Kabul. When I got there Kabul's airport was deserted, with no trace of the chaos that had prevailed in August, when U.S. troops were withdrawing. The Taliban had put up a large blue plastic banner on the terminal that proclaimed, in flowery language, the new Islamic emirate's ardent wish for peaceful relations with the outside world. Dozens of U.S.-made combat helicopters were parked on the tarmac, in neat rows. Departing U.S. forces had sabotaged them so they wouldn't fly, and the Taliban were trying to get them up and running again.

In town, an old man sold white, gold-fringed Taliban flags out of a tricycle in front of the abandoned U.S. embassy. The building, protected behind high concrete walls, was now an empty shell.

The people of Kabul were suffering. Most had lost their jobs when the economy collapsed suddenly after the United States and its allies left. The devastating economic sanctions the West imposed on the country that had frozen the banking sector were only making matters worse. Crowds gathered in front of the banks in town, women to one side and men on the other, waiting long hours to access cash from their accounts. The Taliban had limited bank withdrawals to the local currency equivalent of $200 a week to avoid capital flight, but the currency had crashed anyway. Some people were so desperate that they were selling their belongings—appliances, rugs, anything—to buy food. Snow had appeared on the mountains that ring the city, a harbinger of a long winter of cold and hunger.

I spent the next weeks working with my Afghan counterparts to estimate the number of people in the country who needed food. We concluded that more than half the population, nearly 23 million people, would soon face acute food insecurity. The people I worked with struck me as some of the bravest and most committed individuals I'd ever met. Their country was coming apart, but they came to the office and did their jobs all the same. After work, they would go home to jobless neighbors, anxious relatives, desperate friends.

The country was in a tailspin. It had already been on the verge of a food crisis before the U.S. withdrawal. There had been a bad drought the previous winter. But it was the sanctions designed to punish the Taliban that suffocated Afghanistan's economy. The sanctions froze the country's foreign currency reserves and made international bank transfers extremely difficult. Even the relatively well-off urban middle class couldn't feed itself anymore. Journalists documented cases of people giving up or selling their own children. We have seen sanctions hurt regular people before—in Cuba, in Haiti, in Iraq. Drought and conflict are bad enough, but sanctions can be the death knell. Punish the Taliban, but don't sentence an entire nation to famine. The international community should systematically exempt basic needs, starting with food, from economic sanctions.

Until recently, food security projects have largely focused on farming, but I am now seeing an increasing—and appropriate—emphasis on the next step in the chain: processing. This is the essential step that turns a crop of coarse grain and roots into flour, semolina, and other products that can be sold, stored, or readily prepared. Income from family food processing businesses can sustain entire communities. As a Malian colleague once told me, "It's where the money is." I learned a lot from working with food processors in southern Congo, a place that has a unique culinary tradition that can be leveraged to support broader food security goals.

Congo's food culture was profoundly influenced by the extraordinary and violent dislocations of the colonial era. The construction of the Congo–Ocean Railway in the 1920s and 1930s stands out as a particularly bloody colonial enterprise. The project was meant to connect Brazzaville, on the Congo River, to Pointe-Noire, a new deepwater port on the South Atlantic, thus opening central Africa to commerce. To build it, the French pressed thousands into service, shipping in workers from as far away as Indochina and Chad. Journalist Albert Londres traveled to Congo to investigate reports of abuses on the construction project. In *Terre d'ébène,* published in 1929, he painted a horrific picture of the working conditions. "I have already seen railroads being built, and there were machines on the site. Here, only negroes! The negro replaced machines, trucks, cranes and explosives."

The poor diet, lack of hygiene, and brutal treatment caused mass illness and death along the five-hundred-kilometer-long railroad. It is commonly said that as many African workers died as ties were laid between Brazzaville and Pointe-Noire. For the contingent of a few thousand brought in from Chad, the annual death toll stood near 50 percent in the first years of construction.

In 1934, this new railroad connected Congo to the outside world. While it would eventually make the nation's burgeoning cities dependent on food imports, it also led to the emergence of new local foods. With men forced to labor away from home for days on end, women invented a portable, pre-cooked, tasty, and nutritious meal that is equal parts cassava and peanut butter. The snack is known as a *mbala pinda*—a savory bar about the size of a Snickers. Cassava and peanuts are so common in central African cooking that it's easy to forget they are New World crops the Portuguese brought to Africa in the sixteenth century. All over the continent, the entire cassava plant is eaten, from its nutrient-packed leaves to its starchy roots, while peanuts are ubiquitous in African stews.

In June 2020 I met Misette, an imposing woman of about fifty who is renowned as a master mbala pinda producer. Misette is from the town of Madingou, a bustling stop on the Congo–Ocean railroad. She makes the cassava and peanut bars in an open-air kitchen in the back of her redbrick house. One day, she showed me how it was done. First, she ground the cassava into a paste, and the peanuts into peanut butter. Once she had mixed the two ingredients into a basketball-sized loaf, she tasted the dough, adjusted the salt, and added dried fish or the chilies that give the bars a kick. Her group of helpers scooped small handfuls of dough from the ball and shaped each into a bar, which they carefully wrapped in a fresh dark green marantaceae leaf. Then they placed the bundles in a large pot, steamed them for half an hour, and let them cool. The mbala pinda are good for a week.

Many Congolese from the city remember the taste of mbala pinda from visits to the countryside as children, when visiting grandmothers or aunts. This handmade, homemade snack is loaded with nutrition. The cassava's carbs offer energy, while the peanuts supply fat, vitamins, and minerals—enough to tide people over while they're out working for the day. Misette sells her mbala pinda bars every market day for 100 francs, the equivalent of 20 cents apiece. Because they're hand-wrapped in biodegradable leaves that grow nearby, a mbala pinda produces none of the plastic waste that commonly litters the cities of Africa.

Misette handed me a freshly made bar, wrapped like a present. I undid the package and took a bite. The dark, moist bar tasted nutty, and its texture was dense, like whole wheat bread. As I chewed, I could see that Misette and her friends, who stood ten feet away, were laughing at me. Clearly, there was something hilarious about this lanky foreigner sampling their home cooking in their own backyard.

In 2020 WFP put together a project to promote the recipe and began working with sixteen cooperatives near Madingou involving two hundred women like Misette to produce mbala pinda. The co-ops deliver mbala pinda to nearby schools, where they are served to children as a nutritious snack. Groups like Misette's do all of the work, from the cooking to the delivery. The project is a success.

We had initially reached out to Misette because in early 2020, the COVID-19 pandemic had dramatically slowed the flow of food imports to Congo. By supporting Congo's food processors, we hoped we might still be able to run a school meals program despite these setbacks.

Of course, we had concerns. Our Canadian donor asked us whether we were sure that the women could deliver at the scale needed. It was a legitimate question: Could poor women in rural Congo crank out thousands of snack bars each week? But we were sure that Misette and her friends knew the business. We gave them a hand by providing grinders to help boost their volume. We also organized courses in food safety. When Misette and the Congolese food processors delivered their mbala pinda bars to schools, we paid them the next week in mobile money. By creating the market, supply followed. The women fed thousands of schoolchildren with a nutritious local snack, all in the midst of a pandemic. As I write in 2023, Misette and the sixteen cooperatives have made more than a million individual bars for Congo's school feeding program. All from locally grown cassava and peanuts.

Rediscovering forgotten foods such as the mbala pinda, and supporting the home-based processors who make them, is one of the ways we can build resilience, inclusivity, and nutrition into food systems. In the West we have coddled our farmers for decades through subsidies; we now need to support our artisanal food processors. Craft food processors can do much more than produce fine foods for the elites. They can help feed all of us, as long as we give them a chance and don't stifle their work through heavy-handed regulations.

Interestingly, something similar to what I saw in Congo has been playing out in the United States in recent years, as a boom in home cooking and home food processing is taking place. In 2018, California legalized home-based restaurants—many of which are owned by women of color or immigrants. Utah followed suit in 2021. Home restaurant owners are allowed to go through a simplified certification process involving a weeklong food safety course and a health inspection, after which they can obtain insurance and begin selling food from their homes. Home-based food processing and preparation can allow food deserts to come back to life and bring income and opportunity to small-scale entrepreneurs. And technology is enabling this change, too: we're seeing apps that connect consumers with homemade meals. The budding home restaurant movement shows there is growing recognition that small players—not just large corporations—should play a role in feeding us all.

Centuries ago, King Henry promised the people a hearty *Poule au Pot*. What we've ended up with is Costco's $4.99 rotisserie chicken. Mechanized agriculture and supermarkets have undermined small farmers, brought us cheap foods of dubious nutritional value, and created overextended supply chains. And they have harmed us: poor diets are one of the reasons why my home state of West Virginia suffers from high rates of obesity and cardiovascular disease. As in other parts of America, improving access to food in the Mountain State must involve making healthy, fresh foods available to everyone.

Supporting our farmers' markets can help. America's 8,600 farmers' markets bring healthy local foods back to the neighborhoods they'd disappeared from in the mid-twentieth century with the advent of supermarkets. They have become a weekend fixture for millions of consumers, and a lifeline for small farmers who get a chance to sell their produce directly. Like many other places, my hometown of Charles Town has long had a farmers' market. But unlike many other towns and cities in the United States, its farmers' market has been a first step in a more ambitious journey toward ensuring the community is able to feed itself.

Fiona Harrison, the market manager, remembers how the Charles Town farmers' market struggled for years. The market had no permanent home. For a time, it was held on a sloping street, where gravity would snatch tomatoes and apples right off the farmers' tables and send them rolling down the gutter. Fiona thought: This market will shut down if we don't do something about it.

Fiona teamed up with Todd Coyle, who played guitar at the market, and a number of other food vendors, to create the Jefferson County Growers, Artisans and Producers Association—

the GAP. She took over as market manager in 2014, changed the market hours, secured a flat location, and brought in more vendors. After just a few seasons, the Charles Town farmers' market had become the largest in the county. Some of the vendors have thrived and gone from weekend hobbyists to established food businesses, with their own storefronts and full-time employees. Black Dog Coffee, Tabb's Fruits and Vegetables, and Mountaineer Popcorn have all grown out of the farmers' market.

There is a general sense that farmers' markets are elitist, and it's hard to deny that when heirloom cantaloupes go for $6 apiece and organic cherries cost $10 a pint, as they do in Charles Town. But as Fiona is quick to point out, the Charles Town farmers' market has not only taken SNAP since 2015, it also matches those dollars with top-up grant funding arranged through donors—meaning that people with SNAP cards double or even triple their credit when they buy fruits and vegetables at the market. Thanks to the subsidy, Jefferson County's farmers help feed people in the community who would not otherwise have been able to afford healthy local food.

In 2015, Fiona and Todd decided to open a brick-and-mortar version of the market—a locally sourced, nonprofit community food store that would operate five days a week. They wanted to offer food producers a place to sell year-round and help the five thousand people of Charles Town buy local food right on Main Street.

With support from the city, the Bushel & Peck opened in October 2017. It sells seasonal fruits and vegetables, organic or free-range meat and chicken, local kombucha, and maple syrup from the Appalachians. The food they stock is either grown or processed within a fifty-mile radius. Todd and Fiona set it up to feel like the general stores of old. While it is much smaller than any supermarket, the Bushel & Peck is a bright and friendly alternative to shopping at Kroger, Costco, or Walmart.

The GAP also is working with schools to bring healthy local

foods back into the school lunch program. The GAP's "Farm 2 School" project helps children in middle schools learn about farming and food, and establishes school gardens.

With its weekly farmers' market and its Main Street store, the GAP is at once an outlet for Jefferson County's farmers, an incubator of food startups, and a purveyor of healthy food to everyone. The GAP now intends to set up a Main Street "food hub" that would expand the Bushel & Peck's retail space and include a community kitchen, a fully equipped shared area that local food processors could rent. People could also take classes on how to process fruits and vegetables, making the most of the fresh foods grown in nearby community gardens.

Fiona Harrison and Todd Coyle are not firebrand socialists. Like Misette in Congo, they aren't interested in the latest trends in food security theory. Creating a nonprofit that does retail in addition to community outreach just happened to be the best way forward for Charles Town. Still, the approach is unexpected for West Virginia, one of the reddest states in the nation. Their approach has distinct echoes of the interlinked, highly inclusive local food programs that helped Belo Horizonte beat back hunger. What the Jefferson County GAP also shows is that a small, motivated group, without millions of dollars or political clout, can change the food trajectory of a community using their own common sense.

As Fiona and Todd focus on building a Main Street food hub, others are working to preserve Jefferson County's farmland. The farmers who sell at the Saturday market are paying higher and higher rents for the land on which they grow their crops. It's easy to see why: every winter, it seems another cornfield becomes a construction site, and plywood houses emerge in the spring like snowdrops. Between 2012 and 2017, more than 850 acres of Jefferson County farmland—an area the size of New York's Central Park—was entombed in asphalt and concrete for subdivisions and strip malls.

The state and county are attempting to counteract this trend. After local authorities bought development rights from landowners, nearly 6,000 acres of land have already been designated to remain farmland forever. Land set aside in this way now accounts for 10 percent of all farmland in the county, and the goal is to protect 20,000 acres over time. We need space for housing, and for development, but let's not pave over the land that feeds us.

There is reason to be optimistic about our ability to fight hunger: stories from around the world show that it's possible to do a better job of feeding families and communities. We can create a world in which food security and food justice don't come down to the luck of geography or the whims of an administration. Unexpectedly, I found hope at a time of despair, after the WFP warehouse in Gonaïves, Haiti, was ransacked and torched in 2022. The situation had gotten so desperate that some people expected WFP to quit the country.

As soon as I could, I went to the town to comfort my team. During the helicopter flight from Port-au-Prince to Gonaïves, I pondered the words I'd say. In the heat of the cargo hold, my body covered in sweat as the engine roared overhead, I wondered about my colleagues' state of mind, considering the violence and destruction they had just experienced. After a dusty landing at Gonaïves's airstrip, I hopped into a Toyota Land Cruiser for the short drive to the place where I'd meet the team. The town was in a state of torpor. Shops were closed. Stone block barricades stood everywhere. Debris littered the deserted streets.

All of my colleagues in town that day turned up to meet me. We exchanged hugs and handshakes and sat down to talk. "We want to get back to work as soon as possible," said Rony, a clerk, as soon as the meeting began. The rest of the group voiced their approval. They were emphatic that even though we had been attacked, our work in Gonaïves would go on. We would not give up, we would not run. There was confidence and determination all around. Even though all that remained of our office were scorched cinder block walls and a pile of broken glass.

In the weeks that followed, we cleared the rubble and set up a new office. We got our programs up and running again, with a renewed focus on outreach to the community that had just attacked us. Without holding any grudges, we set out to resume our school meals program and our projects to support local farming cooperatives. All along, we worked with a heightened sense of our great vulnerability: the area was still very dangerous, and the threat of another attack on our office hung over our heads.

Months later, I visited a rural community outside Gonaïves and asked them what they thought of what had happened. The response was immediate: "You come here to help us, and someone attacks you? It's shameful," an elderly farmer told me. It was heartening to hear such clarity from those we help.

In the aftermath of the incidents, we did something Haitian authorities and civil society had long called for: we sourced more food for our school meals program from the country's farmers. Because we bought small batches at a time from dozens of cooperatives through the year, we were less exposed to pilferage than when we stored stacks of imported food in a central warehouse. The effort was a godsend for the country's beleaguered farmers, who earned a steady income, and for the children who benefited from fresh, locally grown foods at their schools.

There is no risk-free path to helping a vulnerable community feed itself, especially in contexts as unforgiving as Haiti. For those who work on the front lines, like my colleagues in Gonaïves, a big part of fighting hunger means being ready to take your licks. And being able to forgive, forget, and move on.

My team's resolute response to a devastating attack also speaks to a deeper truth. To end hunger, we'll need good kings, like

Henry IV of France, and good presidents and prime ministers. We will need bold leaders who will hold others accountable for starvation in war, and who will build food systems that are fair to small farmers, and resilient to climate change and mass disease. But our food security comes down to much more than policy choices. It's fundamentally about our individual attitudes.

To end hunger, we need to end the dissonance between our stated values and our actions. Mass hunger has been a problem we have chosen to ignore, that we've conveniently banished to the arid tropics or tucked away in our inner cities and trailer parks. Feeding everyone should be the business of everyone, down to the individual. We need to get to the point where each of us steps up when there is a need. "You're in front of someone who's suffering, and you have the tools at your disposal to alleviate that suffering or even eradicate it, and you act," as physician and humanitarian Paul Farmer put it.

We need to make hunger anathema.

Pétion-Ville, October 2023

Acknowledgments

My mother, Marie-José, helped me navigate the byzantine detail of our family history. My father, Jean François, offered suggestions as this book came together. Johanne Picard, my cousin, shared her insights into her parents' lifelong effort to grow rice in southern Haiti. My friend and colleague Anna Law kindly went through some of the more challenging material in this book. My partner, Emily Umpleby, offered welcome reality checks.

Many colleagues, friends, and neighbors shared their stories. They include Susan Sebatindira, Sandra Uwantege Hart, Taylor Quinn, Robert Walsh, and George Rutherford. There are also many others who preferred their stories remain anonymous.

Molly McCloskey helped turn my personal notes into the book you are now reading. Lucy Luck took an early interest in this project. Kris Dahl's encouragements kept me going. Andrew Miller, Maris Dyer, Helen Maggie Carr, Nicole Pedersen, Ed Lake, and Nick Humphrey were there, on my shoulder, as this book came together. Thank you all.

Notes

Introduction

4 half of the country's population: Integrated Food Security Phase Classification, "Haiti: Acute Food Insecurity Situation September 2022–February 2023 and Projection for March–June 2023."

6 more than 250 million people would be facing: Global Network Against Food Crises, "Global Report on Food Crises, 2023."

6 more than 13 million families are food insecure: USDA, "Household Food Security in the U.S.," 2021.

7 "No famine has ever taken place": Sen, *The Idea of Justice,* 343.

8 "There's no way Michael Jackson": Tupac Shakur, quoted in MTV News, "Tupac Talks."

10 "related, ultimately, to economic disparity": Sen, "Apocalypse."

Chapter 1 Young Haiti: *From Failed Rebellion to Mass Hunger*

12 "Can a man": Roumain, *Gouverneurs de la rosee,* 107. Author's translation.

13 It was November 12, 1964: Picard, *Jérémie: La Hantise d'un Passé Révolu,* 183.

14 dropping them off like packages: Picard, *Jérémie,* 190.

15 fighting off Duvalier's soldiers with stones: Picard, *Jérémie,* 193–96.

15 · the assassins were seen driving: Picard, *Jérémie.* 201.

16 "social and economic apartheid": Danticat, "The Fight for Haiti's Future."

16 a modified version of the Lord's Prayer: Krebs, "Papa Doc, a Ruthless Dictator, Kept the Haitians in Illiteracy and Dire Poverty," 44.

16 her fur coat collection: "Jean-Claude Duvalier," *The Times*.

16 pockets of famine-like conditions: Wyss, "Haiti Suffers Famine-Like Conditions as Chaos Paralyzes Economy."

16 100,000 children suffer from malnutrition: DiPierro Obert, "Hunger in Haiti: Ten Years After Catastrophe Struck, a New Crisis Looms."

18 Corrupt members of the Haitian elite: Gamio, Méheut, Porter, Gebrekidan, McCann, and Apuzzo, "Haiti's Lost Billions."

18 along with 167 other political opponents: Joseph, "A Brief History of Presidential Deaths."

20 the *Neptune*—the *Agnes*'s sister ship—went down: Young, "1,000 or More Feared Dead, Haitian Vessel Held Up to 1,500."

21 the country became self-sufficient: Borlaug, "The Green Revolution, Peace and Humanity."

22 "she comes back in the door": "The Permaculture Project," quotes from Masanobu Fukuoka.

22 "Miami Rice": Bell, "'Miami Rice': The Business of Disaster in Haiti."

23 "Now it's one meal every other day": Booth, "Embargo Leaves Haiti's Economy Down but Not Out."

25 the "shock doctrine": Klein, *The Shock Doctrine*.

26 now imports half its food: Cochrane, Childs, and Rosen, "Haiti's U.S. Rice Imports."

26 "I have to live every day": Doyle, "US Urged to Stop Haiti Rice Subsidies."

27 "Blood will flow in Haiti": Heinl and Heinl, *Written in Blood*, 362.

28 The recording is posted on the ICRC website: International Committee of the Red Cross, "Discours du Dr. Jacques Fourcand."

29 the country would be ruled by heroes: Diederich and Burt, *Papa Doc and the Tonton Macoutes*.

30 wiping out that season's rice crop: Garcia-Navarro, "Haiti Still Struggling to Recover from Hurricane Jeanne."

30 nearly 1 million people required: World Food Programme, "Food

Security of 800,000 Seriously Threatened After Passage of Hurricane Matthew."

30 only six permanent houses: Sullivan, "In Search of the Red Cross' $500 Million in Haiti Relief."

Chapter 2 Desert Blues: *Generational Hunger in the Sahel*

32 "The food speculators": Roumain, *Masters of the Dew*, 74.

32 Ultimately, starving people die: Canadian Broadcasting Corporation, "How a Hunger Strike Affects the Body."

33 "He couldn't eat without dying": Duras, *The War*, 56.

33 A quarter of a billion people: Global Network Against Food Crises, "Global Report on Food Crises, 2023."

33 affects more than 700 million people: Food and Agriculture Organization, "The State of Food Insecurity and Nutrition in the World 2022."

33 research has brought to light a correlation: Seligman et al., "Food Insecurity Is Associated with Diabetes," 1018.

33 "may be the key": Chilton and Rabinowich, "Toxic Stress and Child Hunger," 6.

34 At least 20 million of its people: Food Crisis Prevention Network, Policy Brief, April 2023.

34 malnutrition remains a leading cause of: Médecins Sans Frontières, "Malnutrition in the Sahel."

34 With 80 percent of the region's land: World Economic Forum, "The Sahel Is Engulfed by Violence."

35 "accelerator of history": Lenin, *Letters from Afar*. First letter.

35 pilfering food aid: Walker, "Military Coup in Niger."

35 killed 75 percent of the country's livestock: *New York Times*, "Mauritania Coup Ousts President," 12.

35 One of the worst droughts: Held, "Sahel Drought."

37 their importation into West Africa: Duteurtre and Corniaux, "Local or Imported."

38 in Malthus's view: Wrigley and Smith, "Malthus and the Poor Law," 33.

45 76 percent of girls are married before age eighteen: UNICEF, "End Child Marriage."

45 Only 14 percent of women can read and write: UNICEF, "Children in Niger."

47 The workers recovered nearly 35,000 hectares: Food and Agriculture Organization, "Approche territoriale du projet KEITA."

48 influence over the lower caste: Rossi, "From Slavery to Aid."

49 more than 40 million people: Food Crisis Prevention Network, Policy Brief, April 2023.

49 $14 billion in funding: Toulmin and Scoones. "The Sahelian Great Green Wall."

Chapter 3 To Deal with the Devil: *The Global Rush to Grab Land*

50 "And farmers, are there farmers": Roumain, *Gouverneurs de la rosee*, 42. Author's translation.

50 "Few of the larger cities": Casson, "The Role of the State in Rome's Grain Trade," 21.

50 laden with precious grain: Casson, *The Ancient Mariners*, 207–208.

51 "The Campanians are glad": Seneca the Younger, *On Suicide*, 1.

51 a startling story: Song et al., "Daewoo to Cultivate Madagascar Land for Free."

52 "Food can be a weapon in this world": Ibid.

52 140 million acres: Deininger et al., *Rising Global Interest in Farmland*.

52 an area larger: U.S. Department of Agriculture, "Agriculture Counts."

53 nearly one in three humans: International Fund for Agricultural Development, "Smallholders Can Feed the World."

53 they produce one-third of the world's food: Food and Agriculture Organization, "Small Family Farmers Produce a Third of the World's Food."

53 $2 a day or less: World Bank, "A Year in the Lives of Smallholder Farmers."

53 rationed until 1954: Adams and de Zwarte, "Rationing in Britain During World War II," 2.

54 "lakes of milk and mountains of butter": Durisin et al., "Europe's Butter Mountain Has Melted Away."

54 "risk society": Beck, *Risk Society*.

55 fears that global food scarcity looms: Brown, "The New Geopolitics of Food."

55 80 million more people each year: Ibid., 3.

55 will reduce grain yields by 10 percent: Ibid., 4.

55 caused a 40 percent drop: Ibid., 4.

55 "water-based food bubbles": Ibid., 5.

55 in arid parts of India and China: Ibid., 5.

56 "From the mid-twentieth century until 1995": Ibid., 2.

56 "Few things are more likely": Ibid., 7.

56 In 2017, Qatar: British Broadcasting Corporation, "Qatar Crisis."

59 from 4 to 8 percent of families: United Nations, "Liberia: The Impact of High Food Prices on Food Security."

59 abuzz with talk about a *Washington Post* article: Timburg, "In Postwar Liberia, Paradise Amid the Poverty."

60 a whopping 220,000 hectares of land: Toweh and Inveen, "Sime Darby to Sell Liberia Plantation to Local Manufacturer."

61 "Pity the nation": Gibran, "Dead Are My People."

64 nearly 40 percent of children: U.S. Aid for International Development, "Mali: Nutrition Profile."

65 selling it to Black Africans: Lahiff and Li, "Land Redistribution in South Africa."

66 "They need every foodstuff": Maritz, "Commercial Farming in the Congo Not for the Faint-Hearted."

66 land they had used for hunting and foraging: Bergen, "On the Map: Charting a Path for Sustainable Development in the Republic of Congo."

67 " 'You have a camp for your workers' ": Bergen, ibid.

Chapter 4 Starving in a Land of Plenty:
Misrule and Greed in the Central African Republic

69 "You don't have to invite misfortune": Roumain, *Masters of the Dew,* 164.

69 "Reasons of State prevail over family reasons": Condom, "Notre Ami L'Empereur Bokassa 1er."

69 he once ordered his uniform strengthened: Cathcart, "Obituary, Jean-Bedel Bokassa."

70 plumed busbies: Condom, "Notre Ami L'Empereur Bokassa 1er."

70 Valery Giscard d'Estaing: Ibid.

70 "a roughneck": Bigo, *Pouvoir et obéissance en Centrafrique,* 341.

70 "an idiot": Carayannis and Lombard, *Making Sense of the Central African Republic.*

70 the splendid white horses that collapsed: Condom, "Notre Ami L'Empereur Bokassa 1er."

70 "Surely no public occasion": Cathcart, "Obituary, Jean-Bedel Bokassa."

71 the waiters who served the gargantuan meal: Condom, "Notre Ami L'Empereur Bokassa 1er."

71 The event cost about $50 million: Association for Diplomatic Studies and Training, "The Man Who Would Be Emperor."

71 America canceled its aid: Condom, "Notre Ami L'Empereur Bokassa 1er."

71 mass protests broke out: Cathcart, "Obituary, Jean-Bedel Bokassa."

71 "You did not realize it": *Le Monde*, "Bokassa Ier avait-il servi de la chair humaine à M. Galley?"

71 fed his enemies to wild animals: Lazareva, "In the Central African Republic, Nostalgia for a Leader Who Is Said to Have Fed His Critics to Crocodiles."

71 a high point for the country: Ibid.

73 between 20 and 30 percent of the population: Vangroenweghe, "The Leopold II Concession System," 325.

74 More than 700,000 square kilometers of land: Ibid., 325.

74 crossed the river: See Vangroenweghe, "The Leopold II Concession System," 323–72.

74 A private army of four hundred *touroucous*: Vangroenweghe, "The Leopold II Concession System," 346.

75 "there was wilderness and hunger": Ibid., 331.

75 "they killed passers-by with their guns": Ibid., 357.

76 "they will not harvest rubber anymore": Ibid., 348.

76 "a miraculous increase in production": Polanyi, *The Great Transformation*, 80.

76 A helping of hunger, he explained: Christine Baumgarthuber, "Hunger as an Instrument of Social Control." Baumgarthuber, writing in 2016, commented that "this attitude, as inhumane as it seems today, struck many of Townsend's fellow Victorians as eminently reasonable. And its widespread adoption heralded a new era, one in

which countrymen could be categorized not as fellow Britons, but as something subhuman and therefore exploitable."

80 smashed through South African lines: Langlois, "13 South African Soldiers Killed in Central African Republic."

82 Mpoko airport camp held more than 100,000 people: Lazareva, "'Now We're Back It's Even Worse.'"

82 800,000 Central Africans: U.S. Agency for International Development, "Central African Republic Complex Emergency FactSheet #2."

82 2.6 million people: UN Office for the Coordination of Humanitarian Affairs, "Central African Republic: Multi-Cluster/Sector Initial Rapid Assessment."

83 stay and face starvation or disease: Human Rights Watch, "Central African Republic: Muslims Trapped in Enclaves."

84 ministers occupied penthouse suites: Associated Press, "C. African Republic Rebels Refuge at Luxury Hotel."

84 "the good intentions crowd": Lombard, *State of Rebellion.*

85 a shot at the big time: Dubner and Levitt, *Freakonomics.*

86 food scarcity loomed: Food and Agriculture Organization and World Food Programme, "Special Report: FAO/WFP Crop and Food Security Assessment Mission to Central African Republic," 3.

88 CAR's "Green Diamond": Mangan et al., "The 'Green Diamond': Coffee and Conflict in the Central African Republic."

88 "This is the price": Voltaire, *Candide,* 70.

89 a record 3 million people: Integrated Food Security Classification, "Central African Republic. IPC Food Security Snapshot," November 2022.

90 starvation and cold killed a million Soviet citizens: Bivens, "New Facts Point Up Horror of Nazi Siege of Leningrad."

90 rats migrated en masse: Ibid.

90 "a belligerent commander": U.S. Military Tribunal, Nuremberg, "High Command Trial: The United States of America vs. Wilhelm Von Leeb et al.," 75.

91 "with washed-out ribs": Achebe, "Refugee Mother and Child."

91 "Starvation is a legitimate weapon of war": Mudge, "Starvation as a Means of Warfare," 228.

91 "I want to see no Red Cross": Ibid.

91 Two million people died: Vestergaard, "Biafra, 1967–1970."

92 where most acute hunger occurs: Global Rights Compliance, "The Crime of Starvation and Methods of Prosecution and Accountability."

92 to amend international humanitarian law: Global Rights Compliance, "The Netherlands Accepts Starvation Amendment: One Year On."

92 UN Security Council passed Resolution 2417: United Nations, "Adopting Resolution 2417 (2018)."

Chapter 5 Forever Famines: *The Middle East's Descent into Hunger*

93 "If a man won't think with his head": Roumain, *Masters of the Dew,* 126.

93 a graphic photo: Walsh, "The Tragedy of Saudi Arabia's War in Yemen."

93 "Amal Hussain, 7": Ibid.

94 "The tragedy in Yemen": Nagourney and Slackman, "Why We Are Publishing Haunting Photos of Emaciated Yemeni Children."

95 At least 100,000 people: Taylor, "Bobby Sands."

95 an increasing share of the vote: Ibid.

95 12.4 million: World Food Programme, "Global Report on Food Crises," 2021, 18.

95 13.5 million: Ibid.

95 relief organizations raised more than $6 billion: Kweifio-Okai, "Where Did the Indian Ocean Tsunami Aid Money Go?"

95 more than $100 million on its hands: Médecins Sans Frontières, "Asian Tsunami: Three Months Financial Overview."

96 MSF asked their donors: Philanthropy News Digest, "Doctors Without Borders Caps Tsunami Relief, Directs Donors to General Fund."

96 only $1 billion was raised: extracted from UN Office for the Coordination of Humanitarian Affairs, Financial Tracking System.

96 Britain, France, and Russia blockaded Syria's ports: Schilcher, "The Famine of 1915–1918 in Greater Syria," 229, 231.

97 "They perished from hunger": Gibran, "Dead Are My People."

97 the famine killed up to 500,000 people: Schilcher, "The Famine of 1915–1918 in Greater Syria," 229, 231.

97 lost a third of its population: Ibid.

97 "For the Assads": Ciezadlo, "The Most Unconventional Weapon in Syria: Wheat."

97 3 million tons of grain: Ibid.

98 a loss equivalent: World Bank. "Arable Land."

98 a morsel of life: Ciezadlo, "The Most Unconventional Weapon in Syria: Wheat."

98 ample supply to all its citizens: Kim, "Syria, Country Policy Brief."

98 40 percent of the calories: Martínez and Eng, "Struggling to Perform the State."

98 regarded as a right: Slackman, "Egypt's Problem and Its Challenge: Bread Corrupts."

98 "streamline the extensive subsidy system": International Monetary Fund, "Syrian Arab Republic," 3.

99 the worst in at least nine hundred years: Cook et al., "Spatiotemporal Drought Variability in the Mediterranean over the Last 900 Years," 121.

99 forcing the country to start importing wheat: Polk, "Understanding Syria."

99 up to 1.5 million people moved: Ciezadlo, "The Most Unconventional Weapon in Syria: Wheat."

99 a ready target for recruiters: Polk, "Understanding Syria."

99 As Syria's decades-old systems teetered: Zevenhuizen, "Land, Conflict and Agriculture in Syria."

100 "bread, freedom, and social justice": Tadros, "Where's the 'Bread, Freedom and Social Justice' a Year After Egypt's Revolution?"

100 2.2 million in 2019: El Dahan, "Syria's Wheat Crop Almost Doubles but Food Security Still a Challenge: U.N."

100 Four million Syrians had fled the country: United Nations, "Humanitarian Needs Overview, Syrian Arab Republic."

100 7 million people inside Syria: Food and Agriculture Organization and World Food Programme, "Crop and Food Security Assessment Mission to the Syrian Arab Republic," 33.

102 "the fear of all fears": Wiam Simav Bedirxan and Ossama Mohammed, "Silvered Water."

102 350,000 lives: United Nations, "Syria, 10 Years of War Has Left 350,000 Dead."

103 profound demographic impacts: United Nations, "Syria War."

105 seven thousand Yazidi girls and women: Kolstad, "5 Things You Should Know About the Yazidis."

107 WFP called for a ceasefire: World Food Programme, "Pauses in Syrian Fighting During Harvest Vital to Meet Country's Food Needs."

108 one of the most serious food emergencies in the world: World Food Programme, "Global Report on Food Crises," 2022.

109 It reached Britain around five thousand years ago: Wetherell, "A Brief History of Wheat."

109 wheat is the world's most traded crop: USDA, "World Agricultural Supply and Demand Estimates." July 2023.

109 they had managed to transfer: Simon, "These Rare Seeds Escaped Syria's War."

109 the first-ever withdrawal: Ibid.

109 more than 110,000 acres of land burned: Parker, "As Crops Burn in Syria Conflict Zone, Hunger Warnings for Civilians."

109 a third of all agricultural land: Sherlock, "How Crop Fires Have Become the Latest Weapon of War in Syria."

110 Incendiary weapons were used: Ibid.

110 "eat out Virginia clear and clean": U.S. National Park Service, "The Burning: Shenandoah Valley in Flames."

111 "What is the worst in war": Ibid.

111 "Reduction to poverty": Ibid.

Chapter 6 Not War, Not Peace: *Feeding a Nation After a Conflict*

112 "What do you think": Roumain, *Masters of the Dew*, 153.

120 whose ministry began in the 1990s: Coyault, "The Warrior Prophetism of the Reverend Pastor Ntumi."

121 "a hulking monster bristling with fetishes": Quoted in Coyault, "Warrior Prophetism," from Ntumi (révérend pasteur), *Une longue nuit. La demeure du silence* (Essonnes, France: Éditions ICES, 2010).

121 "their sticks started firing": Coyault, "Warrior Prophetism."

121 "My reign is eternal": Ibid.

122 He remained a hermit in Mpangala country: Ibid.

Chapter 7 Going Viral: *The Relationship Between Disease and Hunger*

130 "There are fevers that consume you": Roumain, *Masters of the Dew*, 170–71.

130 25 million people: *Encyclopaedia Britannica*, "Black Death."

130 recover to pre-plague levels: Ibid.

130 introduced the plague to the continent: Ibid.

131 a malnourished population: Powell, "Did Famine Worsen the Black Death?"

131 270 million people: World Food Programme, "WFP Chief Calls for Urgent Funds to Avert Famine."

132 In a seminal 2003 article: de Waal and Whiteside, "New Variant Famine."

132 much less labor-intensive: Ibid.

133 or to earn the money needed: Ibid., 1235.

133 their parents had died of AIDS: Ibid.

133 "We must face the prospect": Ibid., 1236.

141 a lower COVID death rate: Nolen, "Trying to Solve a Covid Mystery."

141 get by on reduced budgets: Robins, "False Things You Believe About the Great Depression."

142 14.9 percent of households: Coleman-Jensen et al., "Household Food Security in the United States in 2020."

142 the pre-recession range of 10–11 percent: National Institute of Food and Agriculture, "Food and Nutrition Security."

142 plowed back into fields: Yaffe-Bellany and Corker, "Dumped Milk, Smashed Eggs, Plowed Vegetables: Food Waste of the Pandemic."

142 unemployment reached 14.7 percent: Feeding America, "The Impact of the Coronavirus on Food Insecurity."

142 Experts feared the worst: Schanzenbach and Pitts, "Food Insecurity Triples for Families with Children During COVID-19 Pandemic."

142 the 2020 "stimmies": Alpert, "A Breakdown of the Fiscal and Monetary Responses to the Pandemic."

143 The level of food insecurity in late 2020: Coleman-Jensen et al., "Household Food Security."

143 indicators worsened for African American households: Ibid., vi.

145 more than five hundred men and women who once worked: Associated Press, "Hundreds of Furloughs Become Permanent at WVa. Casino."

148 infected 28,000 people and killed more than 11,000: Rogers, "Ebola Outbreak of 2014–16."

149 "medieval": Roberts, "Ebola in West Africa: A Medieval Quarantine in the Modern World."

149 "Today I work your field": Roumain, *Masters of the Dew*, 26.

149 or cutting back on essentials: CILSS, "Cadre Harmonisé for the Identification of Areas and Populations in Food Insecurity in Guinea, Liberia and Sierra Leone."

149 people began to ask: Centers for Disease Control and Prevention, "2014–2016 Ebola Outbreak in West Africa."

150 while humanitarians distributed cash or food: Dahl et al., "CDC's Response to the 2014–2016 Ebola Epidemic"; and L. M. Mobula, J. H. Nakao, S. Walia et al., "A Humanitarian Response to the West African Ebola Virus Disease Outbreak."

Chapter 8 "P" Is for Pygmy: *Indigenous Peoples and the Right to Food*

152 "We ordinary folks": Roumain, *Masters of the Dew*, 51.

155 between 370 and 500 million Indigenous people: World Bank, "Indigenous Peoples Overview."

155 before the arrival of other ethnic groups: Amnesty International, "Indigenous Peoples."

156 an area the size of New Jersey or Israel: Olam, "Republic of Congo," 2022.

157 essential to nutrition throughout central Africa: Food and Agriculture Organization, "Edible Insects, Important Source of Protein in Central Africa."

157 took up arms in 2016: British Broadcasting Corporation, " 'Caterpillar Tax': DR Congo Ethnic Clash Sees 16 Killed."

158 "wildest, most isolated": Kamba, "African Rainforest Experiences."

158 $9,670 for a four-night stay: Congo Conservation Company, "International Discovery Rates, 2022."

159 a complaint denouncing abuse: Vidal, "Armed Ecoguards Funded by WWF 'Beat Up Congo Tribespeople.' "

160 The UNDP investigated: UNDP. "Final Investigation Report."

160 died shortly after being released: Vidal, "Armed Ecoguards Funded by WWF."

160 "They think of the Baka as animals": Ade Adepitan, "Congo: The Tribe Under Threat."

160 "colonial conservation": Survival International, "The Baka."

160 "they're in way over their head": Schiffman, "Green Violence: 'Eco-Guards' Are Absusing Indigenous Groups in Africa."

162 huckleberries were plentiful: Marangione, "Evicted from the Mountains."

163 five hundred families were dispossessed: U.S. National Park Service, "The Displaced—Shenandoah National Park."

163 "humanitarian act": Ibid.

163 "supported by a primitive agriculture": Ibid.

164 "not of the 20th century": Ibid.

164 to remove the man from his property: Michaels, "Man Sings National Anthem as He Is Evicted from His Home."

164 were sterilized at the hands of the government: Marangione, "Evicted from the Mountains."

166 "We can't defend ourselves": Ngokia, "Scolariser les Pygmées de la Sangha, Congo Brazzaville."

170 "the worst mistake": Diamond, "The Worst Mistake in the History of the Human Race."

170 2,140 kilocalories (kcals) and 93 grams: Ibid.

170 "that enabled us to build": Ibid.

170 dropping from five foot nine for men: Ibid.

171 more likely to have anemia: Ibid.

171 Life expectancy fell from twenty-six to nineteen years: Ibid.

171 with lethal effect: Ibid.

Chapter 9 Digital Food:
The Ambiguous Promise of Technology and Innovation

172 "Trust is almost a mystery": Roumain, *Masters of the Dew,* 86.

172 In a 2017 interview: Pilling, "UK Company Develops Edible Drones to Feed Hungry."

172 "Our food technologist guys": Ibid.

173 "absolutely irrelevant for resolving acute hunger": Ibid.

174 a "Fourth Industrial Revolution": Schwab, *The Fourth Industrial Revolution*.

174 played on information asymmetries: Aker and Fafchamps, "Mobile Phone Coverage and Producer Markets: Evidence from West Africa."

175 25,000 individual farmers: GSM Association, "The Rise of Agri E-Commerce During COVID-19."

175 more than 1.2 billion people worldwide: Mureithi, "Half of the World's Mobile Money Services Are in Africa."

175 rising sharply in sub-Saharan Africa and South Asia: Ibid.

176 before food or water: Kane, "Refugees in Greece Need Internet So Badly They'll Stop a Riot to Let the Wifi Guys Work."

177 $5.6 billion in 2019: Jodar et al., "The State of the World's Cash."

181 Pharaoh once dreamed: Genesis 41 (New International Version).

181 "the sand of the sea": Genesis 41:49.

184 our social and political structures: Kissinger et al., *The Age of AI*.

185 almost instantly on their phone: Give Directly, "Study: AI Targeting Helped Reach More of the Poorest People in Togo."

185 outperformed alternatives: Aiken et al., "Machine Learning and Mobile Phone Data Can Improve the Targeting of Humanitarian Assistance."

187 increase by 60 percent by 2050: Graziano Da Silva, "Feeding the World Sustainably."

187 $17 a serving: Stevens and Ruperti, "Lab-Grown Meat Is on the Rise. It's Time to Start Asking Tough Questions."

187 not genetically modified: Manning, "Here's How Eat Just's GOOD Meat Will Spend Its Latest $170m Funding."

189 a food uniquely suited: van Huis et al., "Edible Insects: Future Prospects for Food and Feed Security."

189 100,000 tons of mealworms: Ledsom, "Insect Market to Explode: EU Gives Green Light to Eating Mealworm."

192 "this approach can ensure": Quinn, "Low Tech, High Impact."

192 quoted critics calling the product: Dewey, "The Silicon Valley Food Start Up Best Known for Its Vegan Mayo Thinks It Can Cure Malnutrition in Africa."

192 DuPont, Danone, and Pepsi had tried before and failed: Ibid.

Chapter 10 The Black Humanitarian: *Race and the Aid System*

195 "You damned Haitian! You black hunk of dung!": Roumain, *Masters of the Dew,* 43.

196 describes how British authorities: Davis, *Late Victorian Holocausts.*

196 between 5.6 and 9.4 million people: Dyson, *A Population History of India,* 137.

196 "a salutary cure for overpopulation": Davis, *Late Victorian Holocausts,* 32.

197 offered less than half the calories: Ibid., 38.

197 the infamous concentration camp of Buchenwald: Ibid., 38–39.

197 "Nor will many be inclined": Ibid., 41.

197 largely excavated by hand: Césaire, "Discours sur le Colonialisme."

198 only about a third: Chakamba, "Has WFP Failed to Tackle Racism in Its Ranks?"

198 one in five: United Nations, "Review of Measures and Mechanisms for Addressing Racism and Racial Discrimination in United Nations System Organizations."

198 a lightning rod for anti-Western protests: France 24, "French Centre in Niger Set Ablaze in Charlie Hebdo Protests."

200 or by groceries and supermarkets: Milkman, "The Radical Origins of Free Breakfast for Children."

200 it expanded to forty-five schools: Ibid.

200 "I mean, nobody can argue against free grits": Blakemore, "How the Black Panthers' Breakfast Program Both Inspired and Threatened the Government."

201 "potentially the greatest threat": Ibid.

201 urinated on the food supplies: Ibid.

201 14.5 million American children: Ibid.

201 "almost all of the major food assistance programs": Quoted in Urbi, "The Government Cheese Phenomenon and the American Cheese Stockpile Today."

202 highly processed, shelf-stable bars: Karp, "WTF Happened to Government Cheese?"

202 couldn't stomach the stuff: Ibid.

207 Blacks wearing "white masks": Fanon, "Peau Noire, Masques Blancs."

209 technology they need to industrialize: Dumont, *L'Afrique Noire est mal partie.*

209 a mausoleum of gleaming marble: Atlas Obscura, "De Brazza's Mausoleum."

210 "He wears a mask, and his face grows to fit it": Orwell, *Shooting an Elephant and Other Essays,* 3.

Chapter 11 Real Food: *Grassroots Solutions to Feed Us All*

217 "Then one morning": Roumain, *Masters of the Dew,* 45.

217 "I want every laborer in my Kingdom": Vitaux, "La poule au pot du bon roi Henri IV."

218 "Finally the chicken": Ibid.

218 redistributed it to freedmen: Gates, "The Truth Behind '40 Acres and a Mule.'"

219 A crop of wheat: *Encyclopaedia Britannica,* "Italy—Economic Policy."

220 monopolistic food system: Patel, *Stuffed and Starved.*

221 "the right of peoples": La Via Campesina, "The International Peasants' Voice."

221 our globalized food supply chains: Henderson and Natsoulas, "José Bové and Food Sovereignty: An Interview."

221 dismantled a McDonald's restaurant: Agence France-Presse. "Bové Loses McDonald's Attack Case."

221 Two million Mexican farmers: Johnson and Fromartz, "NAFTA's 'Broken Promises': These Farmers Say They Got the Raw End of Trade Deal."

221 increase in migration to the United States: Alexander, "Want to Understand the Border Crisis? Look to American Corn Policy."

223 a compelling critique: Pollan, *The Omnivore's Dilemma.*

223 discrimination that has crushed minority farmers: Hurt, "The USDA Is Set to Give Black Farmers Debt Relief."

223 the equivalent of $250 billion to $350 billion: Francis et al., "Black Land Loss: 1920–1997," 38.

223 by 2017 that number had dropped to 2 percent: Tabuchi and Popovitch, "Two Biden Priorities, Climate and Inequality, Meet on Black-Owned Farms."

223 excluded from government programs: Fidler, "Ask the Expert: Building upon a Family Legacy."

224 involved the food industry, consumer groups: Makri, "How Belo Horizonte's Bid to Tackle Hunger Inspired Other Cities."

225 72 percent drop in child mortality: Ibid.

225 reached 48 million people: World Bank. "Implementation Completion and Results Report."

225 fell by more than half: Food and Agriculture Organization, International Fund for Agriculture Development, and World Food Programme, "The State of Food Insecurity in the World, 2014," 23.

225 travel from south to north: Bosman, "City Will Stop Paying the Poor for Good Behavior."

225 from the Bolsonaro administration: Alves, "Pandemic Puts Brazil Back on the World Hunger Map."

226 "We only came here": Severson. "José Andrés Fed Puerto Rico, and May Change How Aid Is Given."

227 "real food, not emergency rations": Andrés, "How We've Served 1 Million Meals to Hurricane Dorian Survivors in the Bahamas."

227 Brillat-Savarin's 1825 treatise: Brillat-Savarin, *La Physiologie du Goût.*

228 "When we couldn't safely establish": Andrés, "How We've Served 1 Million Meals to Hurricane Dorian Survivors in the Bahamas."

228 the 2022 conference on food security: Andrés, "What the Pandemic Can Teach Us About Treating Hunger."

228 appointment of a "food czar": Andrés, "Our People Are Hungry, We Need a Leader Who Will Feed Them."

228 More than 80,000 Afghans: Alvarez et al., "Afghan Evacuees Abroad and at US Bases Still Wait to Be Resettled."

232 nearly 23 million people: Integrated Food Security Phase Classification, "Afghanistan IPC Acute Food Insecurity Analysis: September 2021–March 2022."

232 people giving up or selling their own children: Associated Press, "Parents Selling Children Shows Desperation in Afghanistan."

233 "I have already seen railroads": Londres, *Terre d'ébène.*

234 the annual death toll stood near 50 percent: Daughton, *In the Forest of No Joy,* 215.

236 Utah followed suit in 2021: Baylen Linnekin, "Utah Second State to Adopt Microenterprise Home Kitchen Operations Law."

237 high rates of obesity and cardiovascular disease: West Virginia Department of Health and Human Resources, "Fast Facts."

240 the goal is to protect 20,000 acres over time: West Virginia Farmland Protection System, "Jefferson County's Protected Farmland Grows to 5,866 Acres with 51st Farm."

242 "You're in front of someone": Farmer, quoted in *New York Times*, "Q&A; Health Care for the Poorest as a Central Human Right."

Bibliography

Achebe, Chinua. "Refugee Mother and Child." In *Beware, Soul Brother.* Portsmouth, NH: Heinemann Educational Books, 1972.

Adams, Robin J. C., and Ingrid de Zwarte. "Rationing in Britain During World War II." University of Oxford, Faculty of History. 2020.

Adepitan, Ade. "Congo: The Tribe Under Threat." *Unreported World,* June 2, 2019. Channel 4. Available on YouTube.

Agence France-Presse. "Bové Loses McDonald's Attack Case." March 22, 2001.

Aiken, Emily, Suzanne Bellue, Dean, Karlan, Christopher R. Udry, and Joshua Blumenstock. "Machine Learning and Mobile Phone Data Can Improve the Targeting of Humanitarian Assistance." National Bureau of Economic Research Working Paper 29070, July 2021.

Aker, Jenny C., and Marcel Fafchamps. "Mobile Phone Coverage and Producer Markets: Evidence from West Africa." *World Bank Economic Review* 29, no. 2 (2015): 262–92.

Alexander, Renée. "Want to Understand the Border Crisis? Look to American Corn Policy." *The Counter,* July 24, 2018.

Alpert, Gabe. "A Breakdown of the Fiscal and Monetary Responses to the Pandemic." *Investopedia,* April 12, 2022.

Alvarez, Priscilla, Kylie Atwood, and Ellie Kaufman Ellie. "Afghan Evacuees Abroad and at US Bases Still Wait to Be Resettled." CNNPolitics, December 29, 2021.

Alves, Lise. "Pandemic Puts Brazil Back on the World Hunger Map." *The New Humanitarian,* July 19, 2021.

Amnesty International. "Indigenous Peoples." www.amnesty.org.

Andrés, José. "How We've Served 1 Million Meals to Hurricane Dorian Survivors in the Bahamas." *Washington Post,* October 11, 2019.

———. "Our People Are Hungry, We Need a Leader Who Will Feed Them." *Washington Post,* April 20, 2020.

———. "What the Pandemic Can Teach Us About Treating Hunger." *Washington Post,* December 7, 2020.

Associated Press. "C. African Republic Rebels Refuge at Luxury Hotel." *USA Today,* April 17, 2013.

———. "Hundreds of Furloughs Become Permanent at Wva. Casino." *AP News,* August 18, 2020.

———. "Parents Selling Children Shows Desperation in Afghanistan." National Public Radio, December 31, 2021.

Association for Diplomatic Studies and Training. "The Man Who Would Be Emperor—CAR's Jean Bokassa." *Huffington Post,* December 2, 2015.

Atlas Obscura. "De Brazza's Mausoleum." August 12, 2012.

Baumgarthuber, Christine. "Hunger as an Instrument of Social Control." *The New Inquiry,* April 7, 2016.

Beck, Ulrich. *Risk Society: Towards a New Modernity.* Translated by Mark Ritter. Washington, DC: Sage, 1992.

Bedirxan, Wiam Simav, and Ossama Mohammed. *Silvered Water, Syria Self Portrait* (film), 2014.

Bell, Beverly. "Miami Rice: The Business of Disaster in Haiti." *Huffington Post,* December 9, 2010.

Bergen, Molly J. "On the Map: Charting a Path for Sustainable Development in the Republic of Congo." *Trees of Life* (blog), June 4, 2019.

Bigo, Didier. *Pouvoir et obéissance en Centrafrique.* Paris: Editions Karthala, 1988.

Bivens, Matt. "New Facts Point Up Horror of Nazi Siege of Leningrad." *Los Angeles Times,* January 27, 1994.

Blakemore, Erin. "How the Black Panthers' Breakfast Program Both Inspired and Threatened the Government." *History,* February 6, 2018.

Booth, William. "Embargo Leaves Haiti's Economy Down but Not Out." *Washington Post,* August 10, 1994.

Borlaug, Norman. "The Green Revolution, Peace and Humanity." Nobel Peace Prize acceptance speech, December 11, 1970.

Bosman, Julie. "City Will Stop Paying the Poor for Good Behavior." *New York Times,* March 30, 2010.

Brillat-Savarin, Jean Anthelme. *La Physiologie du Goût.* Paris: Gabriel de Gonet, 1848.

British Broadcasting Corporation. "'Caterpillar Tax': DR Congo Ethnic Clash Sees 16 Killed." BBC News, October 18, 2016.

———. "Qatar Crisis: Air-Lifted Cows Start Arriving in Doha." BBC News, July 12, 2017.

Brown, Lester. "The New Geopolitics of Food." *Foreign Policy,* April 25, 2011.

Canadian Broadcasting Corporation. "How a Hunger Strike Affects the Body." CBC News, January 4, 2013.

Carayannis, Tatiana, and Louisa Lombard. *Making Sense of the Central African Republic.* London: Zed Books, 2015.

Casson, Lionel. *The Ancient Mariners: Seafarers and Sea Fighters of the Mediterranean in Ancient Times.* 2nd ed. Princeton, NJ: Princeton University Press, 1991.

———. "The Role of the State in Rome's Grain Trade." *Memoirs of the American Academy in Rome* 36 (1980): 21–33. 21.

Cathcart, Brian. "Obituary, Jean-Bedel Bokassa." *The Independent,* November 5, 1996.

Centers for Disease Control and Prevention. "2014–2016 Ebola Outbreak in West Africa."

Césaire, Aimé. "Discours sur le Colonialisme." Lecture Analytique Numéro 2, 1950.

Chakamba, Rumbi. "Has WFP Failed to Tackle Racism in Its Ranks? Some Employees Say Yes." Devex, March 31, 2023.

Chappell, M. Jahi. *Beginning to End Hunger: Food and the Environment in Belo Horizonte, Brazil, and Beyond.* Oakland: University of California Press, 2018.

Chilton, Mariana, and Jenny Rabinowich. "Toxic Stress and Child Hunger over the Life Course: Three Case Studies." *Journal of Applied Research on Children* 3, no. 1.

Ciezadlo, Annia. "The Most Unconventional Weapon in Syria: Wheat." *Washington Post,* December 18, 2015.

CILSS. "Cadre Harmonisé for the Identification of Areas and Populations in Food Insecurity in Guinea, Liberia and Sierra Leone." February–March 2015.

Cochrane, Nancy, Nathan Childs, and Stacey Rosen. "Haiti's U.S. Rice Imports." U.S. Department of Agriculture, February 2016.

Coleman-Jensen, Alisha, Matthew P. Rabbitt, Christian A. Gregory, and Anita Singh. "Household Food Security in the United States in 2020." U.S. Department of Agriculture, September 2020.

Condom, Cédric. "Notre Ami L'Empereur Bokassa 1er." Docs Interdits, September 19, 2011.

Congo Conservation Company. "International Discovery Rates." 2022.

Cook, B. I., K. J. Anchukaitis, R. Touchan, D. M. Meko, and E. R. Cook. "Spatiotemporal Drought Variability in the Mediterranean over the Last 900 Years." *Journal of Geophysical Research: Atmospheres* 121 (2016): 2060–74.

Coyault, Bernard. "The Warrior Prophetism of the Reverend Pastor Ntumi: The Origin and Development of the Nsilulu Movement in the Republic of the Congo (1998–2019)." *Afrique Contemporaine* 267/268, no. 3/4 (2018): 11–45.

Dahl, B. A., M. H. Kinzer, P. L. Raghunathan, et al. "CDC's Response to the 2014–2016 Ebola Epidemic—Guinea, Liberia, and Sierra Leone." *Morbidity and Mortality Weekly Report Supplements* 65, no. 3 (2016): 12–20.

Danticat, Edwidge. "The Fight for Haiti's Future." *The New Yorker,* October 21, 2022.

Daughton, J. P. *In the Forest of No Joy.* New York: W. W. Norton, 2021.

Davis, Mike. *Late Victorian Holocausts.* New York: Verso, 2001.

Deininger, Klaus, and Derek Byerlee, with Jonathan Lindsay, Andrew Norton, Harris Selod, and Mercedes Stickler. *Rising Global Interest in Farmland.* Washington, DC: World Bank, 2011.

de Waal, Alex, and Alan Whiteside. "New Variant Famine: AIDS and Food Crisis in Southern Africa." *Lancet* 362 (2003): 1234–37.

Dewey, Caitlin. "The Silicon Valley Food Start Up Best Known for Its

Vegan Mayo Thinks It Can Cure Malnutrition in Africa." *Washington Post,* February 24, 2018.

Diamond, Jared. "The Worst Mistake in the History of the Human Race." *Discover,* May 1987.

Diederich, Bernard, and Al Burt. *Papa Doc and the Tonton Macoutes.* Princeton, NJ: Markus Wiener Publications, 1970.

DiPierro Obert, Jess. "Hunger in Haiti: Ten Years After Catastrophe Struck, a New Crisis Looms." *The New Humanitarian,* January 13, 2020.

Doyle, Mark. "US Urged to Stop Haiti Rice Subsidies." BBC News, October 5, 2010.

Dreyfuss, Joel. "Haiti in U.S. History: A Timeline." *The Root,* March 31, 2010.

Dubner, Stephen J., and Steve Levitt. *Freakonomics.* New York: William Morrow, 2011.

Dumont, René. *L'Afrique Noire est mal partie.* Paris: Editions du Seuil, 1962.

Duras, Marguerite. *La Douleur.* Paris: Folio, 1985.

———. *The War.* New York: Pantheon, 1986.

Durisin, Megan, Isis Almeida, and Innocent Anguyo. "Europe's Butter Mountain Has Melted Away." *Bloomberg News,* July 27, 2017.

Duteurtre, Guillaume, and Christian Corniaux. "Local or Imported: What Is the Most Sustainable Option for Milk in the Sahel?" CIRAD, December 8, 2020.

Dyson, Tim. *A Population History of India: From the First Modern People to the Present Day.* Oxford: Oxford University Press, 2018.

El Dahan, Maha. "Syria's Wheat Crop Almost Doubles but Food Security Still a Challenge: U.N." Reuters, September 5, 2019.

Encyclopaedia Britannica. S.v. "Black Death." August 13, 2022.

———. S.v. "Italy—Economic Policy." August 2022.

Fanon, Frantz. *Peau Noire, Masques Blancs.* Paris: Editions du Seuil, 1952.

Feeding America. "The Impact of the Coronavirus on Food Insecurity." March 2021.

Fidler, Kathryn. "Ask the Expert: Building upon a Family Legacy, a Q&A About Heirs' Property with J. Latrice Hill," May 5, 2021.

Food and Agriculture Organization. "Approche territoriale du projet KEITA."

————. "Edible Insects, Important Source of Protein in Central Africa." November 8, 2004.

————. "Small Family Farmers Produce a Third of the World's Food." April 23, 2021.

————. "The State of Food Insecurity and Nutrition in the World 2021."

Food and Agriculture Organization and World Food Programme. "Crop and Food Security Assessment Mission to the Syrian Arab Republic." July 23, 2015.

————. "Special Report: FAO/WFP Crop and Food Security Assessment Mission to Central African Republic." October 29, 2014.

Food and Agriculture Organization, International Fund for Agriculture Development, and World Food Programme. "The State of Food Insecurity in the World, 2014."

Food Crisis Prevention Network (RPCA). Various Analytical Bulletins, 2012–2022. www.food-security.net. Accessed April 2023.

France 24. "French Centre in Niger Set Ablaze in Charlie Hebdo Protests." January 16, 2015.

Francis, Dania V., Darrick Hamilton, Thomas W. Mitchell, Nathan A. Rosenberg, and Bryce Wilson Stucki. "Black Land Loss: 1920−1997." *AEA Papers and Proceedings* 112 (2022): 38–42.

Fukuoka, Masanobu. *The One-Straw Revolution.* Emmaus, PA: Rodale Press, 1978.

Gamio, Lazaro, Constant Méheut, Catherine Porter, Selam Gebrekidan, Alisson McCann, and Matt Apuzzo. "Haiti's Lost Billions," *New York Times,* May 20, 2022.

Garcia-Navarro, Lulu. "Haiti Still Struggling to Recover from Hurricane Jeanne." *All Things Considered,* October 8, 2004.

Gates, Henry Louis, Jr. "The Truth Behind '40 Acres and a Mule.'" *The Root,* January 7, 2013.

Gibran, Kahlil. "Dead Are My People." www.poemhunter.com.

Give Directly. "Study: AI Targeting Helped Reach More of the Poorest People in Togo." July 28, 2021.

Global Network Against Food Crises. "2022 Global Report on Food Crises, 2023."

Global Rights Compliance. "The Crime of Starvation and Methods of Prosecution and Accountability." June 13, 2019. starvationaccountability.org.

———. "The Netherlands Accepts Starvation Amendment: One Year On." December 11, 2020. starvationaccountability.org.

Graziano Da Silva, Jose. "Feeding the World Sustainably." *The Future We Want?* 49, nos. 1 & 2 (June 2012).

GSM Association. "The Rise of Agri E-Commerce During COVID-19: Opportunities for Smallholder Impact." August 31, 2020.

Heinl, Robert Debs, and Nancy Gordon Heinl. *Written in Blood.* Boston: Houghton Mifflin Harcourt, 1978.

Held, Isaac. "Sahel Drought: Understanding the Past and Projecting into the Future." NOAA Geophysical Fluids Dynamics Laboratory. 2016.

Henderson, Elizabeth, and Andrianna Natsoulas. "José Bové and Food Sovereignty: An Interview." *The Natural Farmer.* 2022.

Human Rights Watch. "Central African Republic: Muslims Trapped in Enclaves." December 22, 2014.

Hurt, Emma. "The USDA Is Set to Give Black Farmers Debt Relief. They've Heard That One Before." National Public Radio, June 4, 2021.

Integrated Food Security Classification. "Central African Republic. IPC Food Security Snapshot." November 2022.

Integrated Food Security Phase Classification. "Afghanistan IPC Acute Food Insecurity Analysis: September 2021–March 2022." October 25, 2021.

———. "Haiti: Acute Food Insecurity Situation September 2022–February 2023 and Projection for March–June 2023." October 14, 2022.

International Committee of the Red Cross. "Discours du Dr. Jacques Fourcand." Audio recording, July 20, 1965.

International Fund for Agricultural Development. "Smallholders Can Feed the World." February 2011.

International Monetary Fund. "Syrian Arab Republic: 2009 Article IV Consultation—Staff Report; and Public Information Notice." February 12, 2010.

Jodar, José, Anna Kondakhchyan, Ruth McCormack, Karen Peachey, Laura Phelps, and Gaby Smith. "The State of the World's Cash." *The CALP Network.* July 23, 2020.

Johnson, Kristina, and Samuel Fromartz. "NAFTA's 'Broken Promises': These Farmers Say They Got the Raw End of Trade Deal." National Public Radio, August 7, 2017.

Joseph, Celucian J. "A Brief History of Presidential Deaths." *Haitian Times*, July 11, 2021.

Kamba Africa. "African Rainforest Experiences." kambaafrica.com. Accessed October 2023.

Kane, Madeline. "Refugees in Greece Need Internet So Badly They'll Stop a Riot to Let the Wifi Guys Work." *Quartz*, June 20, 2016.

Karp, Myles. "WTF Happened to Government Cheese?" *Vice News*, February 19, 2018.

Kim, Sunae. "Syria, Country Policy Brief." Food and Agriculture Organization. December 2010.

Kissinger, Henry, Eric Schmidt, and Daniel Huttenlocher. *The Age of AI*. New York: Little, Brown & Company, 2021.

Klein, Naomi. *The Shock Doctrine*. New York: Metropolitan Books, 2007.

Kolstad, Kristine. "5 Things You Should Know About the Yazidis." Norwegian Refugee Council. December 10, 2018.

Krebs, Albin. "Papa Doc, a Ruthless Dictator, Kept the Haitians in Illiteracy and Dire Poverty." *New York Times*, April 23, 1971.

Kweifio-Okai, Carla. "Where Did the Indian Ocean Tsunami Aid Money Go?" *The Guardian*, December 25, 2014.

Lahiff, Edward, and Guo Li. "Land Redistribution in South Africa—A Critical Review." The World Bank. May 28, 2012.

Langlois, Jill. "13 South African Soldiers Killed in Central African Republic." *GlobalPost*, March 25, 2013.

La Via Campesina. "The International Peasants' Voice." 2021.

Lay, Jann, Ward Anseeuw, Sandra Eckert, Insa Flachsbarth, Christoph Kubitza, Kerstin Nolte, and Markus Giger. *Taking Stock of the Global Land Rush: Few Development Benefits, Many Human and Environmental Risks: Analytical Report III*. Bern, Montpellier, Hamburg, Pretoria: Centre for Development and Environment, University of Bern; Centre de coopération internationale en recherche agronomique pour le développement; German Institute for Global and Area Studies; University of Pretoria; Bern Open Publishing, 2021.

Lazareva, Inna. "In the Central African Republic, Nostalgia for a Leader Who Is Said to Have Fed His Critics to Crocodiles." *Washington Post*, June 22, 2017.

———. "'Now We're Back It's Even Worse': The Bangui Residents

Who Preferred a Refugee Camp to Their Home City." *The Guardian,* July 15, 2017.

Ledsom, Alex. "Insect Market to Explode: EU Gives Green Light to Eating Mealworm." *Forbes,* January 13, 2021.

Le Monde. "Bokassa Ier avait-il servi de la chair humaine à M. Galley?" September 29, 1979.

Lenin, Vladimir. "First Letter: The First Stage of the First Revolution." In *Letters from Afar,* www.marxist.com.

Linnekin, Baylen. "Utah Second State to Adopt Microenterprise Home Kitchen Operations Law." *Reason,* May 29, 2021.

Lombard, Louisa. *State of Rebellion: Violence and Intervention in the Central African Republic.* London: Zed Books, 2016.

Londres, Albert. *Terre d'ébène.* Paris: Albin Michel, 1929.

Makri, Anita. "How Belo Horizonte's Bid to Tackle Hunger Inspired Other Cities." *Nature Index,* September 24, 2021.

Mangan, Fiona, Igor Acko, and Manal Taha. "The 'Green Diamond': Coffee and Conflict in the Central African Republic." Special Report 464. United States Institute for Peace. www.usip.org.

Manning, Lauren. "Here's How Eat Just's GOOD Meat Will Spend Its Latest $170m Funding." *AgFundNews,* May 24, 2021.

Marangione, Margaret. "Evicted from the Mountains." Audio. *With Good Reason Radio,* May 3, 2014.

Maritz, Jaco. "Commercial Farming in the Congo Not for the Faint-Hearted." How We Made It in Africa (website), October 26, 2012.

Martínez, José Ciro, and Brent Eng. "Struggling to Perform the State: The Politics of Bread in the Syrian Civil War." *International Political Sociology* 11, no. 2 (June 2017): 130–47.

Médecins Sans Frontières. "Asian Tsunami: Three Months Financial Overview," April 8, 2005.

———. "Malnutrition in the Sahel Requires Long-Term Solutions." Press release, July 17, 2012.

Michaels, Denver. "Man Sings National Anthem as He Is Evicted from His Home." DenverMichaels.net (website), April 20, 2021.

Milkman, Arielle. "The Radical Origins of Free Breakfast for Children." Eater (website), February 16, 2016.

Mobula, L. M., J. H. Nakao, S. Walia, et al. "A Humanitarian Response to the West African Ebola Virus Disease Outbreak." *International Journal of Humanitarian Action 3*, no. 10 (2018).

MTV News. "Tupac Talks Donald Trump & Greed in America in 1992 Interview." YouTube video. April 19, 2016.

Mudge, George Alfred. "Starvation as a Means of Warfare." *International Lawyer 4*, no. 2 (1970).

Mureithi, Carlos. "Half of the World's Mobile Money Services Are in Africa." *Quartz*, March 30, 2021.

Nagourney, Eric, and Michael Slackman. "Why We Are Publishing Haunting Photos of Emaciated Yemeni Children." *New York Times*, October 26, 2018.

National Institute of Food and Agriculture. "Food and Nutrition Security." 2021. https://nifa.usda.gov.

New York Times. "Mauritania Coup Ousts President." December 13, 1984.

———. "Q&A; Health Care for the Poorest as a Central Human Right." March 29, 2003.

[Ngokia, Melaine]. "Scolariser les Pygmées de la Sangha, Congo Brazzaville." Blog. June 29, 2017.

Nolen, Stephanie. "Trying to Solve a Covid Mystery: Africa's Low Death Rates." *New York Times*, March 23, 2022.

Observer, The. "Bushel & Peck Receives Grant to Expand Operations." January 2021.

Olam Agri. "Republic of Congo." 2022. www.olamagri.com.

Orwell, George. *Shooting an Elephant, and Other Essays*. New York: Harcourt, Brace & World, 1950.

Parker, Ben. "As Crops Burn in Syria Conflict Zone, Hunger Warnings for Civilians." *New Humanitarian*, June 7, 2019.

Patel, Raj. *Stuffed and Starved*. London: Portobello, 2007.

Philanthropy News Digest. "Doctors Without Borders Caps Tsunami Relief, Directs Donors to General Fund," January 5, 2005.

Picard, Jean Serge. *Jérémie: La Hantise d'un Passé Révolu*. Montréal: Papyruz, 2018.

Pilling, David. "UK Company Develops Edible Drones to Feed Hungry," *Financial Times*, March 2017.

Polanyi, Karl. *The Great Transformation*. New York: Farrar & Rinehart, 1944.

Polk, William. "Understanding Syria: From Pre-Civil War to Post-Assad." *The Atlantic,* December 10, 2013.

Pollan, Michael. *The Omnivore's Dilemma: A Natural History of Four Meals.* New York: Penguin Press, 2006.

Powell, Alvin. "Did Famine Worsen the Black Death?" *Harvard Gazette,* January 5, 2016.

Quinn, Taylor. "Low Tech, High Impact: An Affordable, Hand-Powered Innovation Aims to Boost Food Production in Africa." *Next Billion.* July 25, 2018.

Roberts, Jacob. "Ebola in West Africa: A Medieval Quarantine in the Modern World." Glimpse from the Globe (website). September 1, 2014.

Robins, Becki. "False Things You Believe About the Great Depression." *Grunge,* April 19, 2020.

Rogers, K. "Ebola Outbreak of 2014–16." *Encyclopaedia Britannica.* August 28, 2019.

Rossi, Benedetta. *From Slavery to Aid.* Cambridge: Cambridge University Press, 2015.

Roumain, Jacques. *Gouverneurs de la rosée.* Montréal: Mémoire d'encrier. 2007.

———. *Masters of the Dew.* Oxford; Portsmouth, NH: Heinemann, 1997.

Schanzenbach, Diane, and Abigail Pitts. "Food Insecurity Triples for Families with Children During COVID-19 Pandemic." Northwestern Institute for Policy Research (website). May 13, 2020.

Schiffman, Richard. "Green Violence: 'Eco-Guards' Are Abusing Indigenous Groups in Africa." *Yale Environment 360,* March 17, 2020.

Schilcher, Linda. "The Famine of 1915–1918 in Greater Syria." In *Problems of the Modern Middle East in Historical Perspective: Essays in Honour of Albert Hourani,* edited by John P. Spagnolo. Oxford: Oxford University Press, 1992.

Schwab, Klaus. *The Fourth Industrial Revolution.* New York: Crown, 2013.

Seligman, H. K., A. B. Bindman, E. Vittinghoff, A. M. Kanaya, and M. B. Kushel. "Food Insecurity Is Associated with Diabetes Mellitus: Results from the National Health Examination and Nutrition Examination Survey (NHANES), 1999–2002." *Journal of General Internal Medicine* 22, no. 7 (July 2007): 1018–23.

Sen, Amartya. "Apocalypse Then." *New York Times,* February 18, 2001.

———. *The Idea of Justice.* Cambridge, MA: Belknap Press of Harvard University Press, 2011.

Seneca the Younger. *On Suicide,* Letter 77.

Severson, Kim. "José Andrés Fed Puerto Rico, and May Change How Aid Is Given." *New York Times,* October 30, 2017.

Sherlock, Ruth. "How Crop Fires Have Become the Latest Weapon of War in Syria." National Public Radio, June 28, 2019.

Simon, Matt. "These Rare Seeds Escaped Syria's War—to Help Feed the World." *Wired,* November 17, 2020.

Slackman, Michael. "Egypt's Problem and Its Challenge: Bread Corrupts." *New York Times,* January 17, 2008.

Song Jung-a, Christian Oliver, and Tom Burgis. "Daewoo to Cultivate Madagascar Land for Free." *Financial Times,* November 18, 2008.

Stevens, Hallam, and Yvonne Ruperti. "Lab-Grown Meat Is on the Rise. It's Time to Start Asking Tough Questions." *The Guardian,* June 17, 2021.

Sullivan, Laura. "In Search of the Red Cross' $500 Million in Haiti Relief." *All Things Considered,* National Public Radio, June 3, 2015.

Survival International. "The Baka." Survival (website). Accessed 2021.

Tabuchi, H., and N. Popovitch. "Two Biden Priorities, Climate and Inequality, Meet on Black-Owned Farms." *New York Times,* February 18, 2021.

Tadros, Mariz. "Where's the 'Bread, Freedom and Social Justice' a Year After Egypt's Revolution?" *The Guardian,* January 25, 2012.

Taylor, Peter. "Bobby Sands: The Hunger Strike That Changed the Course of N. Ireland's Conflict." BBC News, May 1, 2021.

Timburg, Craig. "In Postwar Liberia, Paradise amid the Poverty." *Washington Post,* May 29, 2008.

Times (London). "Jean-Claude Duvalier." October 6, 2014.

Toulmin, Camilla, and Ian Scoones. "The Sahelian Great Green Wall: Start with Local Solutions." International Institute for Environment and Development. February 4, 2021.

Toweh, Alphonso, and Cooper Inveen. "Sime Darby to Sell Liberia Plantation to Local Manufacturer." Reuters, December 6, 2019.

United Nations. "Adopting Resolution 2417 (2018), Security Council Strongly Condemns Starving of Civilians, Unlawfully Denying

Humanitarian Access as Warfare Tactics." 826th Meeting of the Security Council, May 24, 2018.

———. "Humanitarian Needs Overview, Syrian Arab Republic." March 2021.

———. "Liberia: The Impact of High Food Prices on Food Security." July 31, 2008.

———. "Review of Measures and Mechanisms for Addressing Racism and Racial Discrimination in United Nations System Organizations: Managing for Achieving Organizational Effectiveness." Note of the Joint Inspection Unit. 2023.

———. "Syria, 10 Years of War Has Left 350,000 Dead." September 24, 2021.

———. "Syria War: Average of One Child Injured or Killed Every Eight Hours over Past 10 Years." UN News, March 10, 2021.

UNICEF. "End Child Marriage." March 2020.

———. "Children in Niger." Undated.

UN Office for the Coordination of Humanitarian Affairs. "Central African Republic: Multi-Cluster/Sector Initial Rapid Assessment." January 2014.

United Nations Development Programme. "Final Investigation Report Investigating Allegations of Non-Compliance with UNDP Social and Environmental Commitments Relating to the Following UNDP Activities: Integrated and Transboundary Conservation of Biodiversity in the Basins of the Republic of Congo, TRIDOM II (October 2017– March 2023)." June 4, 2022.

Urbi, Jaden. "The Government Cheese Phenomenon and the American Cheese Stockpile Today." CNBC, February 16, 2019.

U.S. Agency for International Development. "Central African Republic Complex Emergency FactSheet #2." November 7, 2014.

———. "Mali: Nutrition Profile." June 2014.

U.S. Department of Agriculture. "Agriculture Counts." June 28, 2019.

———. "Household Food Security in the U.S." 2021.

———. "World Agricultural Supply and Demand Estimates." July 2023.

U.S. Military Tribunal, Nuremberg. "High Command Trial: The United States of America vs. Wilhelm Von Leeb et al." October 27, 1948.

U.S. National Park Service. "The Burning: Shenandoah Valley in Flames." July 21, 2022.

———. "The Displaced—Shenandoah National Park." February 26, 2015.

Vangroenweghe, Daniel. "The 'Leopold II' Concession System Exported to French Congo with as Example the Mpoko Company." *Journal of Belgian History* 36, nos. 3–4 (2006).

van Huis, Arnold, Joost Van Itterbeeck, Harmke Klunder, Esther Mertens, Afton Halloran, Giulia Muir, and Paul Vantomme. "Edible Insects: Future Prospects for Food and Feed Security." FAO Forestry Paper 171. Food and Agriculture Organization of the UN, 2013.

Vidal, John. "Armed Ecoguards Funded by WWF 'Beat Up Congo Tribespeople.' " *The Guardian,* February 7, 2020.

Vitaux, Jean. "La poule au pot du bon roi Henri IV." *Canal Académies,* May 9, 2010.

Voltaire. *Candide.* Electronic Scholarly Publishing Project, 1998.

———. *Candide ou l'Optimisme.* Paris : Bibliothèque Nationale de France, 1759.

Waite, Tori, and Olivia Thoelke. "3 Devastating Effects of Hunger on the Body." Feeding America (website). May 18, 2021.

Walker, Martin. "Military Coup in Niger." *The Guardian,* April 16, 1974. *Candide.* Electronic Scholarly Publishing Project, 1998

Walsh, Declan. "The Tragedy of Saudi Arabia's War in Yemen." *New York Times,* October 26, 2018.

Westergaard, Mie. "Biafra, 1967–1970: Ethical Dilemmas of Humanitarian Relief." In *Online Atlas on the History of Humanitarianism and Human Rights,* edited by Fabian Klose, Marc Palen, Johannes Paulmann, and Andrew Thompson.

West Virginia Department of Health and Human Resources. "Fast Facts." 2022.

West Virginia Farmland Protection System. "Jefferson County's Protected Farmland Grows to 5,866 Acres with 51st Farm." July 19, 2021.

Wetherell, Steph. "A Brief History of Wheat." Sustainable Food Trust. November 22, 2019.

World Bank. "Arable Land (Hectares)." 2021.

———. "Implementation Completion and Results Report IBRD 7841-BR on a Loan in the Amount of US$200 Million to the Federative Republic of Brazil for the Second Bolsa Familia Project." August 29, 2019.

———. "Indigenous Peoples Overview." April 14, 2022.

———. "A Year in the Lives of Smallholder Farmers." February 25, 2016.

World Economic Forum. "The Sahel Is Engulfed by Violence. Climate Change, Food Insecurity and Extremists Are Largely to Blame." January 23, 2019.

World Food Programme. "A Global Food Crisis."

———. "Food Security of 800,000 Seriously Threatened After Passage of Hurricane Matthew." October 24, 2016.

———. "Global Report on Food Crises–2021." May 5, 2021.

———. "Pauses in Syrian Fighting During Harvest Vital to Meet Country's Food Needs." May 26, 2015.

———. "WFP Chief Calls for Urgent Funds to Avert Famine." March 11, 2021.

Wrigley, E. A., and Richard Smith. "Malthus and the Poor Law." In "Malthusian Moments," Special Issue 1, *The Historical Journal* 63 (February 2020): 33–62.

Wyss, James. "Haiti Suffers Famine-Like Conditions as Chaos Paralyzes Economy." *Bloomberg,* October 14, 2022.

Yaffe-Bellany, David, and Michael Corker. "Dumped Milk, Smashed Eggs, Plowed Vegetables: Food Waste of the Pandemic." *New York Times,* April 11, 2020.

Young, Michael E. "1,000 or More Feared Dead, Haitian Vessel Held Up to 1,500." *South Florida Sun Sentinel,* February 19, 1993.

Index

A Note About the Author

Jean-Martin Bauer is a humanitarian worker with two decades of experience with the World Food Programme. He has served in the western Sahel and central Africa and has responded to food emergencies in Afghanistan and Syria. Bauer has led WFP country offices in the Republic of Congo and in Haiti. His work has also focused on leveraging digital tech and analytics to fight hunger. A Washington, D.C., native, Bauer holds degrees from the London School of Economics and the Harvard Kennedy School.

A Note on the Type

This book was set in Monotype Dante, a typeface designed by Giovanni Mardersteig (1892–1977). Although modeled on the Aldine type used for Pietro Cardinal Bembo's treatise *De Aetna* in 1495, Dante was originally cut for hand composition by Charles Malin, the famous Parisian punch cutter, between 1946 and 1952. Its first use was in an edition of Boccaccio's *Trattatello in laude di Dante* that appeared in 1954. The Monotype Corporation's version of Dante followed in 1957.

Composed by North Market Street Graphics
Lancaster, Pennsylvania

Printed and bound by Berryville Graphics,
Berryville, Virginia

Designed by Betty Lew